Advance Praise

"With masterful skill, Sandler pulls the reader into a scenario of the horrors of war and the invincibility of love and courage. This is more than a biography. It is a lesson in history not to be forgotten."

-Barbara Marriott, author of *Banana River* and *The Fleet Angels of Lakehurst*

"Len Sandler has skillfully combined the stories of two extraordinary people who, individually, had novel-worthy lives. Now, prepare yourself for an amazing journey filled with dedication, love, service, courage and family that brought George and Simone Stalnaker together."

-Mike Lowe, iHeart Media Program Director

"Colonel Stalnaker's exploits after bailing out of a crippled B-26 bomber are stirring and make him a warrior in my opinion. He is equaled, though, by his wife, Simone de Cruzel, a member of the French Underground. For both, it's a story of intrigue and ingenuity behind the lines during World War II."

-Marine Major Harry Johnson, WWII pilot, Pappy Boyington's Black Sheep Squadron, VMF 214

"I thoroughly enjoyed reading this book. Len has masterfully weaved World War II history with an inspiring story. The soldiers who fought as part of 'America's Greatest Generation' stand as a shining example of sacrifice and bravery. Len also offers insight into the critical role that civilians, such as Simone de Cruzel, played in the war effort. He perfectly describes the unbreakable bond that was established between so many both in and out of uniform as they risked their lives in an all-out effort to achieve victory."

-Medal of Honor Recipient Marine Major General James Livingston (Ret.)

"The book is GORGEOUS, incredible, amazing, wonderful. I have been crying so much over it. This real story is so beautiful. Thanks so much for writing it. I'm proud of George and Simone's life!!!! I'm also proud of my American family and of all those soldiers who gave their lives for our country."

"This is much more than just an escape and evasion story. It's very interesting reading from beginning to end, but I particularly liked the background material that introduced the personalities and events that led to the Second World War in Europe. I also found the details of the German occupation of France, the activities of the French Resistance, and the references to French collaboration fascinating."

"I am deeply touched by the fact that you have written a book about George and Simone. It's an initiative that I truly applaud. We still cherish the wonderful memory of this whole epic story that was such a special moment in our childhood."

"Because of You, We Live!"

The Untold Story of
George & Simone Stalnaker

Pocol Press

Clifton, VA

POCOL PRESS
Published in the United States of America
by Pocol Press
6023 Pocol Drive
Clifton, VA 20124
www.pocolpress.com

Publisher's Cataloguing-in-Publication

Title: "Because of You, We Live!" the untold story of George & Simone Stalnaker / Len Sandler.
Description: Includes bibliographical references and index. | Clifton, VA: Pocol Press, 2017.
Identifiers: ISBN 978-1-929763-71-9 | LCCN 2016960904
Subjects: Stalnaker, George. | Stalnaker, Simone de Cruzel. | Women spies--France--Biography. | World War, 1939-1945--Underground movements--France. | France--History--German occupation, 1940-1945. | World War, 1939-1945--Aerial operations, American. | Fighter pilots--United States--Biography. | BISAC HISTORY / Military / World War II.
Classification: LCC D739 .S73 2017 | DCC 940.53092—dc23

Library of Congress Control Number: 2016960904

Photos courtesy of the Stalnaker family
Additional photos on www.becauseofyouwelive.com

Table of Contents

Dedication

A valiant group of people calling themselves "The Resistance" or "The Underground" operated in secrecy during the time of the German occupation of France in World War II. Fighting against their own oppressive government, which collaborated with the Nazis, approximately 100,000 of them gave their lives in the effort.

Among those they helped were Lt. Col. George Stalnaker and his flight crew who were shot down behind enemy lines. They returned to France many years later to present those who aided them with plaques that proudly proclaimed, "Because of You, We Live!"

Supreme Allied Commander General Dwight D. Eisenhower praised the Resistance at every opportunity declaring they were of "inestimable value" to the Allied cause. Their spirit is celebrated in the stirring words of Commandant le Baron de Vomécourt who served both with the British Army and the French Resistance as quoted in the "London Daily Mail" on February 4, 1947:

"Had all of us in France meekly, lawfully carried out the orders of the German master, no Frenchman could have ever looked another man in the face. Such submission would have saved the lives of many - some very dear to me - but France would have lost its soul."

Thankfully, France never did lose its soul. This book pays tribute to two courageous individuals, Simone de Cruzel and George Stalnaker, and to the brave French civilians who fought for their country's freedom. The world is a better place because of them.

The information in this book is taken from declassified military records and first-hand accounts of those who were involved in the events. There are many others who contributed but, in particular, I'd like to thank George and Simone's four surviving children – Jerry, Marc, Eric, and Claire – as well as Stub Miller's wife Bess for sharing their memories. I'd also like to acknowledge the contributions of Michel Gaglio, a former member of the Armée de l'Air (French Air Force), who graciously translated many documents from French into English for this book.

In addition, I'd like to express my appreciation for my wife Marilyn who provided her usual outstanding assistance, support, and advice.

George Stalnaker

Simone Stalnaker

Foreword

By the time I was 9 or 10 years old, I began to understand what my parents meant to their respective countries. It was obvious that my dad was a big deal. As a full Colonel, he commanded troops and was treated with great respect on Air Force bases. The stories he told about his time as a World War II pilot were fascinating. My father made an amazing escape from enemy territory after bailing out of his crippled bomber.

I also started asking my mother about her time with the French Resistance. Not a professional soldier and just a teenager when she began to do things such as carry explosives undercover, she was imprisoned and threatened with death every day. Her story was not the same as the stories about the moms of my friends.

I am very proud of both my parents. As I went to college and decided that I would make the Air Force a career, I felt like I could never live up to the standards they had set. It was only when I was sent to Viet Nam, flew in the F-4 Phantom, was getting shot at, and was losing friends to enemy fire that I felt like my contributions to our country began to approach, although never equal, theirs. My father earned the Silver Star and my mother several of the French equivalents. I was fortunate enough to have been presented with the Distinguished Flying Cross.

My brothers and sisters and I always felt like the story of our parents' actions during World War II deserved a book. It's an amazing story told by Len Sandler. I will never forget what they did and what he has done.

-Jerry Stalnaker
Colonel, USAF (Ret.)

Chapter 1 – Heroism was in their DNA

Some call it a "Winter Playground" while others refer to it as a "Summer Playground." They're all correct. The operative word is "Playground." The sun-splashed French Riviera, also known as the "Côte d'Azur" or "Azure Coast," is more than 115 kilometers (71 miles) of picturesque paradise in southern France. The city names evoke romance – Cannes, Nice, and Saint-Tropez. The air temperature ranges from a moderate 13 degrees Celsius (55 degrees Fahrenheit) on average in the winter to a balmy 27 degrees Celsius (80 degrees Fahrenheit) in the summer.

In July and August, the water stays at about 20 degrees Celsius (68 degrees Fahrenheit) while the sun shines an average of 300 days of the year. You can walk right into the ocean without feeling a chill or you might choose, instead, to sit and sip Bordeaux on the balcony of one of the luxury hotels and simply watch the aristocrats, politicians, actors and actresses, artists, playwrights, millionaires, and European royalty on their yachts. Maybe you'll want to lounge at an outdoor café and plan an evening at a casino or nightclub.

In the 1920's and 1930's, France was a country of individualism, surrealism, materialism and plenty of other "isms" that influenced world culture. The Charleston, shimmy, cabaret, and jazz clubs were the rage as Josephine Baker scandalized the nation by dancing in scantily-clad outfits. Money and champagne flowed freely. In Riviera high society, gentlemen were expected to wear morning dress and evening tails with opera cloaks. The women were adorned in custom-made gowns, carried fancy parasols, and accessorized with the finest furs and jewels. There were parties before major social events and, of course, parties afterwards. Perhaps whole rounds of parties if you were well-connected.

Born into this upper-class, privileged lifestyle on August 6, 1920, Simone de Cruzel fit right in. She enjoyed skiing in the French Alps, boating and snorkeling in the Mediterranean, and cavorting on the beaches of the Riviera with friends such as Prince Ranier III of Monaco, son of the Duke and Duchess of Valentinois. The Prince later married American film star Grace Kelly in a wedding capturing the world's attention and producing a media frenzy.

One of Simone's many prized possessions was a sky blue sports car that she received for her birthday. She loved to drive the convertible as fast as she could with the top down and her long light brown hair flowing in the breeze. The electric hair dryer had yet to be invented which was not a problem at all for her because she really didn't need one. Following her favorite route on the steep, twisting mountain roads

1

Simone de Cruzel, socialite

Simone relaxes by the family pool

that overlook the pristine ocean, she tested her beloved car's acceleration and handling. It passed the test every time.

A Horse Calvary Officer in World War I, her father Etienne was a judge and member of the Provincial Supreme Court. As you would expect, he had a stern demeanor and was a strict disciplinarian so Simone and her sisters, Jacqueline and Monique, learned to live within boundaries and limits. They weren't going to do anything to embarrass their father, one of the most respected members of the community.

There were times when her parents, particularly her father, felt they had to remind the girls of the family rules. When he wanted to intimidate them, he'd grab one of them by the hair or gather his sabers and swords and put them around his place at the dinner table. Both acts managed to get their attention.

Marie-Ange, their mother, was known as a sophisticated and cultured woman. The family lived in Nice in a luxury apartment building they owned about two blocks from the sparkling waters of the Mediterranean. Their huge courtyard was frequently used to host parties and other social gatherings. It was as close to an idyllic existence as can be imagined.

That life quickly changed as Nazi Swastikas blighted the landscape of most of Europe during World War II in one of the darkest periods of human history. The continent was in shambles with many cities reduced to rubble as destruction occured on an enormous scale. Acts of unprecedented cruelty were taking place that make the most frightening scenes depicted in horror movies seem tame. France fell on June 22, 1940.

Although just 19 years old, Simone joined the struggle to free her country from its occupiers by becoming a spy for the British and taking to the streets with a rifle in hand as a member of the Resistance. After many successful missions, her identity was compromised and she was captured by the Gestapo, imprisoned, and put on Death Row. Suffering through torture and starvation, she awoke every morning for months wondering if this day would be her last.

In contrast to the French Riviera, few people have referred to the state of Iowa as a "playground" of any sort. The climate is less than ideal with an average annual temperature of 49.9 degrees Fahrenheit (10 degrees Celsius.) Typically, 134 days of the year are below freezing. There are 164 cloudy days and 97 partly cloudy days per year. That doesn't leave many more for sunshine. The mean annual snowfall is over 33 inches. The city names are not known for evoking romance -

4

Cedar Rapids, Dubuque, and Davenport. The tallest mountain is Hawkeye Point, reaching an elevation of just 1,670 feet (509 meters.) Frankly not much of a tourist attraction, it's more of a hill than a mountain. If you wanted to spend a day at the beach, you'd have quite a drive because the coastline is pretty far away. You certainly won't find many members of royalty in Iowa. The seat of Polk County and the capital of the state, Des Moines is the perfect definition of "Middle America." Located 1,551 miles (2,496 kilometers) from Los Angeles and 1,159 miles (1,865 kilometers) from Boston, the city would eventually become a center for the insurance industry and a national focus of attention as home to the first American presidential primary caucuses every four years. Iowa is best known for being America's top corn-producing state, generating 2.3 billion bushels on 12.6 million acres of land.

Born the son of a minister named Luther who preached at the Des Moines Congregationalist United Church of Christ and his wife Margaret, George Winfield Stalnaker had a fraternal twin sister Josephine. It was before the days of ultra-sound imaging so they were surprised on May 23, 1917 when she emerged after George. Exhausted, Margaret asked the doctor, "Are there any more?" She was relieved to hear him say, "No, that's it!" They went on to have a second son named Howard on June 6, 1919. The children were all born at home at 3103 University Ave. House calls were made in the case of approximately 95% of all births at the time.

The preacher's kids were very polite but full of mischief as they went wading in the baptismal font, soaping windows of homes, and tipping over outhouses. George's favorite expression would turn out to be, "By golly!" while continually pushing his glasses back up on his nose as they fell down. It was reminiscent of a Jimmy Stewart movie. In fact, George, with his dark brown hair and hazel eyes, resembled the thin, athletic-looking Stewart. You say the words, "American World War II pilot" and you immediately picture someone who looked like him.

During George's early childhood in the 1920's, the U.S. stock market was on an historic run that saw the Dow Jones Industrial Average increase tenfold in value. The exuberance was evident in

5

Luther Stalnaker

economist Irving Fisher's prediction the day before the market crash that "Stock prices have reached what looks like a permanently high plateau." The "Roaring Twenties" ceased its roar on "Black Friday," October 24, 1929. The market lost 11% of its value by the opening bell and the slide continued with a drop of nearly 13% on "Black Monday" and 12% on "Black Tuesday." The "Great Crash" ushered in "The Great Depression" which lasted for the next decade. Industrial production dropped by 46% and international trade by 70%. Although it originated in America, the "Great Depression" had global impact as the world's Gross Domestic Product fell 15% by 1932. The stock market did not return to its September 3, 1929 peak of 381 until November 23, 1954.

U.S. President Herbert Hoover indicated the economic crisis was "just a passing incident in our national lives" and urged people to be patient and not rely on the federal government for assistance. By 1933, nearly half of the country's banks had failed. Of the 52 million people in the work force, close to 13 million of them had lost their jobs, an all-time high rate of over 25%. Some of the unemployment rates in American cities were staggering, such as 80% in Toledo, Ohio and 90% in Lowell, Massachusetts. Shantytowns consisting of makeshift cardboard box and scrap wood homes were sarcastically called "Hoovervilles." The "Great Depression" described not just the economic downturn but the mood of the country. People were in no frame of mind to worry about the problems in Europe, thousands of miles away in distance and thought. They saw in newsreels or listened on the radio to the dreadful things happening but the most common response was, "Hey, we've got our own problems to worry about." News about the German atrocities taking place in death camps was buried deep in the pages of American newspapers.

With the country mired in the Great Depression, the American public grew increasingly dissatisfied with President Herbert Hoover's hands-off economic policies and was ready to look to the federal government for leadership. In accepting the Democratic Party nomination in 1932, Franklin Delano Roosevelt pledged "A New Deal for the American people."

After graduating from Harvard University, Roosevelt attended Columbia Law School and began working for the firm of Carter, Ledyard, and Milburn. At age 28, he was elected State Senator from New York's 26th District, which had been held by Republicans for 32 years. He served only a few months of his second term when President Woodrow Wilson named him Assistant Secretary of the Navy. He was on the national ticket for Vice-President in 1920 but he and Presidential candidate and Ohio Governor James Cox lost to Warren Harding and

Calvin Coolidge. Roosevelt was then elected New York's Governor in 1928, serving for four years.

The President delivered his inauguration speech on March 4, 1933 declaring, "The only thing we have to fear is fear itself." He claimed he would "wage a war against the emergency as though we were invaded by a foreign foe." His speech resonated with the American people who were confident they had elected someone willing to take bold action. Over the next eight years, he put a massive government stimulus program into action.

Putting people back to work buoyed consumer confidence and gave Americans a sense of optimism. The role of the federal government was re-defined as initiator of massive social programs. Where did the money come from? FDR took the dangerous gamble of gutting the defense budget, leaving the country to pursue its isolationist stance out of necessity.

In the meantime, young George Stalnaker rose early before school every day and shoveled coal into downtown church furnaces to earn a few dollars of spending money. Few American children were fortunate enough to be given an "allowance" during those days.

One of his earliest hobbies was making small clay sculptures and drawings. His mother Margaret bragged to people about how artistic he was, yet George didn't agree. He made a clay statue of himself that she raved about. George was so displeased with the end result that he broke it and threw it away, which really upset his mother. He was not going to invest time and effort in art or sculpture. George would make his mark on the world in a different way.

After graduating from West Point, he was named a Squadron Commander, flew 35 combat missions, and rose to the rank of Lieutenant Colonel. He was piloting a B-26 Marauder twin-engine bomber when it was hit by enemy fire over Nantes, France, losing its right engine. With the left engine failing and the plane rapidly losing altitude, the mission of destroying the last remaining bridge the Germans could use to reinforce their troops at Normandy was completed before the crew was forced to bail out. The aircraft banked sharply, stalled, spun out of control, and exploded upon impact with the ground. Trapped behind enemy lines, he and his flight crew were declared Missing in Action.

Simone De Cruzel and George Stalnaker may have been born worlds apart but they were alike in one important way – heroism was in their DNA. This is the epic true story of how they survived, met, and fell in love.

Chapter 2 – The Blighting of the Landscape

Born in Austria on April 20, 1889 to a poor peasant family, there was a man who failed as a student and was unable to complete a grade school education, dropping out at age 15. However, he was fascinated with theater, literature, opera, and drawing. Hoping to attend the Vienna Academy of Art or the Vienna School of Architecture, his application was rejected by both schools.

The man avoided military service in Austria by escaping to Munich, Germany, claiming he didn't want to serve in an army that had "a mixture of races." Living off a small inheritance from his father, he tried to sell watercolors and sketches but few people were interested. After the death of his mother, he was forced to live in homeless shelters. Uncertain, alone, and lacking direction, he volunteered for the German infantry during World War I.

There are plenty of stories about deeds that changed the world. There aren't many about missed opportunities to change the world. A lowly British Army Private named Henry Tandey's decision not to take action on September 28, 1918 turned out to be one that would have a profound impact on history.

Born in Leamington Spa in 1891, the former hotel boiler engineer enlisted in the Green Howards in 1910. When World War I broke out, Henry joined the British Expeditionary Force in France. Arriving in Ypres on October 14, 1914, he took part in the first battle there and helped evacuate the injured at the Menin Crossroads.

Wounded at the Battle of the Somme in October of 1916, he was given the Distinguished Service Medal two years later at the Battle of Cabrai for storming an enemy post with two comrades, killing several Germans and capturing twenty.

Two weeks later, he earned the Military Medal for rescuing wounded men under fire and leading a bombing party into German trenches. As part of the Duke of Wellington's Regiment, Henry was awarded the Victoria Cross at the Battle of Marcoing in France. When his platoon was halted by heavy machine-gun fire, he crawled forward to locate the gun post and lead fellow soldiers in destroying it. He then rebuilt a plank bridge, crossing the canal under a hail of bullets.

Later that day, Henry, though badly wounded, led a bayonet charge and 37 of the enemy were trapped. During the ensuing close combat, he aimed his rifle at a wounded German corporal who had come into his line of fire. Their eyes met and Henry made the immediate decision to lower his gun and let the downtrodden soldier limp away.

"I took aim but couldn't shoot a wounded man so I let him go," admitted the 27-year-old Tandey, claiming he had a personal honor code of never shooting injured, unarmed, or retreating Germans, even though he did everything he could to kill them in battle.

The German soldier nodded in thanks and then disappeared. In that moment of compassion, Henry had unknowingly spared the life of 29-year-old Adolf Hitler.

After becoming German Chancellor, Hitler had his staff obtain a print of an Italian painting called "The Menin Crossroads" which showed Private Tandey carrying an injured Allied soldier on his back. An Italian war artist had portrayed the Green Howards evacuating the wounded at the Battle of Ypres in 1914. Not forgetting that pivotal moment, Hitler recognized Tandey as the man who had spared him and hung the print on the wall at his mountain top retreat at Berchtesgaden in Bavaria.

In 1938, British Prime Minister Neville Chamberlain was worried about the prospect of Great Britain having to fight a two-front war against the Germans and Italians. He was intent on trying to get an agreement of peaceful co-existence with one or the other. He claimed, "From the first, I have been trying to improve relations with the two storm centers of Berlin and Rome. It seemed to me that we were drifting into worse and worse positions with both with the prospect of having ultimately to face two enemies at once."

Chamberlain then paid a cordial visit to Hitler who proudly showed him the print and explained its significance. He told Chamberlain, "That man came so near to killing me I thought I should never see Germany again. Providence saved me from such devilishly accurate fire as those English boys were aiming at us." The Führer then asked to have his personal gratitude conveyed to Tandey, which Chamberlain did by telephone after returning to London. Henry was sickened to learn that Hitler was the soldier he let walk away.

Henry's war wounds prevented him from re-enlisting in World War II. Instead, he worked as a security guard in an automobile plant in Coventry during the day and an air raid warden at night. His "good deed" continued to haunt him, especially when Nazi bombers destroyed Coventry's factories in 1940, killing 560 people in the process. He had spent the previous 10 hours fighting his way into blazing houses, rescuing victims, and pulling out bodies. Nothing he did, though, was able to ease his guilt.

"If only I had known what he would turn out to be. When I saw all the people, women and children, he had killed and wounded that night I was sorry to God I let him go," he confessed in anguish before his death in 1977 at age 86. He was buried in the British Cemetery at Marcoing alongside fallen comrades and close to the spot where he spared Hitler's life.

Henry might have been able to stop the terror wreaked by the Nazis and prevent the deaths of the 58 million people who lost their lives during World War II.   He could have been remembered as the most highly decorated British Private of World War I. Instead, he'll always be known as "The Man Who Didn't Shoot Hitler."

Benito Mussolini's actions in Italy directly influenced Hitler, creating the road map that he followed. Although he admired Mussolini, Hitler privately scoffed at Italians and other non-Aryan races.

Born on July 29, 1883, Mussolini joined the Army in 1915 and fought on the front lines in World War I as a corporal before being wounded.   After the war, Mussolini resumed political activities organizing several right-wing groups into a single force and, on March 23, 1919, formed the ultra-nationalist Fascist Party, claiming that "Italy will be raised to levels of its great Roman past."

Capitalizing on public discontent, Mussolini organized a para-military known as the "Black Shirts," who terrorized political opponents. When Italy slipped into political chaos on October 27, 1922, he seized authority "to restore order."   He then dismantled all democratic institutions, and in 1925 became dictator, declaring himself *Il Duce* or "Supreme Leader."

Ever mindful of his public image, Mussolini carefully orchestrated things to literally portray himself in the best possible light. He was always careful to leave the light on in his office to give the impression that he was working 24 hours a day.

Promoted to corporal after fighting in France and Belgium, Hitler was temporarily partially blinded in a mustard gas attack near Ypres in Belgium on October 13, 1918. He regained his sight five days later and, while still recovering in a military hospital, was furious to hear the news of the November 11, 1918 surrender of Germany. He believed surrender is for cowards.

Wanting to remain in the army, Hitler was appointed to the Intelligence/Propaganda Section where he undertook political training and gave speeches advocating German nationalism and anti-socialism to the troops. He also served as a confidential informant and, in that capacity, attended a beer hall meeting of the DAP (an acronym from *Deutsche Arbeiterpartei* or "German Workers' Party.")   While monitoring their activities, he was attracted to their nationalistic, anti-Semitic, anti-capitalist, and anti-communist ideology.

11

While still drawing a paycheck from the Army, he became a card-carrying member of the DAP and the party's most effective speaker. Crowds began to gather to hear his fiery, hate-filled oratory. On February 24, 1920, the organization was renamed the *Nationalsozialstische Deutsche Arbeiterpartei* (National Socialist German Worker's Party) in at attempt to give it broader appeal. The name "Nazi" came from the first syllable of "NAtional" and the second of "soZIalistische."

Following World War I, The Treaty of Versailles exacted heavy reparation payments from Germany, handicapping its economy and fostering an angry nationalist climate that allowed for the rise of the Nazis. The $33 billion Germany was required to pay the Allies caused the government to print enormous amounts of paper money, resulting in the German Mark essentially losing its value. An item costing 100 marks in July of 1922 cost 944,000 marks just a year later.

Many Germans were resentful and ready to "restore Germany's place." They felt the Versailles treaty had crippled Germany unfairly. The setting, regrettably, was conducive to the rise of extremism.

Allied Supreme Commander French General Ferdinand Foch had recognized the dangerous risk of not demilitarizing Germany. He warned, "This is not peace. It is an armistice for 20 years." His prediction, unfortunately, came true as the first shot of World War II was fired almost 20 years to the day after the signing of the Versailles Treaty.

Hitler became Party Chairman, introducing "Brown Shirts" and the Nazi Swastika, a religious symbol derived from the Sanskrit name for a hooked cross, used by ancient civilizations as a symbol of fertility and good fortune. The name itself comes from the Sanskrit, combining the words *su* (good) and *asti* (to be).

Demonstrating a vanity that rivaled that of Mussolini's, Hitler never took his coat off in public, even on the hottest days, believing that it added to his military bearing. He was advised by his Press Secretary in 1923 to shave off his strange little moustache only to have him smugly respond, "If it is not the fashion now, it will be later because I wear it!" Hitler didn't think he needed a public relations campaign. He was confident he could do a good enough job on his own.

On November 8, 1923, along with right wing factions, Hitler attempted to overthrow the Bavarian government with an armed uprising known as The Beer Hall Putsch. He was one of 2,000 Nazis who brazenly took to the streets of Munich and attempted to take over a meeting conducted by major figures in national politics.

The following day, the Nazis marched again and the police opened fire. Hitler was captured, tried for treason, and sentenced to nine months in Landsberg prison. During his incarceration, he wrote the book *Mein Kampf* (My Struggle) which defined his political ideology.

After being released, Hitler re-formed the Nazi party and in the general election of September of 1930, they increased their representation in Parliament from 14 to 107 members. Now leading the second largest political party, he became a German citizen, enabling him to run in the Presidential election against Paul von Hindenburg. He lost, but on January 30, 1933, was named Chancellor of a coalition government with the Nazis holding a third of the seats in the Reichstag, the German version of the Parliament, which subsequently was destroyed by a mysterious fire. The communists were blamed and a state of emergency called to "stabilize" the situation. The accusation allowed him to arrest the communist members of the Reichstag and thereby eliminate much of his political opposition.

Membership in the Nazi Party grew from 129,583 in 1930 to 849,009 in 1933. During the war years, it exploded to more than five million. Even at its highest level, it still represented only 7% of the German population. It's a group, though, that was particularly powerful and influential.

The "*Gesetz zur Behebung der Not von Volk und Reich*" (Law to Remedy the Distress of People and Reich), more commonly called the "Enabling Act," was passed on March 24, 1933, giving powers of legislation to Hitler's cabinet for four years, making him a virtual dictator. The act eliminated civil liberties and proclaimed the Nazis would be the only political party permitted in Germany. All trade unions were disbanded. Individual German states lost their autonomous powers and Nazi officials were installed as governors of those states.

Hitler used the term "Third Reich" (meaning "regime" or "empire") to describe the Nazi rule. The First Reich was the Holy Roman Empire of the German Nation from 962 to 1806 and the Second Reich the German Empire of 1871 to 1918. He boasted that his Reich would last a thousand years while forming a "New World Order."

On May 10, 1933, in a precursor to the censorship to come, students at the University of Berlin burned over 25,000 volumes of what were termed "un-German" or "subversive" books. They were defined as "representing ideologies opposed to Nazism," including books by Jewish, socialist, communist, liberal, anarchist, and pacifist authors. More than 40,000 people gathered at the State Opera to hear Dr. Joseph Goebbels declare in a speech, "No, to decadence and moral corruption!

13

Yes, to decency in family and state! I consign these books to the flames." The crowd cheered wildly.

Goebbels, with his flair for the dramatic, so impressed Hitler that he later named him to be his Minister of Propaganda. There would be a number of additional book burnings conducted by the German Student Union in Germany and Austria. A century before the Nazis, a prophetic German poet Heinrich Heine claimed, "Where one burns books, one will, in the end, burn people."

On June 30, 1934, the "Night of the Long Knives" occured when Hitler purged all opposition within his own party. Estimates are that from 85 to several hundred people were murdered and more than one thousand imprisoned. The SS and *Gestapo* were responsible for carrying out the slaughter. The "SS," an abbreviation of *SchuftzStaffel* or "Protective Echelon," was Hitler's personal protection service. The word "Gestapo" was an acronym derived from "GEheime STAatsPOlizie." or "Secret State Police."

Fearing for their lives, those on the German courts and in the political establishment openly expressed support for Hitler. In a speech to the Reichstag on July 13, 1934, he claimed to be "the supreme judge of the German people." There was no one left who was willing to disagree. The following month, he declared himself *Führer* (Leader) and Reich Chancellor (Head of Government) and began to build a fearsome military force.

On March 12, 1938, Germany annexed Hitler's home country of Austria. World leaders signed the Munich Agreement on September 30 in an attempt to appease the growing threat. It allowed Germany to annex the Czechoslovakian Sudetenland Region where three million ethnic Germans lived. A year later, Nazi troops poured into Bohemia and Moravia. The Czechoslovakian provinces offered no resistance and were turned into what was called a German "protectorate." That same evening, Hitler made a triumphant entry into Prague.

The Munich Agreement, which British Prime Minister Neville Chamberlain claimed would mean "peace in our time," turned out to have the opposite effect.

The *Kristallnacht* (Crystal Night,) also referred to as the "Night of Broken Glass," occured on November 9, 1938 when Nazis openly attacked Jews and their property, littering the streets with the windows of shops smashed in the pogroms. The pretext was the Paris shooting of Ernst von Rath, a German diplomat, by a Polish-Jewish student, Herschel Grynszpan two days earlier. Hitler conferred with Joseph Goebbels who arranged to have the violence staged to appear as "spontaneous demonstrations." A total of 7,500 Jewish shops were destroyed, 400 synagogues burned, and approximately 20,000 Jews sent to concentration camps.

Crystal Night was the beginning of the Holocaust, derived from the Greek word *holokaustos* for "burned whole." There have been other holocausts throughout history but only the one during World War II is spelled with a capital "H" signifying that it is THE Holocaust, mass murder on an unimaginable scale.

There was a widespread emigration of Jews from Germany during the Nazi rise to power. Starting at 500,000 in 1933, the population shrunk to just 220,000 by 1939. Of those who stayed, only 10% survived the war. Perhaps the most horrifying statistic was the deliberate targeting of children. It's estimated that 1.5 million of the 1.6 million Jewish children living in territories occupied by the Nazis were exterminated. Hardest hit was Poland where only 5,000 out of one million Jewish children survived.

According to historian Emmanuel Ringelblum, "Even in the most barbaric times, a human spark glowed in the rudest heart, and children were spared. But the Hitlerian beast is quite different. It would devour the dearest of us, those who arouse the greatest compassion - our innocent children."

Poles were massacred in huge numbers over the next five weeks as Hitler marched across the country virtually unchallenged. In a precursor to the inhumane acts to follow, some 50,000 Polish children that the Nazis thought "looked German" were taken from their homes and given to German parents. It is believed that as many as six million Poles, half of them Jews, were killed in World War II.

Hitler named Heinrich Himmler as head of the SS, divided into the *Allgemeine-SS* (General SS) and the *Waffen-SS* (Armed SS), to carry out executions of political opponents and ethnic minorities. The Nazis also began a "Euthanasia" program in which 80,000 to 100,000 physically disabled, mentally challenged, or mentally ill Germans were murdered. Based in Berlin at No. 4 Tiergartenstrasse, it became known as the T-4 program.

With military pacts in place that commited France and Great Britain to aid the Polish government, both declared war on Germany September 3, 1939, yet no Allied military forces were deployed.

Eight months passed while France and Great Britain publicly denounced Hitler's actions while privately debating the appropriate course to take. The Allied powers were engaged in what satirically became known as the "Phoney War," using the British spelling. Critics also dubbed this period of stagnation the "Twilight War" and the "Sitzkrieg" or "Sitting War," as opposed to the *Blitzkrieg*. Others called it the "Bore War," rather than the "Boer War." It was termed the *Drôle de Guerre* ("Joke of a War") in French. In truth, there was nothing funny about it. The deadliest threat the free world had ever known was growing stronger and bolder.

The United States continued to pursue a policy of isolationism saying, "It's the war in Europe. It's not our war." The U.S. Congress passed a Neutrality Act on August 31, 1935 to help keep the country out of European affairs by prohibiting the export of "arms, ammunition, and implements of war" to foreign nations at war. American citizens traveling in war zones were advised that they must do so at their own risk. A second Neutrality Act in 1937 forbid Americans from traveling on belligerent ships, prevented American merchant ships from transporting arms or war materials to belligerents, and barred all warships from U.S. waters.

At the urging of President Franklin D. Roosevelt and in a deliberate attempt to assist Great Britain and France, a "cash and carry" provision was included in the second act that permitted the acquisition of non-military items such as oil if they were paid for in advance and transported on non-American ships. A third and final Neutrality Act was passed in November of 1939 that lifted the arms embargo and allowed all items to be sold under cash and carry terms.

After beefing up its military during the eight months of the Phoney War, Germany's appetite became insatiable. It began to swallow countries whole, quickly devouring the armies of Denmark, Norway, Belgium, the Netherlands, Luxembourg, Yugoslavia, Greece, Estonia, Latvia, and Lithuania.

In Great Britain, Prime Minister Neville Chamberlain was replaced by Winston Churchill who galvanized political and popular support for the all-out fight to come. He had little respect for the efforts that had taken place up to that point to appease the Germans stating, "An appeaser is one who feeds a crocodile, hoping it will eat him last."

In his first speech as Prime Minister to the House of Commons on May 13, 1940, Churchill told them, "I have nothing to offer but blood, toil, tears, and sweat." Then, in response to the question on the mind of every British citizen, he declared, "You ask, what is our aim? I can answer in one word. It is victory. Victory at all costs. Victory in spite of all terrors. Victory, however long and hard the road may be, for without victory there is no survival."

The "Miracle of Dunkirk" occurred later that month. The British Army was sent to fight in France but they were no match for the Nazis and their Panzer Tank Divisions who backed them up to the sea at

Dunkirk. The Germans rushed in reinforcements and were poised to complete the overwhelming victory when, surprisingly, Hitler ordered his troops to halt, creating an opportunity for escape.

Thirty-nine British Naval ships were dispatched but were capable of rescuing only a fraction of those who were trapped, some of whom walked into shoulder-deep water to meet their rescuers. Virtually all pieces of military equipment, weapons, and vehicles had to be abandoned. Word spread that the troops needed help. A huge ad-hoc civilian navy of merchant marine, pleasure craft, fishing boats, and even rowboats filled the English Channel. Over an eight-day period, a total of 338,226 troops were rescued as the German Army awaited further orders from Berlin.

There was little cause for celebration. Winston Churchill reminded the nation in a speech to the House of Commons on June 4 that this was not a victory. He called it a "colossal military disaster" and proclaimed, "Wars are not won by evacuations." As bleak as things looked, he vowed, "We shall not flag or fail. We shall go on to the end. We shall fight in France, we shall fight on the seas and oceans, we shall fight with growing confidence and growing strength in the air. We shall defend our island, whatever the cost may be. We shall fight on the beaches, we shall fight on the landing-grounds, we shall fight in the fields and in the streets, we shall fight in the hills. We shall never surrender!"

Colonel Charles de Gaulle was in charge of the French Fifth Army tank regiment at the outbreak of World War II and then given command of the 4e Division Cuirassée. With 200 tanks, he attacked German forces at Montcornet and forced them to retreat to Caumont. In recognition of one of the rare battle victories for the French, de Gaulle was promoted to Brigadier General. He was part of a force that attempted unsuccessfully to rescue the Allies trapped at Dunkirk and then named "Under Secretary of State for National Defence and War" to coordinate with British Forces.

To this day, military analysts debate why Hitler allowed the British to escape from Dunkirk. He may have expected them to surrender or may have been wary of heavy losses being inflicted on his troops. Some theorize his real interest in gaining *lebensraum* or "living space" for Germany was to take territory from Russia and he believed the British Army had been effectively neutralized. He may have thought he could pound English cities into submission with bombings without risk to his troops. Whatever the reason, Great Britain remained in the war.

17

While France was under attack, Marshal Henri-Philippe Pétain, a World War I hero, was appointed Premier by the National Assembly of the Third Republic. He rejected the invitation of Winston Churchill to form an "indissoluble" union to fight the Germans. Pétain saw Britain as close to collapse, angrily calling their proposal a request for "marriage with a corpse."

The Battle of France was hardly a battle at all. It's also known as the Fall of France which is probably more descriptive. It wasn't a case of a vastly superior army overpowering the French. Only 16 out of Germany's 135 Divisions were even mechanized. The vast majority depended on horses and foot soldiers. France alone had 10,700 artillery pieces and 3,254 tanks compared to 7,378 artillery pieces and 2,439 tanks for the Germans.

After just six weeks, the vaunted French Army was ready to capitulate. During the course of the short campaign, they adopted a careful, defensive posture. They simply attempted to hold their positions, relying on a series of newly-built steel and concrete fortifications known as the Maginot Line to ward off the invasion. Bold, aggressive action might have changed the course of the war.

Why were the French so cautious? It's likely the devastating cost of World War I was still on their minds. Of the 8.4 million French soldiers who fought, more than 1.3 million died, nearly 4.3 million were wounded, and 537,000 taken POW or MIA. Those numbers represent a staggering total of 73% of those who served in uniform during "The Great War." The French grossly overestimated how much protection the Maginot line provided them. Author Raoul Aglion admitted, "I, like most men my age, was not drafted, since the French government considered itself invulnerable behind the mighty Maginot Line, the massive chain of fortifications that lined the frontier with Germany. Proud of our impregnable border, we were absolutely confident of an eventual victory."

Even the Nazis were surprised by the ease of their conquest. After the surrender, Goebbels wrote, "A historic moment. Now the guns fall silent throughout France. A victory, such as we could not have imagined in our wildest dreams, is ours."

Italy entered World War II by declaring war on both Britain and France on June 10, 1940, launching the Battle of the Alps the same day. Mussolini saw it as an opportunity to reclaim the "Italia Irredenta" region of southeastern France that borders the two countries. A demilitarized zone was created on the French side with an Armistice Control Commission created in Turin to ensure adherence to its terms.

An armistice with the Germans was signed in Compiègne on June 22, 1940 causing "The City of Lights" along with the rest of France to go dark and allowing an occupation of the country following their decisive victory. Sometimes called "The Second Compiègne Treaty," it followed Germany's document of surrender on November 11, 1918 and was signed in the same building. The symbolism was a deliberate attempt by Hitler to atone for what he regards as the humiliating World War I defeat.

Pétain formed a pro-Axis government based in Vichy. One of his ministers, Jean Ybarnegaray, claimed, "Better to be a Nazi province. At least we know what that means." Another, Jean Pozzi, echoed, "The war is over, the Nazis have won. The defeat is complete. Hitler is so clever. We must accept defeat and abide by the terms of the surrender. A Nazi Europe may endure for hundreds of years. It will be painful for us, but our grandchildren will be able to live in the great Nazi empire of Europe."

The new country was called the "État Français" (French State.) The Germans occupied northern France while Hitler allowed the day-to-day administration of the government of the mostly rural south to be handled by the collaborationist regime, with Vichy as its capitol.

When German forces ceremoniously marched into Paris to occupy the city, the French cut the lift cables on the Eiffel tower so soldiers would have to walk up to fly the Swastika. During his visit, Hitler chose to stay on the ground rather than take the steps. It was really little consolation.

France's government was not the only one to partner with the Nazis. Norway's leader, Vidkun Quisling, for example, actively collaborated with Germany during its occupation, making *quisling* popular as a new word in the Norwegian language meaning "traitor."

Originally a tactic for land war, the air "Blitz" (for "lightning") with a second syllable of "krieg" (for "war") often added was begun on September 7, 1940. A total of 652 bombers dropped an estimated one million bombs at the rate of 150 to 200 tons per day. Approximately 40,000 civilians were killed in the next six months and more than a million homes in London alone destroyed.

Air raid shelters provided the most protection against the Blitz. The "Tube" subway stations were also open to the public beginning at 4 p.m. each day with an estimated 150,000 people slepping in them every night. Other cities targeted by the bombings included Birmingham, Liverpool, Plymouth, Bristol, Glasgow, Southampton, and Portsmouth.

On September 27, Germany, Italy, and Japan signed a tripartite agreement officially forming the Axis powers.

The Battle of Britain was fought during the summer and fall of 1940. The RAF (Royal Air Force) performed brilliantly, preventing a ground invasion that could have given Germany complete control over Europe. Winston Churchill famously claimed, "Never was so much owed by so many to so few." British industry then went into all-out production mode, increasing the RAF from just 75 planes at the beginning of the war to 132,500 by the war's end.

Sounding like something from a "Star Wars" plot, British engineer Robert Watson-Watt had begun working on a "Death Ray" in 1935 to try to discover a practical method of destroying enemy aircraft using radio waves. It evolved into "RDF (Range and Detection Finding) four years later, as World War II began. Independently, German scientists had developed a similar *Funkmessgerät* (radio measuring device.) The Americans were also working on the new scientific advance with the U.S. Navy, developing a ship-based system. They used the acronym RADAR (RAdio Detection And Ranging) and that turned out to be the name that stuck.

By the time the Battle of Britain occured, the British radar system was fully operational, giving them a temporary tactical advantage over the Germans who had failed to realize the potential of the technology. Many feel that was because of Hitler's preference for offensive rather than defensive devices. Radar helped the RAF to successfully repel the Luftwaffe attacks.

The British military then began what seemed to be a frivolous attempt to explain the effectiveness of their pilots. They started a rumor that their prowess in aerial combat came from remarkable vision, aided by a high-carrot diet. While there is no evidence that the Germans bought into this explanation, it actually produced a boom in carrot sales in Great Britain at a time when the government was stressing the importance of raising home-grown vegetables as an alternative to food rationing. The myth that carrot consumption improves vision persists to this day.

In the meantime, the "Act to Promote the Defense of the United States," commonly known as the "Lend-Lease Act," was passed on March 11, 1941 which allowed the "borrowing" of ships, planes, and war material by Allied nations with the stipulation that military base leases be granted to America free of charge. More than $50 billion worth of badly-needed military equipment was sent to Allied nations engaged in the war.

The diabolical plan to implement the *Die Endlosung* (Final Solution) of murdering Europe's Jews was formulated by the Germans at the Wannsee Conference in a suburb of Berlin on January 20, 1942.

Fifteen attendees agreed upon the methods to answer "The Jewish Question."

Reinhard Heydrich began the conference to "Inform and secure support from government ministries and other interested agencies relevant to the implementation of the Final Solution." He declared that the decision to proceed had already been made by Hitler himself so the participants did not discuss whether such a plan should be undertaken. Their task was simply the implementation. Hitler had already authorized the Reich Railroads to transport German, Austrian, and Czech Jews to concentration camps to be killed.

Heydrich indicated that not only Jews residing in Axis-controlled Europe, but also the Jewish populations of the United Kingdom and all of the European neutral nations, a total of 11 million people, would be targeted. He gave this explanation, complete with chilling euphemisms, as to why ALL Jews needed to die:

"During the course of the Final Solution, the Jews will be deployed under appropriate supervision at a suitable form of labor deployment in the East. In large labor columns, separated by gender, able-bodied Jews will be brought to those regions to build roads, whereby a large number will doubtlessly be lost through natural reduction. Any final remnant that survives will doubtless consist of the elements most capable of resistance. They must be dealt with appropriately, since, representing the fruit of natural selection, they are to be regarded as the core of a new Jewish revival."

Six million of Europe's nine million Jews were killed during the Holocaust. An additional six million were exterminated from groups defined as "racially inferior" including Poles, Czechs, Greeks, Gypsies, Serbs, Ukranians, Russians, homosexuals, mentally and physically handicapped persons, trade unionists, Jehovah's Witnesses, and others.

At the heart of Hitler's political philosophy was the idea of Aryan blood remaining "pure and strong." Neither Hitler nor any of the participants in the Wannsee Conference were the first to exhibit extreme prejudice against minority groups. They were born into an environment in which the notion of racial superiority was already present. Many would say that Hitler was an opportunist who simply used this to his political advantage to gain the support of the German people. It is certainly noteworthy that Hitler did not attend the Wannsee Conference nor did he ever visit any of the concentration camps.

Chapter 3 – The Woman from the French Riviera

The Compiègne Peace Treaty proved disastrous for the French. They were required to pay the expenses for the 300,000 Nazi troops occupying their country. There were food shortages, rampant inflation, soaring unemployment, and widespread malnutrition. Both the Germans and the Vichy Regime terrorized the French to keep them subservient. There was widespread censorship and nightly curfews. Simply listening to the BBC (British Broadcasting Corporation) on the radio was declared illegal.

General Charles de Gaulle denounced the armistice with Germany saying that they had "lost the battle but not the war" and began building the Free French Forces. He encouraged the French to resist the German occupation and work against the Vichy. He challenged the people to take action declaring, "Silence is the ultimate weapon of power" and "The flame of French resistance must not die and will not die."

De Gaulle's rallying cry earned him both praise and notoriety. He inspired many French citizens to fight but was tried for treason in absentia in an August 2, 1940 court martial and sentenced to death. Those who joined him in acts of resistance were labeled as "terrorists." Fleeing the country, he set up headquarters in London. Until July 3, 1944, he served as President of the Free French Republic as a man without a country.

At first the French Resistance was not organized and consisted of individual, ad-hoc acts of sabotage, then groups such as telephone, postal, and railway workers started to band together. Finally, large groups of diverse people formed and formalized their connections with Great Britain, which contributed weapons, explosives, communication devices, and other supplies.

Thierry d'Argenlieu proposed the "Croix de Lorraine" (Cross of Lorraine) be used as the symbol of the Free French Forces to invoke nationalism and as a counterpoint to the Nazi Swastika. Part of the heraldic arms of Lorraine, the cross consisted of one long vertical and two shorter horizontal bars superimposed on the French Flag, or tricolor.

Between 1871 and 1918, the northern third of Lorraine was annexed by Germany, along with Alsace. During that period the Cross served as a rallying point for French ambitions to recover its lost provinces. This historical significance lent it considerable weight as a symbol of French patriotism. During World War II, the cross was displayed on the flags of Free French warships and military vehicles and as nose art on Free French aircraft. The medal of the Order of Liberation bears the Cross of Lorraine. De Gaulle himself was memorialized by a

141-foot Cross of Lorraine in his home town of Colombey-les-Deux-Églises.

The French National Anthem, *La Marseillaise* (the Song of Marseille), was also invoked as a call to inspire citizens to resist the occupiers. Originally written in 1792 after the invasion of France by Prussia and Austria, *La Marseillaise* acquired its name after being sung by volunteers from Marseille while marching on Paris. It fit perfectly the mood of the Resistance fighters, who used it as a patriotic call for the citizenry to raise arms. Many French hearts were stirred by the anthem which opens with:

> "Let's go children of the fatherland,
> The day of glory has arrived!
> Against us tyranny's
> Bloody flag is raised! (repeat)
>
> In the countryside, do you hear
> The roaring of these fierce soldiers?
> They come right to our arms
> To slit the throats of our sons, our women!
>
> To arms, citizens,
> Form your battalions,
> Let's march, let's march!
> Let an impure blood
> Water our fields!"

Written by Claude-Joseph Rouget de Lisle

An estimated 200,000 to 400,000 civilians joined the Resistance to engage in acts of defiance. They provided military intelligence to the Allies, published underground newspapers, and helped soldiers caught behind enemy lines. They also waged guerilla warfare, sabotaged electrical power lines, stole military equipment and supplies, dynamited transportation facilities, and interrupted lines of communications.

At the same time, French pro-Vichy police teamed with members of the Gestapo to specialize in intimidation and brutality and routinely executed those who were suspected of disloyalty. The Vichy regime created the *Milice Française* or "French Militia" to seek out and destroy the Resistance. Prime Minister Pierre Laval was officially in charge but Chief of Operations Secretary General Joseph Darnand carried out the day-to-day work of execution, torture, and deportation of Jews,

23

Resistance members, and others to concentration camps. The Milice were considered even more dangerous than the Gestapo or SS because they were members of the local citizenry who had in-depth knowledge of villages, customs, dialects, and influential leaders.

Whole villages were routinely destroyed because they were suspected of harboring members of the Resistance or engaging in other subversive activities. No proof was necessary. A mere suspicion was enough to bring a massacre.

Even after the French surrender, there were still Free French forces scattered around Europe. During Operation Torch, the Algeria-Morocco military campaign that began on November 8, 1942, Vichy forces fought against invading Allies. The stiff Vichy resistance produced three hundred British and 700 Free French troop casualties.

In an angry response to Operation Torch, Germany seized all of France, including the *Zone Libré* or "Free Zone" in the south, which then became known simply as *Zone Sud* or "South Zone." The Vichy puppet government remained in existence in theory, although it had virtually no authority. Germany now had a vise-like grip on the entire country.

FDR reacted by severing diplomatic relations with France and recalling American Ambassador Admiral William D. Leahy who returned to Washington as Chairman of the Joint Chiefs of Staff.

In February of 1943, the "*Service du Travail Obligatoire*" or "Compulsory Work Service" was established which required all French men between 18 and 20 to be deported to work in Germany. A total of 600,000 to 650,000 workers were sent there over the next two years but, faced with that prospect, there were many thousands who disappeared into the hills to join the Resistance.

Simone de Cruzel's uncle and mentor, Brigadier General Édouard Corniglion-Molinier, was a national hero in France. Few people deserved more to be called a "Renaissance Man." A World War I flying ace, he was one of only three pilots to shoot down at least 40 enemy airplanes. A founder of the Resistance, he went on to be one of the original 60 members of Charles de Gaulle's *Compagnon de la Liberation* (Free French National Council).

A section of Nice Airport, the extension of the Promenade des Anglais toward the west to Saint-Laurent-du-Var, was named "Promenade Courniglion Molinier." A commemorative coin was issued with his likeness. Holder of a Doctorate in Law, he held a number of high-level government positions including Minister of Public Works,

Brigadier General Édouard Corniglion-Molinier

Transportation, and Tourism as well as Minister of Justice. If that isn't a diverse enough background, he also became a film producer with such pictures as *The Brighton Twins, Drama Funny, Mollenard*, and *Hope* to his credit.

Simone hated what was happening to her country. After she privately shared those feelings with her uncle, he paused for a few seconds, looked her straight in the eyes, and asked if she would be willing to do something that could make a difference. Admiring her intelligence, tenacity, and ingenuity, the Brigadier General saw something very special in her. He wanted to know if she'd be willing to join the Resistance as well as spy for Britain.

A difficult person to refuse, he told her simply, "France needs you!" She looked around the room to see if he was talking to someone else. "Yes, you!" he asserted. "But I'm just a teenager," she exclaimed. He responded, "I know. The question is whether you want to REMAIN just a teenager."

She then asked, "Can I discuss this with my mother and father?" "Absolutely not," he insisted, "No one can know, not even your sisters." Simone indicated that she understood and then added, "But, if I make a mistake, the lives of everyone in my family could be in danger." He gave her a steely-eyed stare, paused again, and then said clearly and slowly, "Then don't make any mistakes."

For the first time, she saw her uncle in an entirely different light. Not as the kindly, nurturing person she'd always gone to for advice but as the no-nonsense, battle-hardened Brigadier General. There would be many times that she'd recall that exchange and remember his emphatic words - "Then don't make any mistakes."

There's no way she could refuse him. It's as if she matured into a woman on the spot. Simone accepted his offer and was ready to devote her life to help liberate her country. "Yes, I'll do it," she declared. "Good, someone will contact you," he said. "Who will it be?" she asked naively." He smiled and responded, "It doesn't matter what they call themselves. It won't be their real name." Their conversation over, he put one of his large hands over her two folded delicate hands and patted them. He didn't have to say anything more. Simone knew he had wished her good luck.

What exactly did the Brigadier General see in her? The young socialite didn't fit the image of the savvy spy portrayed in movies. In truth, the best kind of operative is one who doesn't look like and act like one. In other words, it's someone who can blend in and not arouse suspicion. Other classic characteristics he identified in her include:

High native intelligence. There's a good reason that a spy is always a member of an "Intelligence" organization. A prerequisite is the ability to outsmart others. An excellent memory, quick decision-making ability, and unusually good attention to detail are mandatory. **People skills.** Being able to read and understand people, gain their trust, quickly recognize their weaknesses, and in many cases deceive them is critical. Some of this can be learned but a lot of it is having good instincts and being willing to trust those instincts. **Adaptability.** A spy has to be able to make use of existing resources, react quickly in changing circumstances, and be or do whatever the situation requires. It involves being used as an "asset" like a chess piece. A knight, rook, or pawn can be used to kill another piece, serve as a decoy, or even be sacrificed for the greater good. An asset is used for whatever purpose is deemed necessary at the time. **Courage.** There's no way around it. A spy is a soldier who is not issued a uniform. It requires a willingness to sacrifice everything you have, including your life, and not betray the cause under any circumstances.

Simone began to learn her trade. She became adept at telling lies. She started by frequently telling her parents that she was simply "going out." They assumed that boys were involved and they were right. Just not the kind of boys they thought.

She was taught how to operate a radio, send as well as receive Morse Code messages, employ surveillance and eavesdropping techniques, utilize information exchange protocols and procedures, etc. This was war-time crisis mode. Her training was given to her as quickly as she was able to absorb it. New operatives were desperately needed to replace those who had been captured or killed.

Did she have what it takes to succeed? She knew that question would have to be answered by her deeds. It's an easy thing to take a stand for or against something by casting a vote in a ballot box. It's quite another to risk your life by carrying weapons and explosives. The same kind of courageous person who actively participated in the French Revolution was likely the one who would have been willing to fight for the French Resistance. It was a hodge-podge of people with very diverse backgrounds willing to do the hard, dirty work required. There was nothing glamorous or romantic about it.

There's one additional factor that led to success - a commitment to do whatever it takes to achieve an objective. Sometimes "whatever it

27

takes" was within the law but in many cases it was not. According to author István Deák, being a member of the French Resistance meant being willing to live a criminal life: "In order to be able to print and distribute illegal newspapers, one had to steal strictly controlled printing paper and machines and to forge or steal ration cards, banknotes, residence permits and identity cards. To fight the enemy, the resisters needed to seize arms from military garrisons or from rival resisters. All this required the talents of a burglar, a forger and a thief."

Jean-Pierre Levy, leader of the *Franc-Tireur* Resistance in southern France, described the life this way: "We lived in the shadows as soldiers of the night, but our lives were not dark and martial. There were arrests, torture, and death for so many of our friends and comrades, and tragedy awaited all of us just around the corner. But we did not live in or with tragedy. We were exhilarated by the challenge and rightness of our cause."

Simone trained as a nurse, not knowing how important that would soon become. She joined the FFI (*Forces Francaises de L'Interior*), the fighting arm of the French Resistance known colloquially as the "Fee Fee." The Resistance in many rural areas was called *La Maquis*, a French word for the "little bushes." Why? "Because we spread everywhere over the mountains and land," she declared proudly.

Also agreeing to spy for the British, she was assigned the Code Name of "SISTER" by the War Office in London and given the torn left half of a five-franc note with the number "283" on it. The iconic "Helmeted Woman" proudly facing the future was pictured on the front of the bill. The watermark was a young male warrior's head which stood for the battle against oppression from *La Marseillaise*. This particular currency was well-chosen for its meaning. The right half of the note was kept in a top secret area of the London War Office to identify her as a member of the intelligence organization known as the SOE (Special Operations Executive.)

Under the direction of Winston Churchill, British Minister of Economic Welfare Hugh Dalton formed the SOE on July 22, 1940. Its mission was to conduct espionage, sabotage, and "irregular warfare," the British equivalent of American "special operations." Nicknamed "The Baker Street Irregulars," "Churchill's Secret Army," and "Ministry of Ungentlemanly Warfare," the agents supported those in Nazi-occupied countries. They were also sent by parachute or small boats to work undercover. There was even a contingent group set up to assist the British Underground in the event the country was over-run by the Nazis.

The SOE depended on its wireless network which, of course, referred to radio communication at the time. Being caught sending or

Simone's Spy I.D.

receiving messages from behind enemy lines would typically lead to torture and a death sentence. It became one of the war's most dangerous occupations. A total of 118 of the 470 British SOE agents sent into France were never heard from again. By 1945, the organization employed more than 13,000 full-time people.

Simone's initial assignment was to deliver a picnic basket filled with explosives. Upon entering a train, she was dismayed to see that the only empty seat was between two German soldiers. Not wanting to look suspicious, she casually sat down between them. She knew if she dropped the basket, her life and the lives of a number of others would be over. Maintaining her composure and only looking down at the floor, she carefully got off and handed the TNT over to her Underground contact. The explosives were used in acts of sabotage against the Nazis. Simone breathed a sigh of relief. She had proven herself to be capable, not only to her handlers but, more importantly, to herself. Her first mission over, she felt energized and ready for more. Working as a courier and radio operator handling communications within her sector in France, Simone's job became more dangerous when the Germans began patrolling the streets with radio vans trying to locate transmission devices. Many people became reluctant after that to have their homes used as part of the communication network. She cleverly snuck a Morse Code machine into an old schoolhouse that the Germans were using as a headquarters. A seemingly-innocent former school principal who had been allowed to stay in her home on the top floor agreed to keep the device. When Simone visited her to transmit communications, the signals picked up by the radio vans were assumed to be messages emanating from the headquarters.

"The Germans were on the first floor of the schoolhouse and we were on the top floor. They are so stupid. They didn't see what was right under their noses," scoffed Simone.

There were other times when things didn't go as well. She worked with a group of Boy Scouts who were caught by the Gestapo with explosives and messages in their hands while they were standing near her. She watched in disbelief while the young boys were shot and their bodies urinated on by the troops. She knew she had to be careful to try to contain her emotions. The Germans glanced in her direction but left her alone. It worried her that they did not seem to pay attention to her. On the other hand, she was relieved that she, too, wasn't killed.

After many successful missions, her luck finally ran out because of a German spy known only as "SIMPSON" who approached French people offering them passage to London on his boat. The unsuspecting victims were led into a German ambush and shot. Simone followed

"SIMPSON," photographing him and taking notes on his actions. During one of the encounters, he suddenly turned to her and asked, "Do you have enough information on me?" She feigned innocence by responding, "I don't know what you're talking about," but realized that her identity had been compromised.

The Underground instructed her to keep moving around the Nice area, knowing that she would be tailed. She bumped into one of her followers to ensure she'd get a good look at him so she could give a description to her handler. Simone nervously awaited her fate in the cat and mouse game.

On Monday, March 13, 1944, she was standing on the sidewalk with her sister Jacqueline when a black Gestapo car suddenly pulled up next to them. Jacqueline protested saying, "Something is wrong. This is a mistake." But Simone knew it was no mistake.

Before they grabbed her, Simone whispered to her sister that she was with the Resistance and she needed Jacqueline to take her journal that was hidden in the family house and burn it because it contained contact information that could cost people their lives. Jacqueline promised she would carry out the task and hugged her sister good-bye. Simone asked her to let their parents and Monique know she loved them. Jacqueline watched as Simone was taken away, wondering if she would ever see her again. Until that moment, no one in Simone's immediate family had known about her clandestine activities.

She was handcuffed and thrown into the back seat of a Mercedes 260D sedan. The sinister-looking black car, rather than becoming famous as the first diesel passenger car, became known as the "Death Mobile" since it was used in hunting down Jews. Simone sat between two burly prison guards while a Gestapo officer occupied the front passenger seat next to the driver. They asked her no questions and she didn't speak, knowing the less she said, the better off she'd be.

She was taken to a dingy three-story concrete building known only as the Nice "Maison d'Arrêt" or literally "Stopping Place" on 12 Rue de la Gendarmerie on the east side of the city. Although it was built in 1887, just 57 years earlier, the three-story dilapidated structure both looked and smelled like it hadn't been cleaned since the Middle Ages. There was no registration process. They didn't have her fill out any forms. There was no trial, no judge, no formal charge filed. Instead, they ripped the clothes off her body and gave her a plain grey prison suit. There was no women's version. All inmates got the same suit. She expected to be put in a prison cell but instead a Gestapo officer came in and bellowed the order, "Take her to THE ROOM!"

Her worst fears were realized. After she was dragged to the basement, she looked around and quickly recognized the frightening fact that "THE ROOM" was a torture chamber.

Chapter 4 – The Man from Middle America

Luther Stalnaker was offered and accepted a position as pastor of the Congregational Church in Brookfield, Connecticut. It came with an opportunity to teach at the prestigious private Curtis School for Boys, which provided free tuition for his three children. Josephine was delighted to be the only girl in a school for boys, enjoying the attention she received from the other students.

During the period the family spent in southeastern Connecticut, Luther earned a Ph.D. from Yale in 1929 to go along with the B.S. degree he received in 1920 from Drake. After four years, he returned home to the United Church of Christ in Des Moines as Head Minister and also conducted services at the Drake University Chapel. Luther began teaching Philosophy at Drake as an Assistant Professor. He went on to receive a full Professorship, became head of the department, and was named Dean of the College of Liberal Arts in 1940. He was also a board member of Iowa's American Civil Liberties Union and was eventually named Chairman of the Board.

After attending Callanan Middle School in Des Moines, George became an outstanding track athlete at Theodore Roosevelt High School, competing in and winning the State Half Mile Championship in 1934. He hoped to attend West Point but was an alternate for two straight years, during which time he attended Drake University.

After completing his third application, he received a letter with a U.S. Military Academy return address. His parents watched him open it. He once again had that look of disappointment on his face as he said, "I didn't get in." "Did they say anything else?" asked Luther. "I came close," responded George dejectedly. "I was the third alternate from Iowa. I'll just complete my last two years at Drake. That's it. I'm done trying." It looked like his dream of flying airplanes as an Army officer might be just that - a dream and nothing more.

Several weeks later, he received further correspondence from West Point. This time, good fortune was on his side. Both of the first two choices got sick and George received his coveted appointment. Excitedly opening the letter, he looked at his parents exclaiming, "I got in!" It was a proud moment in what was to be a lifetime of proud moments. He entered the Academy in 1937 with a double major of English and Civil Engineering, knowing he had to put in a full four years since they did not accept transfer credits from other schools. It didn't bother him at all. The extra two years of maturing would help prepare him for what was to come.

West Point Stamp

George Stalnaker's West Point Class Ring

What does it take to qualify for the U.S. Military Academy? A well-rounded high school background in academics, athletics, and extracurricular activities is a prerequisite. That's only the beginning, though. It also requires being nominated by a member of Congress as someone having the intangibles required to join the ranks of a long list of people who have made important contributions to society, including countless military generals and CEO's along with 18 astronauts, 74 Medal of Honor recipients, and 90 Rhodes Scholars. Up to 10 candidates can be named to compete for a single vacancy. Most members of Congress rank their recommendations, as in George's case, but a few prefer naming a single candidate. There is a restriction that the members of the House of Representatives and the Senate can only have five of their constituents attending the Academy at any one time.

The stated mission of West Point is "To educate, train, and inspire the Corps of Cadets so that each graduate is a commissioned leader of character prepared for a career of professional excellence and service to the Nation as an officer in the United States Army." The honor code of "A cadet will not lie, cheat, steal, or tolerate those who do" is taken very seriously. Those who break it are subject to expulsion. On May 26, 1937, George's first year, the Post Office issued an iconic 5-cent stamp honoring the Academy. It showed several of the classic buildings with the stated values of "Duty, Honor, Country" under the West Point name.

George was thrilled to take the cross-country train ride from Iowa in June of 1937 to begin his military career at West Point. He was greeted on "R-Day" (Reception Day) and then started the grueling 6½ weeks of CBT (Cadet Basic Training), known to those who have endured it as "Beast Barracks." The most physically and emotionally demanding part of the four years at West Point, CBT is designed to jump-start the transition from the civilian to the military world and, at the same time, begin to teach a West Point Cadet how to look, think, and act like a military leader.

There are commonly asked questions about life at the Academy now listed on West Point's web site. One of them is, "How does CBT differ from the basic training for enlisted personnel?" It gives this answer - "Overall, Beast is exciting! The upper class cadets are professional and knowledgeable, and there will be a great focus on overcoming fears and forging a unit." It's a certainty that whoever wrote that did so with a chuckle. It is quite true, however, that after that short time in CBT, a cadet will have few fears left to overcome and a permanent camaraderie will be formed among those who have shared the experience.

After successfully completing Beast Barracks, George joined "The Long Gray Line," the continuum of cadets that have earned the right to gaze at the famous "million-dollar view" of the Hudson River near the parade grounds. One of his favorite stories involved the time he tried to show off for his then-girlfriend on those parade grounds. A Platoon Leader, George left his assigned position at the side of his men calling out marching orders to run to the front, unleash his saber, and march his platoon to the area of the bleachers where she was sitting. At least, that's what he thought he was doing. He heard an instructor call out, "Mr. Stalnaker, take command of your troops!"

It turned out that no one had followed him. His cadets were several hundred yards away marching across the tennis courts. He had to run to catch up with them. The girlfriend was not impressed. It might not surprise you to learn he was not a top student, finishing in the bottom third of his class.

George stated proudly, "At the Academy, we marched to class, to chapel, to the mess hall, etc. We marched everywhere. There was discipline. Our rooms were spartan in nature. There were no women cadets."

The campus, located 50 miles north of New York City, may be called "Hell on the Hudson" by some. For him, though, it was reaching a cherished goal. George claimed, "I was proud to be a military man, a graduate of West Point, to be a member of its Long Gray Line, and to have belonged to the magnificent Class of 'Black 1941.'"

No one knows why this particular class earned that distinctive nickname. The most widely accepted explanation is that the cadets had a lot of black marks against them for an unusual number of infractions, which might include such things as having a piece of lint on a uniform or being late for class. These could bring a penalty of several hours of "Punishment Tours" which are "walked off" by having a cadet in full dress uniform carry a weapon while marching in the central area of the barracks courtyard. Typically, this is done on a Friday night or Saturday. Those who spend a lot of time on "Punishment Tours" are called "Area Birds." Those accumulating over 100 hours carry the dubious distinction of being "Century Men."

Sometimes, "Fatigue Tours" are given which involve latrine duty or other forms of manual labor. If a cadet is in academic trouble, then "Sitting Tours" might be assigned which are like detention in high school with mandatory study time. The cadets must report to a large room on a Sunday and sit on uncomfortable stools with their noses buried in books. All cadets who have punishment hours must march, walk, or sit them off no later than a week before graduation. Many of them look forward to visits to the Academy by Heads of State since those dignitaries have the authority to grant amnesty to all those who have accummuated punishment hours.

Freshmen at West Point are considered fourth class and are called Plebes, which comes from Plebeians, the lowest classification of people in ancient Rome. Sophomores are third class or Yearlings, derived from the term for animals that are a year old. Before their junior year, the second class cadets are granted a summer of leave, leading to the tradition of calling them Cows as in "When the cows come home." The assumption is that when they go home to their mother's cooking, they'll come back fat as a cow. Finally, seniors are Firsties signifying that they are "First Class Cadets."

George cherished his West Point ring which would have special significance in his military career. West Point was the first college in the U.S. to award class rings, given at a dinner and dance called a "Hop" during a cadet's senior year. After the ring ceremony, the Firsties are surrounded by Plebes who must memorize and recite the words of the "Ring Poop." Only after that is a Plebe given permission to touch a Firstie's ring. The Ring Poop goes like this:

"Oh my Gosh, sir! What a beautiful ring! What a crass mass of brass and glass! What a bold mold of rolled gold! What a cool jewel you got from your school! See how it sparkles and shines? It must have cost you a fortune! May I touch it, may I touch it, please, sir?"

This tradition has remained unchanged through the years with the exception of the word "Ma'am" which has now been added following "Sir." Cadets can tap the ring against a hard surface to gain attention. If there is a disagreement on any subject, "Ringknockers" have the right to force underclassmen to adopt their point of view.

One practice that has not survived the passage of time is the final exam that George and his classmates had to take for a class on horsemanship. They were required to transverse a maze while blindfolded. That is, THEY were blindfolded, not the horses. Most of the other West Point traditions are the same as when George attended school there. He and his girlfriend, for example, used to stroll along a wooded lane called "flirtation walk," the same place where cadets court their dates today.

The 424 graduates of the "Class of Black '41" came from every one of the then-48 states, as well as Hawaii and Puerto Rico. On June 11, they listened to the somber graduation speech given by Secretary of War Henry L. Stimson who warned, "Usually commencement is a time of rejoicing and congratulations as we elders give good wishes to the young men who are beginning life's journey. But that is hardly the

37

atmosphere that surrounds our country today. And I have the feeling that I should be false to the responsibility which is laid upon me by the invitation to meet here if I did not try to help you to understand the nature of the crisis which confronts us all today, and to give you encouragement in meeting it. The work of meeting it may fall, in large measure, upon your shoulders."

At the end of the graduation ceremonies, the cadets were told, "Class dismissed!" and the band accompanied them as they sang the Alma Mater:

"Hail, Alma Mater dear,
To us be ever near,
Help us thy motto bear
Through all the years.
Let duty be well performed,
Honor be e'er untarned,
Country be ever armed,
West Point, by thee.

Guide us, thy sons, aright,
Teach us by day, by night,
To keep thine honor bright,
For thee to fight.
When we depart from thee,
Serving on land or sea,
May we still loyal be,
West Point, to thee.

And when our work is done,
Our course on earth is run,
May it be said, 'Well Done;
Be Thou At Peace.'
E'er may that line of gray
Increase from day to day,
Live, serve, and die, we pray,
West Point, for thee."

Words by Paul S. Reinecke (West Point, 1911)
Melody by Friedrich Wilhelm Kuecken

George Stalnaker as student

The Class of '41 cadets tossed their hats in the air and, as 2nd Lieutenants, began their military obligation of five years of active duty in exchange for the four years of education plus room and board they received for free. As of that moment, George became an officer in the U.S. Army. His classmate Paul Skowronek bragged, "We were willing to take chances. West Point was preparation for anything and everything. We weren't afraid of very much."

Black '41 didn't disappoint. They earned the right to be called part of "America's Greatest Generation," a term introduced by news broadcaster and journalist Tom Brokaw decades later, as they fought the brutal two-front wars in Europe and the Pacific. Of the 424 West Point graduates that day, approximately one hundred, close to 24%, would be killed or wounded in combat, clearly a group of people that knew the meaning of the word "sacrifice." Virtually every one of them when asked about their service would say something to the effect of, "I was just doing my job. Doing what was expected of me."

One member of the class, Air Force Gen. George Brown, was named the Chairman of the Joint Chiefs of Staff. Unfortunately, his tenure was during the 1974-78 period when he had to preside over the withdrawal from Viet Nam.

The Class of 1941 also produced World War II's first Medal of Honor recipient, 2LT Alexander R. Nininger, Jr. of the 57th Infantry, who was recognized for his bravery in action near Abucay, Bataan in the Philippine Islands. On January 12, 1942, although wounded three times, the 23-year-old nicknamed "Sonny" single-handedly attacked several groups of Japanese snipers in trees and fox holes with his rifle and hand grenades.

President Roosevelt posthumously presented him with the nation's highest military honor. The First Division of Cadet Barracks at West Point was named after him and the Association of Graduates of the US Military Academy created the "Alexander R. Nininger Award for Valor at Arms" to be given to West Point graduates who have displayed courage in combat and upheld the values of West Point.

Another noteworthy graduate, William T. Seawell, served as Chairman of the Board and Chief Executive Officer of Pan Am World Airways and became the Commandant of Cadets for the U.S. Air Force Academy.

George's classmate Colonel Henry Bodson trained an infantryman named Audie Murphy. After being abandoned by his father and then seeing his mother die, Murphy joined the Army at age 17 and became America's most decorated war hero, receiving every available military combat medal. He was presented with the Medal of Honor for single-handedly holding off a full company of German soldiers near Holtzwihr in France. Despite being wounded and out of ammunition, he led a successful counterrattack by jumping into a still-burning M4 Sherman tank and firing its .50 caliber machine gun. After World War II, he became an actor and starred in the movie, *To Hell and Back*, based on his 1949 autobiography of the same name.

"West Point is not about making soldiers," explained another graduate, Edward L. Rowny, "it's about making leaders." The Lt. General should know. He went on to advise five Presidents and negotiate nuclear disarmament with the Soviet Union as the U.S. representative to the SALT (Strategic Arms Limitation Talks.)

The West Point Class of '15, known as "The Class the Stars Fell On," was largely responsible for leading the auspicious Black '41. Five-star Generals Dwight Eisenhower and Omar Bradley were among the 59 generals from the graduates that formed the core of the World War II U.S. Army leadership.

To meet the demand for new officers, the number of cadets in the Class of 1942 was increased from 1,960 to 2,496; the class of 1943 graduated six months early; and the subsequent four classes graduated a full year early.

The U.S. Army gave birth to the Air Force in three stages. The Army Air Corps was formed in 1926; the Army Air Forces in George's graduation year, 1941; and the autonomous Air Force in 1947. The U.S. Air Force Academy later opened in Colorado Springs, CO on April 1, 1954.

After the sharp reduction in military spending during the Great Depression, just 184 pilots graduated from the Army Air Corps Advanced Pilot Training school in 1937. The entire U.S. Army had only 180,000 soldiers at the time, ranking it as number sixteen in the world. It was smaller than the armies of such countries as Czechoslovakia, Spain, Poland, Turkey, Portugal, and Romania while just slightly ahead of Bulgaria.

After the fall of France in 1940, there was an urgent need to prepare the American military for participation in the war, a possibility which seemed more and more likely. President Roosevelt persuaded Congress to increase annual national defense spending from $1.9 billion to $10 billion. By 1945, the budget swelled to $59.8 billion per year.

In order to attract volunteers, the salary for a private in the U.S. Army was raised from $252/yr. to $600/yr., an increase of 138%. To put that in perspective, a loaf of bread at that time cost 8 cents, a gallon of milk went for 34 cents, the price of a stamp just 3 cents, a pound of butter was 42 cents, a dozen eggs went for 45 cents, a gallon of gasoline would set you back 18 cents, and the minimum wage was 30 cents an hour. The average worker's salary was $1,315/yr.

The demand for pilots quickly expanded to 7,000 to be trained per year. The Air Corps contracted with nine civilian flying schools to help fill the need. By 1941, there were 45 schools involved. That number increased to 63 with 31 airfields providing basic training by 1943. American pilot training schools produced a total of 250,000 graduates in all by the end of World War II.

Several months after George's graduation, December 7, 1941 was a sleepy Sunday morning at Pearl Harbor in Hawaii, home of the American Pacific Fleet. Sailors and Marines were preparing for a softball game on a nearby pier. Others were getting ready for a tennis tournament aboard the battleship *USS Nevada*. Many planned to attend church services. There was limited duty with the usual beautiful weather, good visibility, and only scattered to broken clouds.

Cornelia Fort, a 22-year-old Sarah Lawrence College graduate, was at work early as a civilian pilot instructor conducting a routine training flight with a student in an Interstate Cadet Monoplane. The only other American planes in the air at the time were several other civilian aircraft.

As the Cadet approached the airfield from the southeast about 200 feet above ground, Cornelia saw a military plane heading directly toward them. Grabbing the controls from her student, she pulled up over the oncoming craft. Assuming it was a hot-dogging Army pilot, she looked down, hoping to get the plane's registration number. She blinked in disbelief, however, when she saw the Rising Sun insignia on the wings. Later admitting, "The air was not the place for our little baby airplane," she made an emergency landing at the John Rodgers civilian airport, close to the mouth of the harbor.

She and her student hurriedly taxied to the service hanger and then ran for cover as the Japanese Zero strafed her plane. Cornelia cried out, "The Japs are attacking!" to those working in the hanger but was met with loud laughter because they thought she was joking. Moments later, a mechanic ran in shouting, "That strafing plane that just flew over killed Bob Tyce." The co-owner of K-T Flying Service and his wife were standing outside watching smoke billow from Pearl Harbor when he was hit in the head by fire from the Zero.

Cornelia went on to volunteer for the WAFS (Women's Auxiliary Ferrying Squadron), a precursor to the Women's Air Force Service Pilots. Sadly, she became the first WAFS fatality when another plane struck the left wing of the BT-13 she was ferrying in a mid-air collision near Merkel, Texas. Her tombstone was inscribed, "Killed in the

Service of Her Country." She'll always be remembered as the first American pilot to encounter the Japanese during the Pearl Harbor attack.

Back in Washington, D.C., President Franklin D. Roosevelt was in his study finishing lunch when he received an emergency telephone call from Frank Knox, Secretary of the Navy. He was told that, literally from out of the blue, the Japanese had attacked the American military. Roosevelt called in his top aides as they began receiving reports about the damage done to ships, planes, and buildings.

George was shocked to learn that the Japanese Air Force had destroyed much of the Pacific Fleet in the ninety-minute attack which began at 7:48 a.m., Hawaii time. Like virtually all Americans, he spent the day listening intently to the radio to learn the terrible details. The Japanese had launched 353 fighters, bombers, and torpedo planes from six aircraft carriers. No one outside of the Japanese military knew what a torpedo plane was until that day. The Japanese had developed the technology and rehearsed launching torpedoes from the air for months.

Eighteen ships were sunk, including eight battleships, and 350 aircraft destroyed or damaged. A total of 2,402 Americans were killed and 1,280 wounded. The Japanese were seeking to incapacitate the U.S. Navy to prevent interference with their expansion plans in Southeast Asia.

The following day, the Secret Service tried to obtain a bulletproof car to transport FDR to Congress to deliver his famous "Infamy" speech but government regulations prohibited spending more than $750 per vehicle. He was forced to use Al Capone's armored limousine, seized by the Treasury Department in 1931 after his arrest for tax evasion. The President tried to ease the tension by joking, "I hope Mr. Capone won't mind."

President Roosevelt made the Declaration of War address before Congress saying, "Yesterday, December 7, 1941 – a date which will live in infamy – the United States of America was suddenly and deliberately attacked by naval and air forces of the Empire of Japan. The United States was at peace with that nation and, at the solicitation of Japan, was still in conversation with its Government and its Emperor looking toward the maintenance of peace in the Pacific."

According to Admiral Chester Nimitz, "On December 7, I was attending a concert in Washington, D.C., when I was paged and told there was a phone call for me. It was President Roosevelt who informed me I was being named Commander of the Pacific Fleet."

On Christmas Day, he was given a boat tour of Pearl Harbor and what was left of his fleet. "There was such a spirit of despair, dejection and defeat — you would have thought the Japanese had already won the war," claimed the ever-optimistic Nimitz. A young helmsman asked him what he thought of the destruction and he replied, "The Japanese either made three of the biggest mistakes an attack force could make or God was taking care of America." The Admiral went on to explain to those within earshot what he felt were these costly errors:

Mistake One: The Japanese attacked on Sunday morning. Nine out of every ten crewmen of those ships were ashore on leave. If those same ships had been lured to sea and been sunk, the casualties might have been 38,000 instead of 3,800.

Mistake Two: When the Japanese saw all the battleships lined in a row, they got so carried away sinking them that they didn't bomb the dry docks. If they had been destroyed them, every one of the damaged ships would have to have been towed to America to be repaired. As it was, the ships were in shallow water and could be raised. A tug boat could pull them over to the dry docks, and they could be repaired and at sea by the time it would have taken for them to be towed to America. The Admiral indicated he had already assembled crews anxious to man those ships.

Mistake Three: Every drop of fuel the Americans had in the Pacific theater was on top of the ground storage tanks five miles away. One Japanese plane could have strafed those tanks and destroyed the fuel supply. Instead, they were left untouched.

Realizing the unintended result of the attack, Marshal Admiral Isoroku Yamamoto, Commander-in-Chief of the Imperial Japanese Navy, is reputed to have admitted at the end of the day on December 7, "I fear all we have done is to awaken a sleeping giant and fill him with a terrible resolve."

American commitment to isolationism immediately disappeared. The country was ready for war. It was determined to win, no matter the cost.

Work began on one of the greatest salvage projects in history as all damaged ships were repaired and returned to service with the exceptions of the battleships Oklahoma, Utah, and Arizona. Beneath the Pearl Harbor Memorial, the latter still lies silent but continues to spill up to nine quarts of oil per day. Seeing the oil seep to the surface gives visitors the eerie feeling that the ship has just been sunk and it's still bleeding. There is a plaque that lists the names of those who were killed during the attack, as well as those of the 355 survivors who have subsequently chosen to have their remains interred with their shipmates.

Bullet holes from the Pearl Harbor attack can still be found in the walls of Hickam Army Air Field, Schofield Barracks, and Wheeler Army Airfield on Oahu Island. Repairs were never made as a tribute to those who lost their lives that day.

At the time of the Pearl Harbor attack, the top U.S. Navy command was called "CINCUS" (pronounced "sink us"). It didn't take long for the ill-chosen, embarrassing acronym for "Commander-In-Chief, U.S. Fleet" to be eliminated. President Roosevelt issued Executive Order #8984 on December 18, 1941 establishing the title of "COMINCH," standing for "Commander-in-Chief, U.S. Navy." Admiral Ernest J. King was given the position which included responsibility for the Atlantic, Pacific, and Asiatic Fleets along with naval coastal forces.

Hitler had no advance knowledge of the Japanese attack. The alliance between Germany and Japan was hardly an alliance at all. There was virtually no coordination between the two powers. It was more like a "Let's agree to keep out of each other's way." Three days later, America became the only nation on which Hitler was to declare war, even though he didn't have a compelling reason to do so. His failure to finish the British at Dunkirk, underestimation of the will of the French people to fight back, and assumption that America was not prepared to fight a two-front war are among the strategic errors he would come to regret.

Chapter 5 - The Widow Maker

Soon to become George's radio operator/gunner, tall Texan Jim Clark drawled, "On November 25, 1940, I was mobilized and sent by the Army to a little town by the name of Brownwood. There was no bus, no bars, no women – a bad, bad deal. After we had been there about a year, they came up with an offer that sounded really nice. They said anyone who would like to volunteer to go to California could go. I thought about it but decided not to take the offer. Those boys who went to get away from Brownwood were eventually captured by the Japs and were Prisoners of War for three and a half years."

Known as the "Texas Lost Battalion," the men of the 2nd Battalion, 131st Field Artillery were forced to swim ashore from the cruiser USS Houston when it was sunk on its way to the Philippines. Many managed to survive for 42 months in Japanese Prisoner of War camps in Burma and Thailand along what was called "The Death Railway."

Jim went on to say, "The Army Air Corps, as it was known back then, was grabbing up qualified enlisted men out of all the branches of the service so they could build an air force. At first they didn't have enough schools to send us to, so they just sent us on furlough. I was home 30 days and they sent me a telegram and said you have 30 more days. So, it ended up that I spent 58 days at home on $105 a month. That's quite a sum. It doesn't sound like much now, but $105 a month was a lot of money then. My father worked at the Santa Fe Railroad and only made $100 and he was taking care of a family on it."

As one of the 16.1 million Americans who served in uniform during World War II, George took flight training and earned his wings in March of 1942. At the time, flight school was nine months long and divided into three segments - primary, basic, and advanced training - each lasting three months. Pilots learned to fly using a two-seater training aircraft provided by civilian pilot training schools through the Civil Aeronautics Authority's War Training Service. They were required to take 65 flying hours in Stearman, Fairchild, or Ryan primary trainers.

Basic training stressed flying in formation, utilization of instruments, aerial navigation, flying at night, and long-distance flying. Typically, the cadets received 75 hours in BT-9 or BT-10 trainers. Finally, there was another 75 hours spent in advanced training in either single-engine or multi-engine aircraft. The single-engine pilots flew the AT-6 while multi-engine pilots learned on the AT-9, AT-10, AT-11, or AT-17. There were typically an additional two months of training to prepare pilots for combat. Single-engine pilots were placed in fighters or fighter-bombers and multi-engine pilots, like George, in transports or bombers.

As the need for pilots increased during the war, each phase was reduced first to 10 weeks and then to just nine weeks.

Assigned to Columbia Army Air Base in South Carolina, George began training on the Mitchell B-25 twin engine medium bomber. Manufactured by North American Aviation, the B-25 was named in honor of Major General William "Billy" Mitchell, a World War I pioneer of U.S. military aviation. Most thought the land-based plane was too large to take off from anything but a standard airfield runway. However, there were some high-ranking Navy officials that felt its low take-off speed combined with the lift that could come from the forward movement into the wind off an aircraft carrier would make it a candidate for ocean launch.

Lt. Colonel Jimmy Doolittle began to recruit volunteers for a mission involving sixteen B-25's to engage in a daring bombing raid over Tokyo to avenge the surprise attack on Pearl Harbor that had occurred four months earlier. After learning to get their planes airborne within a 500-foot runway to simulate taking off from the deck of an aircraft carrier, the group was transferred to Eglin Field in Florida and then Naval Air Station Alameda in California.

Their mission was top secret and the pilots were not told of the bombing target until their transport ship, the USS Hornet, had cleared the California coast. There was no practical way to allow the airplanes to land, refuel, and then be brought home. Yet, all the flight crews were willing to proceed.

After successfully dropping their payloads on Tokyo, all but one of the B-25's ran out of fuel before reaching the destination in China. Fifteen of the sixteen crews were either forced to bail out or crash-land their aircraft. Jimmy Doolittle received the Medal of Honor for the mission which captured the imagination and revitalized the spirit of the American public and the military.

Had George stayed with the B-25, there's a strong likelihood he would have been one of the Tokyo volunteers. Instead, he received orders to report to a base located just four miles from downtown Tampa, Florida. "All of South America is east of Tampa," George was fond of telling people. Some wouldn't believe him until they checked it out for themselves on a world map. He began training on the B-26, known as "The Widow Maker," not because of its effect on the enemy but because of the number of pilots it killed in training.

47

Originally established as Southeast Air Base on May 24, 1939, the name was changed to MacDill Field on December 1 of that year. It was eventually re-named MacDill Air Force Base on January 13, 1948. A World War I pilot who was Commander of an aerial gunnery school in St. Jean de Monte, France during World War I, Colonel Leslie MacDill was killed on November 8, 1938 in a crash of his North American BC-1.

Stung by the failure of various intelligence agencies to warn of the attack on Pearl Harbor, President Roosevelt established the OSS (Office of Strategic Services) to collect and analyze information and conduct covert operations. He was convinced that someone was needed to pull together the fractious intelligence services that often competed with one another for resources and jurisdiction.

A year earlier, FDR asked an old political opponent, a Republican attorney from his home state of New York, William J. Donovan, to detail a proposal for an over-arching intelligence service modelled after the British Special Operations Executive and MI6 (The Secret Intelligence Service.) Donovan was appointed as "Coordinator of Information" and had a plan but no staff and no real authority.

"Wild Bill," as he was called, finally got his funding on June 13, 1942 and took his agency from a one-man operation to a world-class organization of more than 10,000 by the end of the war. He employed analysts, field agents, commandos, saboteurs, and scientists in stations across the globe. Many inventions and gadgets are developed that help form the basis of modern spy organizations. There is now a statue of Donovan, often called the "Father of Modern American Espionage" in the main foyer of the Central Intelligence Agency's headquarters building in Langley, Virginia. It stands alongside a book containing the names of OSS personnel killed during World War II.

The surprising names of Wild Bill's "Glorious Amateurs," as he called them, were held secret until 2008. The eclectic group included chef Julia Child, Supreme Court Justice Arthur Goldberg, Chicago White Sox catcher Moe Berg, special assistant to JFK Arthur Schlesinger Jr., President Theodore Roosevelt's sons Quentin and Kermit, Ernest Hemingway's son John, actor Sterling Hayden, and Thomas Braden who was author of the book *Eight is Enough.*

According to Jim Clark, "I was sent to Hondo, Texas where I graduated on December 17, 1942 as a Navigator. I was not satisfied with that so they sent me to Carlsbad, New Mexico and put me through bombardier training. Then, I had a seven-day delay before they sent me to MacDill Field and I spent that time at my hometown in Lubbock where I had a sweet young girl friend waiting for me.

One night I was at South Plains Army Air Field, the only base in Lubbock, for a drink or two. I ran into a Captain out there. I was such a 'green' 2nd Lieutenant. I thought this Captain knew everything and I told him I would be going out to MacDill Field to fly B-26's. He said, 'Son, just turn in your suit. Just quit. Let them put you in jail. Do anything but don't get in one of those things. It's a death trap, sure enough.'

I rode the train from here to Tampa and stood up all the way and the conductors were very rude to everybody. The trains were real crowded. I sat on my luggage sometimes between the cars since there wasn't a seat. I got to MacDill and got to hear about 'One a Day in Tampa Bay.' They swore it was true. The airplane was new and it had a lot of bugs in it." The phrase refers to the frequent crashes during initial pilot training at MacDill which, unfortunately, were, in fact, averaging nearly one per day at the time.

Jim explained, "Most of the problems were in the Curtis Electric propellers. The Pratt & Whitney engines were real good but the propellers had a lot of trouble with them. The ship landed real fast and flew fast for a bomber. Back at that time, anyone who landed a B-26 on a single engine and was able to walk away from it was considered a hero.

I remember one time a guy named 'Peaky' Flat landed one on a single engine and must have been going 200 miles an hour. He knew he wasn't going around so he figured he ought to have plenty of speed when he hit the ground. He just kept going and almost went into the bay off the end of the runway. He ruined the airplane but they all walked away from it. They considered the job he did as good.

In the meantime, I was sitting around MacDill wondering when I was going to have to ride in one of the B-26's and was scared to death. Then one day, they scheduled me for my first flight so I crawled into the thing and up we went. The flight was uneventful until we got ready to come in and land. We slid in at 1,500 feet above the runway and it seemed like we got right near the end of it. Then, the first thing they did was increase the engine rpm for landing. I didn't know what it was but it made a whole lot of noise and vibration. I thought, 'Hell, the engines are blowing up!'

About that time, they dumped the landing gear down. The gear was real heavy and when it hit the bottom, it shook the whole airplane. I thought, 'Now it's falling apart.' They drove it onto the runway and landed about four feet off the ground. We FELL that other four feet and it crunched but didn't bounce because it was too heavy. We taxied over to where we were going to operate and I got listening to the two pilots talking. They said, 'Well, this is my first drive without an instructor, how about you?' The other guy said, 'Yeah, me too.' I had no idea that was the case and just thought, 'OH BOY! I sure was lucky.'

We were just organizing the 391st Bomber Group at that time. Colonel Gerald E. Williams was the Group Commander and Lt. George W. Stalnaker was our Squadron Commander. They were both West Pointers and knew what they were about. I got assigned to a real good pilot, although he was below a 2nd Lieutenant as what they called a 'Flying Sergeant.' Junior Olfson, from Alberton, Wisconsin, had been an instructor pilot on B-26's for several hundred hours and was probably one of the best pilots on the base. He was a big Swede, 6'1" and weighed about 230 pounds, and was strong as an ox. He could really fly that thing.

I soon had lots of confidence in Olfson and more and more in the airplane. Right then, we were training at low altitudes – way, way down. They transferred us to Myrtle Beach, South Carolina, a summer resort on the Atlantic coast, and we trained some more there.

There was a group flying in England and they sent a number of B-26's to bomb submarine pens in Holland. They were flying way down low to get under the German radar. The Germans, though, knew they were coming because the whole lot of them were shot down, except for one airplane. The reason he was not shot down was that he had an engine failure before he got there, had to drop his bombs in the ocean, and went back home before the Germans had a chance to shoot at him. About that time, they grounded all the B-26's. I guess you couldn't blame them."

The Truman Committee held hundreds of hearings and saved millions of dollars. Among the issues they tackled were the problems with the B-26's. Truman made a name for himself on the national stage because of his tireless efforts, personally logging more than 10,000 miles of travel. It served him well as he was chosen to be Roosevelt's Vice-President in 1944.

"By 1943, the 9th Air Force Commander is General Samuel E. Anderson and the African and Italian campaigns had happened," continued Jim, "and I thought surely the war would be over before I got overseas to do my part. We continued to train and they continued to improve the airplane. They lengthened the wing which slowed it down a bit but made it safer. Most of the 391st crews had been flying the plane for nearly a year. I imagine we had about the best trained crews around."

The first flight from MacDill was on February 7, 1941. While the airfield was being built, aircraft and troops were located at nearby Drew

Army Airfield. Troops were housed in "Tent City" until barracks opened on June 16, 1941.

Stanley W. Miller, nicknamed Stub, who would become George's tail gunner/armorer, gave this account of his introduction to the Army and a glimpse of what life was like at Tent City: "I left my bus from the YMCA in Benton Harbor, Michigan headed for Fort Custer and induction into the Army. My wife, mother, father, and sisters were there to see me off. It was a sad day for me as I had never been away from home and was leaving behind Bess, my bride of four months. When we arrived at Fort Custer, we were told to strip down and go through a line in a big warehouse-type of building where we received an examination, inoculation shots, and all the clothing we would have to our names.

I am now Pvt. Miller, 36453560, United States Army Air Corp. If I thought this was bad, I was totally unprepared for our first camp. We boarded a train for St. Petersburg, Florida and our camp was in a swamp area, a place called 'Tent City.' This is where I got my Basic Training. It was working out in the hot sun all day and the food was inedible. I avoided it and only ate when I could get into town on a pass. Then I stocked up on candy bars to take back. It was a real hell-hole and the government closed it down shortly after we left."

It's probably a good thing that Stub didn't eat the food as ptomaine poisoning ran rampant through Tent City. Fortunately, permanent barracks were soon built and the tents in the swamp became nothing more than bad memories for the soldiers.

The primary mission at MacDill was the training of units under the III Bomber Command. A total of 15,000 troops and nine of the twelve combat groups that would fly the B-26 in Europe trained at MacDill.

A Warner Brothers movie simply called "Air Force" was released on February 3, 1943 and regarded as one of the first propaganda films of World War II. It starred John Garfield, Arthur Kennedy, Gig Young, and George Tobias and included scenes shot at Drew Field using six MacDill-based B-26's painted as Japanese bombers. Even though the Tampa Bay air defenses were alerted to this fact, the U.S. Coast Guard mistakenly shot at the planes as they flew over the Gulf. Fortunately, none of them were hit.

That same year, a contingent of WACS (Women's Army Corps) troops arrived. Despite the fact that women were only allowed to participate in non-combat support roles, World War II brought a significant and permanent change to America and other Allied countries regarding their role. Many who didn't serve in uniform did their patriotic duty by helping to fill the labor shortage, particularly in

51

factories producing war material. American industrial output was one of the keys to the victory with 300,000 aircraft, 89,000 tanks, three million machines guns, and seven million rifles produced during World War II.

Virtually every American sacrificed in some way. Due to parts shortages, for example, the United States was able to manufacture only 139 civilian automobiles during the entire period of the war. There was rationing of gasoline, rubber, metal, food and anything else critical to the country's war effort. Even Hollywood did its part. The Academy Awards ceremonies continued but because of the metal shortage, temporary Oscars were given made of painted plaster rather than the customary Britannia metal plated in copper, nickel, silver, and 24-karat gold. After the war, recipients were able to turn in their temporary statuettes for real ones.

In the United States, posters of "Rosie the Riveter" gave tribute to women who performed factory work previously done by men who were deployed overseas. It's believed the real-life "Rosie" was Rose Will Monroe, born in 1920 in Pulaski County, Kentucky, who worked at the Willow Run Aircraft Factory in Ypsilanti, Michigan helping to build B-24 bombers. Other women were used to publicize the same concept in other Allied countries.

Once they left the house, a significant number of women chose to remain in the work force because they liked working and their families certainly benefitted from a two-income household. In fact, it helped produce a postwar economic boom. The thinking began shifting from "women belong in the home" to "women belong wherever they want to be."

George began training on the troubled Martin B-26 Marauder at MacDill. He recalled, "We killed about 80 guys in three months at a time when they couldn't figure out why the B-26 was such a hard plane to fly. The propellers were flattening out on take-off and it just wasn't getting airborne. The B-26 landed at 140 mph at a time when most planes landed between 70 and 100 mph. Some of the new pilots reporting into MacDill actually took their wings off when they learned they were supposed to fly it. The B-26 was a real hot rod but the prop had a tendency to run away on take-off. Once it was fixed, it was fine. I cracked up a couple myself in MacDill and ditched one off Myrtle Beach."

In 1939, the U.S. Army Air Corps realized it was not properly equipped with medium bombers, depending only on aging Douglas B-18's and Martin B-10's, neither of which possessed the necessary performance, bomb load, or defensive armaments. Proposal #39-640 was issued, inviting 86 aircraft manufacturers to bid on the design and construction of a medium bomber capable of both high speed and the ability to carry a heavy bomb load. Until then, most had thought the two requirements were mutually exclusive.

The specifications required the capability to carry 3,000 pounds of bombs over a range of 2,000 miles with a top speed of more than 300 mph at a service ceiling exceeding 20,000 feet. Because of these stringent requirements, only seven manufacturers responded and just four of those met the criteria – the Martin, Douglas, Stearman, and North American companies.

The proposal of the Glenn L. Martin Company of Middle River, Maryland described an airplane assigned the company designation of Model 179. Martin chose a bright but relatively inexperienced 26-year-old aeronautical engineer, Peyton M. Magruder, to take charge of the critical project.

A unique character, Peyton, born at Fort Riley, Kansas, was the son of Army Brigadier General Marshall Magruder. Although the constant moves because of his father's military career caused him to attend four different high schools, he had the distinction of being accepted at both West Point and Annapolis. Choosing the Naval Academy, he was an all-round athlete as a pole vaulter on the track team and a member of the swim team. He also reportedly won $350 in bets by running five miles in an impressive 29 minutes and 37 seconds.

Peyton was so determined to enter the Army's aviation school that he resigned during his final year at the Naval Academy. Clearly, he was someone who blazed his own trails. Prior to joining the Martin Company, he became an engineer at the Naval Air Factory in Philadelphia.

Young Magruder and his team chose a low-drag profile fuselage with a circular cross-section. Since the Army wanted a high maximum speed but hadn't specified any limitation on landing speed, the team selected a high-mounted wing with a span of only 65 feet. Its small area gave a wing loading of more than 50 pounds per square foot. The wing was shoulder-mounted to leave the central fuselage free for bomb stowage. The engines chosen were two 1,850 horsepower Pratt & Whitney R-2800-5 Double Wasp air-cooled radials, the most powerful engines available at the time. They drove four-bladed 13 and one-half foot Curtiss Electric propellers.

The armament included a flexible 0.30-inch machine gun installed in the tip of a transparent nose cone and two 0.50-inch machine guns installed in a dorsal turret located behind the bomb bay, just ahead of the tail. This was the first power-operated turret to be fitted to an American bomber. Another 0.30-inch flexible machine gun was installed in a manually-operated tunnel position cut into the lower rear fuselage. There was also a 0.50-inch manually-operated machine gun installed in a pointed tail cone. The tail gunner had enough room to sit in an upright position, unlike the prone position in the B-25.

There were two bomb bays, fore and aft. The doors were unusual in that they were split in tandem, the forward pair folding in half when opened and the aft set being hinged to open forward. Two 2,000-pound bombs were carried in the main bomb bay and up to 4,800 pounds of smaller bombs could be carried in the aft bay.

Detailed design of the Model 179 was completed and submitted to a Wright Field board on July 5, 1939. Soon after, the twin-engine medium bomber contract was awarded to the Martin Company which later became part of Martin Marietta Corp., eventually merging with Lockheed Corp. to form defense contractor giant Lockheed-Martin.

On August 10, 1939, the Army ordered 201 B-26's with the contract approved on September 10, a record time for the government. Since the design had been ordered off the drawing board, there was no XB-26. In other words, there was no attempt to build a prototype, an unprecedented occurrence. The worsening situation in Europe and the Pacific necessitated taking an aircraft from the paper design stage to working model in such a short time. Critics felt the process was hasty and haphazard. Improvements to the initial design were literally made "on the fly."

The first B-26 flight was November 25, 1940 with test pilot William K. Ebel at the controls, Ed Fenimore as co-pilot, and Al Malewski as navigator. The initial 113 hours of flight testing went well and there were few modifications. The production aircraft were used for test purposes. On February 22, 1941, the first four B-26's were accepted by the Army Air Forces. The 22nd Bombardment Group based at Langley Field, Virginia was the first unit to fly the B-26. They had previously operated Douglas B-18's.

The last base model B-26 was delivered in October of 1941. Later that month, the Martin production line shifted over to the B-26A version. The task of training and manning new flight crews along with maintenance and armament personnel was daunting. It was the fastest bomber with the largest bomb load capacity, carrying more machine guns and cannon than any aircraft ever built. Further, there was no one in any capacity with any experience with the aircraft. No one had ever even seen it before. It was an untested airplane rushed into service.

Speed is usually a good thing for any aircraft in combat. However, the B-26 proved to be hard to handle due to its short wings and fighter plane maneuverability. It, unfortunately, had problems doing two very important things – taking off and landing.

The instruction manual for the aircraft indicated a speed of 150 miles per hour must be maintained on short runway approach or if one of the engines was lost. That was not a sentence to be disregarded. It was significantly faster than what most pilots were used to. Without that precise speed, the bomber tended to stall and crash. Further, most of the available runways weren't long enough for the B-26, weighed down by lots of armament and hampered by its short wings. So the phrase "short runway" in the instruction manual could be translated as "pretty much every runway."

A "Pilot to Pilot" description written by Clyde Harkins for www.b26.com demonstrates how complex it was to fly the plane. It wasn't like driving an automobile. Imagine following these lengthy operations in a high-stress combat situation:

Pre-Flight Procedure

"Check that landing gear lever is down and locked, pilot heater is off; emergency air brake bleeder valve is off; outside power source is connected to outlet in left nacelle, master, ignition and battery switches are off; blowers are in LOW position; oil cooler shutters are open; and carburetor air control lever is in the COLD position. Set mixture controls to IDLE CUT-OFF, set propeller governor control levers full forward to INCREASE RPM, set propeller toggle switches to AUTO CONSTANT SPEED and feather switches to NORMAL, move cowl flap lever to OPEN and then to NEUTRAL, and set inverter selector switch to ON position. Check fuel gage indicator level for all tanks.

For starting engines, turn battery switch on, set throttles approximately 3/4 inch open, clear propellers, notify ground crew, ensure fire guard is posted, turn master switch on, and turn left ignition switch to both magnetos. Switch left hand booster pump on and prime left engine for a few seconds. Hold energizer switch to left position until inertia flywheel reaches maximum RPM and turn primer switch on immediately prior to meshing the starter to the engine. Engage the starter to the engine by holding the mesh switch to the left position, at the same time hold the primer switch down until engine starts and then release both switches.

When engine starts firing, move mixture controls to AUTO RICH position. Manipulate the throttle to keep the engine running at 800 RPM initially until there is an indicated oil pressure and then increase to 1000 RPM. Start the right engine in the same manner. Turn booster pumps off and disconnect auxiliary power source. Check hydraulic pressure for

800 to 1050 pounds, set oil cooler shutters as required and put carburetor air control levers in COLD position. Adjust pilot's seat, tune radios, and contact control tower for taxi clearance and altimeter setting for airport pressure.

Take-Off Procedure

Taxi to take-off position; check brakes for proper functioning, check nose wheel for any shimming characteristic and position aircraft into the wind short of the runway for engine run-up checks. Move throttles to 1700 RPM, pull propeller levers back to observe reduced RPM and then forward to obtain 1700 RPM again, move propeller toggle switches to DECREASE RPM, FIXED PITCH, INCREASE RPM, and to CONSTANT SPEED RPM to observe proper functioning. Move throttles to 2100 RPM and set toggle switch to FIXED PITCH, check left engine magnetos by moving switch to LEFT magneto, then to BOTH, then to RIGHT magneto, then back to BOTH and observe that there is not more than a drop of 75 RPM while doing this. Move toggle switch back to CONSTANT SPEED RPM position. Next, check right engine magnetos in the same way.

Reduce throttles to 1000 RPM and then clear engines by advancing each one to 2700 RPM and observe temperature and pressure instruments to assure all are within green limits. Check operation of feathering switches. Lower flaps down to 1/4 position, turn booster pumps on, remove safety lock from landing gear lever, set trim tabs 5 degrees tail heavy for take-off and contact the tower for permission to move into take-off position on the runway.

Position aircraft on the runway, release brakes, move throttles to 52 inches manifold pressure and 2700 RPM, maintain directional control with coordinated brakes and then rudder control, raise nose wheel slightly off the runway at 80 MPH and hold that attitude until aircraft lifts off runway, raise landing gear immediately to obtain minimum single engine air speed of 140 MPH as soon as possible, retract wing flaps at 500 feet and 170 MPH, and set cowl flaps as required to maintain proper cylinder head temperature. Climb to desired altitude at 170 MPH using 37 inches manifold pressure and 2300 RPM, turn booster pumps off when leveling out, reduce power to 30 inches manifold pressure and 2000 RPM for cruising and move mixture controls to AUTO-LEAN when above 5000 feet.

Landing Procedure

During the preparation for landing, the center of gravity location should be checked if necessary using the Load Adjuster. Notify crew members to prepare for landing. Contact the airport tower to advise of landing intentions and obtain runway number in use, altimeter setting, wind velocity and direction, and any caution notices.

Set altimeter to station pressure, make sure blowers are in LOW position and safety cover is in place, adjust oil cooler shutters to maintain proper oil temperature, set carburetor air control levers to COLD position, move mixture controls to AUTO RICH when below 5000 feet, set propeller toggle switches to AUTO CONSTANT SPEED and propeller levers to 2250 RPM, turn fuel booster pumps ON, reduce speed on downwind leg to 165 MPH, place landing gear control lever in DOWN position and increase power to maintain 165 MPH. Check wheel position indicator on pilot's instrument panel to show gear is down, locked and in the green, and visually check to see that the landing gears are down.

Turn on final approach at 165 MPH and lower flaps while reducing speed to 150 MPH, establish uniform rate of descent to runway, during "flare out" smoothly reduce power while pulling the nose up gradually for landing on the main wheels. After touch down and speed is reduced, lower the nose wheel to the runway, leave cowl flaps open, attach safety lock on landing gear lever, retract wing flaps, turn fuel booster pumps off, push propeller governor levers forward to increase RPM position and taxi back to parking position."

Numerous nicknames were given to the B-26 and none of them were complimentary. It was called *The Baltimore Whore, The Flying Vagrant, One-Way Ticket, Martin Murderer, The Flying Coffin, The Coffin without Handles, and the B-Dash Crash.* It was also known as *The Wingless Wonder* because the plane's small wing area made it appear aerodynamically unstable. It was also popular to call it *The Flying Prostitute* because "it has no visible means of support."

One of the standing jokes at the time was "The newly minted Army Air Corps pilot went to the flight surgeon with a complaint. He complained, "Doc, I'm constipated all the time, what can I do?" After examination, the doctor offered, "I can give you a strong laxative or assign you to a B-26 outfit!" The flight crews would tell that story and laugh nervously afterwards.

There was an ode expressing a similar sentiment hand-written in bold black pen on the back of one of the pilot's seats:

"This is something
You don't see often.

Two engines mounted
On a coffin."

The Marauder was grounded in April of 1941 while the Army Air Forces considered taking it out of service. Jimmy Doolittle, now a General, took a test flight with co-pilot Paul Tibbets to help determine the fate of the aircraft. With a Ph.D. in Aeronautical Engineering from the Massachusetts Institute of Technology, Doolittle was more than qualified to help assess the readiness of the airplane. Colonel Tibbets would later pilot the Enola Gay which dropped the Atomic Bomb on Hiroshima. They decided that the design flaws could be fixed and training for the inexperienced pilots should be intensified. It proved to be a good decision as the B-26 turned into one of the workhorse aircraft of World War II.

In subsequent "A" through "G" models, modifications were made to the aircraft that rendered it safer. Included was an increase of wingspan and wing angle-of-incidence and a bigger vertical stabilizer and rudder. In addition, the dorsal turret, which was under development, was installed. Without it, there was an imbalance of weight across the air frame adding to the instability of the aircraft at lower speeds, causing the stalls on take-off and landing.

Despite the calamitous beginning for the B-26, a total of 5,157 were built and it became an extremely effective and reliable aircraft. Once the bugs were worked out in Peyton Magruder's hot rod, as George liked to call it, and the pilots properly trained how to fly it, the B-26 turned out to have the lowest combat loss rate - less than one half of one percent - of any U.S. aircraft during World War II.

Promoted to 1st Lieutenant in March of 1942 and Captain shortly thereafter in July, George was named a Squadron Commander and became adept at delegating responsibility and assignments. During an inventory of base-wide equipment, for example, the auditor asked about some mess hall items which seem to have a way of disappearing on military bases. George was responsible for the items but didn't know that he had signed for them or even where they were stored at MacDill, and he became concerned. So, he called in one of the NCO's known in the military as a "scrounger." It seems every outfit has one. George designated him as point man for the audit telling him to simply "take care of it."

"Sergeant Scrounger" was able to locate an entire chow hall full of brand new equipment and they passed the audit. George never asked him how he was able to get what was needed or what he had to give up in order to get it. He figured that it's best not to know certain things. The technical term for that is "plausible deniability."

In fact, George often didn't even bother to learn people's names. He compensated by typically using the term "Tiger" to refer to others. He'd rarely use "Buddy" or "Pal" but would fall back on "Tiger." "It just worked for him," commented his son Marc. "That's what he used throughout his life."

Promoted once again, this time to Major on July 30, 1943 while stationed at MacDill, George was ordered to Eglin Army Air Field in Valparaiso, Florida to perform the grim task of identifying the remains of seven B-26 crew members who had crashed into the Gulf of Mexico. The coroners were unable to match their decapitated heads with the mangled bodies and asked him for assistance. Knowing there would be no open caskets at the funerals, the son of a preacher said a silent prayer asking for forgiveness and quickly went up and down the line saying, "This head goes with this body, that head with this body, etc." George then left quickly to return to base before he could be asked any questions.

Chapter 6 – "With Wings and Courage"

The 9th Air Force's 391st Bomber Group was officially activated on January 21, 1943 with an initial force of 5,000 men. From then until October of 1945, more than 60,000 would participate in the war effort. No one could volunteer to get into the 391st. They had to be chosen. They were an elite bunch and they knew it. Their task was to combat the dreaded German military with a new, revolutionary, and untested airplane. They had to learn how to fly, maintain, arm, and patch up battle damage to get their B-26's back into the air again for the next mission. Many of them risked their lives in the process. They did it without hesitation.

The war had begun to turn in favor of the Allies but there was still much fighting left to be done. In its first major defeat, Hitler's army surrendered to the Soviet Union in Stalingrad on January 31, 1943. The devastating five-month battle killed a total of two million people, including half a million civilians. The brutality of the war against the Soviet Union was evidenced by the fact that four of every five Germans who died in World War II did so on the Eastern front. Another somber statistic is that 80% of Russian males born in 1923 did not survive the war.

After remaining at MacDill Field until May 23, 1943, the 391st Bomber Group moved to Myrtle Beach, South Carolina for bombardment training. On September 4, it relocated to Fort Knox's Godman Field, Kentucky, about 30 miles south of Louisville for four additional months of training where flight crews were assembled.

Nicknamed "Black Death," the 391st then received orders for overseas duty and departed Godman Field on January 1, 1944. Its motto was *Virtute Alisque* which stood for, appropriately, "With Wings and Courage." The insignia featured a shield with flight wings on top, a flying Pegasus on the upper right, and three feathers in a cluster on the lower left.

Some of the colorful nicknames given to the group's aircraft included *Steppin' Out, Idiot's Delight, Miss Behaving, Rationed Passion, Scrumptious, Thumbs Up, Tobacco Road, Little Pink Panties, Little Gal, Shady Lady, Dream Queen, Miss Laid, Homesick Papa, Sleepy Time Gal, The Grinning Gremlin,* and *Black Jack.* The frivolous names and colorful nose art on the planes belied the serious task ahead for members of "Black Death."

George was anxious to see action and would get more than his share. "Finally, in January, we went overseas," he recalled. "We were delayed a whole year because the first B-26 group in England was sent over as low-altitude aircraft. In the first two missions over Holland, there were virtually 100% losses. They moved us up to 12,000 feet and then we bombed from there."

A practical reason that many aircraft bomber crews preferred flying at low altitudes despite the risk of being easier targets for anti-aircraft guns was the fact that cabins were not pressurized. It wasn't until the B-29 Superfortress was introduced on May 8, 1944 that pressurization became available and was made standard in all aircraft. Prior to that, air crew members flying at high altitudes were prone to suffer from barotrauma caused by pressure differences, decompression sickness, altitude sickness, and hypoxia due to low oxygen levels in the blood. Planes were equipped with oxygen masks which frequently malfunctioned and restricted movement.

Another common occupational hazard of a World War II air crew member was hearing loss. Many would tell the story about how one of them remarked to his two friends, "Windy, ain't it?" The second one replied, "No. It's Thursday." The third one chimed in, "So am I. Let's have a beer."

The ground echelon of the 391st Bomber Group, composed of 67 officers and 1,078 enlisted men, received classified instructions to report to New York City, the port of embarkation, at exactly midnight on New Year's Eve. Here the group underwent intensive training to prepare for the trip abroad. On January 16, 1944, they boarded the French transport SS Ile de'France and the following morning departed for the British Isles.

A 1,786 passenger luxury ocean liner, the ship was the first built after World War I and was known for being beautifully decorated in the Art Deco style. In October of 1942, it was renovated and converted into a troop transport at St. Elizabeth Port in South Africa and began a five-year military service career.

After World War II, it was re-converted to a luxury liner with a maiden voyage to New York City in July of 1949. On July 26, 1956, it played an important role in a six-hour rescue of 753 passengers after the collision of the SS Andrea Doria and MS Stockholm off the Massachusetts coast near Nantucket Island. Before being scrapped, the Ile de'France was given the stage name of the "SS Claridon" and used in the 1960 movie *The Last Voyage* starring Robert Stack, George Sanders, and Dorothy Malone.

The 391st ground echelon arrived at its final destination in Matching, England on January 27, 1944. The flight echelon, composed of 250 officers and 57 enlisted men, left Godman Field early New

Year's Day for Hunter Field, Georgia, where modifications were made to the aircraft in preparation for its flight to the war zone.

George's closest friend, Stub Miller recounted, "My wife Bess came down to be with me until we left for overseas duty. Living quarters were very difficult to come by and we ended up in a basement apartment in the home of one of the Captains. It was right on base so it was very convenient. Christmas Eve and Day were spent at a hotel in Louisville. Neither of us had ever been away from home at Christmastime and it was the loneliest we had ever experienced – but glad to be together! But it got worse because on New Year's Eve, we spent the evening together for the last time for many months. At midnight, I said goodbye and walked to the barracks where I prepared to leave at 8 a.m. for overseas duty."

Bess commented, "Stub was teased as a kid because he was shorter than the others. They called him 'Stubby' which was shortened to 'Stub.' In our wedding pictures, you can see that we're both the same height – 5'5". We were high school sweethearts. Stub was a Drop Hammer Operator stamping out military equipment parts. At first he was told he wouldn't be drafted because of his occupation so we went ahead and got married. I was just 18 years old and he was 20. Then, he got his draft notice four months later and he had to report for duty. He was willing to go. Everyone was willing to go back then. I was upset, of course, but there was nothing I could do. After we were together in Louisville and he shipped out, I moved back home to be with my parents."

Since eight and one-half hours was the maximum time the B-26's could stay in the air with the amount of fuel they carried, the flight echelon made a number of stops along the way for refueling before landing at the final destination in Matching, England. From Kentucky's Godman Field they went back for a short while to Myrtle Beach and then to West Palm Beach, Florida before leaving for Borinquen Field, Puerto Rico. Taking the southern route to England, they traveled approximately 15,000 miles.

They flew to British Guiana, across the equator and over the mouth of the Amazon to Belem, Brazil. After getting delayed for several days because of heavy aircraft traffic, they went on to Natal, the eastern-most point of the South American continent. Then they flew 1,500 miles across the South Atlantic to Ascension Island which was little more than a runway that wasn't particularly straight. From there, they went to Roberts Field, Liberia. After that, it was on to Dakar and then to Marrakesh, French Morocco.

The next leg of the journey to Land's End in England was north over water. They couldn't go the direct route across Europe because it would have taken them over Spain and Portugal, which were neutral, and France, which was under German occupation. The long way over water was about the limit of their range.

The winds were from the north and there was concern that the armada might not have enough fuel to make it across the ocean. They got stuck in Marrakesh for a while, waiting in vain for the winds to subside. They were sent anyway, hoping to be able to make it. They did, although the gas gauges of most of the planes registered empty or close to it when they landed in England.

"We didn't lose a single plane going from Kentucky to England," boasted George. "With navigation what it was in those days, that was unusual."

Newly opened, the Matching Green airfield was located 5 miles or 8.0 km east of Harlow, Essex and 22 miles or 35 km northeast of London and was used by both the RAF and U.S. Army Air Forces. The air base was actually in the middle of a large farm. The family from the farm never left, staying there throughout the war while the Allies were operating from the field.

Upon arrival in England, the 391st Bomber Group was assigned to the Ninth Air Force. Each squadron consisted of about 20 aircraft and 500 men. The Group, commanded by Colonel Gerald E. Williams, consisted of four squadrons, with Lt. Col. Floyd B. Miller heading the 572nd; Major Joseph E. Dooley, Jr. the 573rd; Lt. Col. Donald K. Brandon the 574th; and George the 575th.

The B-26 Marauder's gasoline tanks, located in the wings, were made up of three self-sealing cells and held a total of 1,200 gallons of fuel. The engines consumed approximately 150 gallons per hour while traveling at 222 miles per hour with a full load of bombs at an altitude of 12,000 feet. To increase the B-26's flying range, there were two auxiliary gas tanks, called ferry tanks, installed in the bomb-carrying section holding about 300 gallons of gas. They were attached to the bomb racks and, in an emergency, could be dropped the same as bombs. Typically, they were not used on combat missions because the added weight would affect speed and maneuverability, two critical assets. Cruising speed was typically from 225 mph to 250 mph.

The limited range of the B-26 confined the group to targets in Northern France, Belgium, and Holland. Their primary purpose was to disrupt transportation and communication systems so the enemy couldn't move troops and machinery to the Normandy coastline which would be the invasion area. Highways, railroad bridges, marshalling yards, fuel and ammunition dumps were among the targets.

A standard squadron of B-26's consisted of 18 airplanes in a box formation, typically flying in three "flights" of six planes, in a grouping that looked like this:

```
                        Box Lead
                Wingman       Wingman

                    Deputy Box Lead
                Wingman       Wingman

        Flight Lead                   Flight Lead
    Wingman       Wingman       Wingman       Wingman

        Deputy Flight Lead          Deputy Flight Lead
    Wingman       Wingman       Wingman       Wingman
```

After bad weather aborted two initial sorties, the first successful mission for the group was on February 23, 1944 when two squadrons of 36 B-26's attacked the Gilze/Rijon Airfield in Holland. There were also three "spare ships" that tagged along after the formation. Upon learning of this after-the-fact, the Ninth Air Force command indicated its displeasure and it turned out to be the last time the 391st was allowed to have planes "go along for the ride."

The first box of planes dropped its payload on Gilze/Rijon from 12,000 feet and the second from 11,500 feet. The official "Summary of Operations" submitted to HQ was "Four and possibly five aircraft standings were hit, as well as were several buildings. The ammunition dump, reported near the west dispersal area, had several near misses. Two small buildings on the southwest dispersal seemed to have hits or near misses. Several hits were made on the north runway." Ten of the 39 planes in the attack suffered damage due to flak over the target area and Staff Sergeant Roy J. McKinney was listed as the first member of the 391st to be wounded.

At long last, though, the Bomber Group had made a contribution, although certainly modest, to the war effort. It was a cause for celebration.

George's flight crew went together to London, their favorite destination when they had a night or two of liberty. One of the stories George loved to tell is about the night they were in a bar which closed at midnight, per the local military emergency war edict. There were, however, "bottle clubs" that remained open longer. The local merchants got around the regulations by selling exclusive memberships to the club for those willing to pay premium prices for liquor and entertainment.

While searching around for one of those bottle clubs, they saw an attractive young lady on the corner. George asked one of his crew members to go up to her and ask where one was located. She looked at him and said indignantly, "Listen, mate, I'm selling ass, not whiskey." George would smile when telling that story saying, "We were so damn naïve. We were just farm boys. None of us had ever seen a prostitute before. We didn't even know what one looked like."

Knowing any flight could be their last, George's crew began the practice of, whenever possible, going out for drinks the night before a mission.

"We made some training flights for a week or two and then we started our serious business of bombing German-occupied Europe," related Jim Clark. "I was plumb stupid when I started out. I really was not scared. I would think, 'Well now, we have got these flak suits and steel helmets and they cover all the vital organs so they would have to hit us in the neck, arms, or legs to hurt us. If worse comes to worse, we have always got a parachute to bail out with. If we got captured by the Germans, we know we are going to win the war anyway so we would get liberated and be home before too long.'

As time went on, I saw some of my best friends shot down. I saw some airplanes get direct hits and be blown in half and on fire and people not parachuting out. I began to get a little nervous and decided my theory was not exactly right.

I'll tell you about a couple of deals that made me feel that way. I was flying on the right wing of Captain William Aldrich. We called him Bill but sometimes Henry was his nickname. As we hit the coast of France, he took a direct flak hit in his right engine and it just blew the thing all to pieces and it caught on fire. When this happened, he made a violent right turn into us. I was sitting in the plastic nose without a parachute. We didn't wear a chute in there because there wasn't an escape hatch and there was no room for a parachute anyway. What you were supposed to do was move back into the airplane and there snap on your chute if you had to bail out.

Aldrich went into a violent right turn and we also went into a violent right turn to avoid a collision. He missed us by inches. In fact, it was so close that our waist gunner, who stood in the open waist gun aperture, had his hair burnt by the fire from the other plane. Aldrich's plane went into a flat spin, on fire, and I didn't see any parachutes come out of it. If we had a collision, I would either have been killed by the impact or I would have fallen out into space without a parachute. Either way would have been sudden death. That really scared me. It was the worst I have ever been scared in my life.

We got into a vertical bank and lost 1,000 feet before recovering and then went ahead and rejoined the formation and bombed the target. The whole crew was so shaken up that we were almost useless, but we did complete the mission and got back to England. After we got back, the pilot told me that his feet were shaking so badly that he had to take them off the rudders because he just couldn't keep them still.

The other deal involved a man by the name of Mike Perich who lived in the hut with me. He had been to London and got a tailor-made battle jacket, some called them the 'Eisenhower Jacket' because he was the one who made the short, comfortable jacket famous. Anyway, it was tailor-made and it was beautiful. I asked him to let me try it on and it fit me just perfectly. I said, 'Mike, when you get shot down, I want that jacket.' He said, 'It's yours.' He got shot down two days before I did, was killed, and I wouldn't touch that jacket with a ten-foot pole. It made me sick just thinking of it.

Most of our bombing was in France. We bombed marshalling yards, rail and road bridges, villages, everything they told us to. Then, there was 'NO BALLS.' That was a code name for something that we didn't know what it was. They would make an 'X' on the map, it would not be near a town, it would not be near anything. It might look like it was a forest, a farm, or wheat field. It never looked like it was a target. They would just mark that 'X' and we would bomb it. Every time we did, they'd shoot our butts off. It seemed like we were doing something for nothing. It just didn't look like we were doing any good and it was very demoralizing.

We bombed those things for six months and got shot up every time we hit one. We couldn't imagine why we were doing it. Finally, we found out that when they turned the bombs loose on London, it was a bomb that looked like a little bitty airplane. All the Germans had to do was point that thing at London, give it enough fuel, and turn it loose. We had been bombing the LAUNCHING SITES of the buzz bombs. If we hadn't, I believe they would have wiped London well nigh off the map. After we found out what we were doing, we were sure glad that we had been doing it.

One Sunday morning I was in London and the fog was there. If you've ever heard one of those buzz bombs, you would know what it was because it didn't sound like an airplane. You knew that when the engine quit, it would be coming down. I was walking along the street when I heard one of these things coming. When it sounded like it was right above me, the engine quit and I knew it was coming right along. I didn't know what to do so I didn't do anything. The thing hit about 100 yards from me, blew one hell of a hole, and scared me pretty good. I walked into a restaurant, ordered a cup of coffee and had to use both hands to hold it steady. I couldn't hold it with just one."

"When we went to London, we often teamed up, and it seems I was usually paired with a very arrogant individual," added Stub. "He enjoyed picking fights, especially with English servicemen, and I didn't appreciate his behavior. After a few of these episodes, I decided to step in and try to stop him. He turned on me and we exchanged a few blows. Then, the M.P.'s stepped in and broke it up. We took the next train back to the base to finish our scrimmage. I worked him over pretty well before some guys broke it up."

Within a couple of days, Stub had to appear before Squadron Commander Lt. Colonel Stalnaker to present his case. George listened attentively and announced, "You behaved exactly as a Non-Com (Non-Commissioned Officer) should." "Needless to say, I was happy to be acquitted," said Stub.

"One day, Pilot Herschel Harkins, Co-pilot Eugene Squier, Radioman Tom Lawson, and I flew a plane that was not our own north to Oxford University to deliver a message," he added. We always wore our parachute harnesses but the parachutes were piled up on the floor of the plane. I sometimes stretched out on them and took a little nap which I proceeded to do this time. The airplane, unlike the one we usually flew, had a trap door about 30 inches square under our parachutes. I was resting comfortably when, all of a sudden, the trap door opened and all our chutes fell out. I was left hanging by my heels and elbows. Tom grabbed me and pulled me back in. What a thrill!

Before each mission, we congregated in the briefing room to talk about where the enemy had gun stations, how many there were, and what we could do to avoid these areas. Also, we received other information which might be pertinent to the success of the mission. Only a couple of times did enemy fighters attack us but we often experienced an abundance of flak. Anti-aircraft guns fired four rounds in one loading. We would see a big black puff of smoke just ahead of us, the next one a little closer, the third a little closer and we knew for sure the fourth one would hit us. Many times we would catch some of the shrapnel in the plane and, on occasion, a crewmember would be hit.

On one mission, we flew to Liege, Belgium which was a long trip for us and we got a direct hit in our right engine while over the target. We couldn't remain in formation so had to fly back alone. That direct hit failed to explode or we probably would have gone down. Our fuel supply was running low and we were losing altitude very rapidly. We had no navigator aboard so we had to find our own way.

As our situation became more critical, we had to radio England and have them send a couple of fighters to lead us across the Channel. There was an emergency air base just on the coast closest to us. When we hit the English coast, we were only 300 feet in the air. If that landing field had been two or three miles further, we couldn't have made it. We got out to survey the damage and saw that the shell had almost cut our wing off. Our plane was hauled to the 'graveyard.'

Another time on a mission over France with things relatively quiet, I was in the top turret talking sign language to a fellow in the plane on our right wing. Suddenly we were in a field of flak so thick you could almost walk across it. Their plane took a direct hit, just about cutting it in half, and the crew went down with the plane.

I remember that we flew our first bombing mission on March 3, 1944. For the 391st Bombardment Group, that was the month when we were battle-tested and found equal to the task. The feeling of unknown expectancy which preceded the first missions gradually wore away as the men began to accept each succeeding mission as a job to be done and knew their training and growing experience would not let them down."

Various types of bombs were dropped by the B-26's. They sometimes carried two 2,000-pounders and other times eight 500-pounders. They also dropped anti-personnel bombs, small cluster bombs that were each the size of a half-dozen hand grenades. There were even occasions when they simply dropped propaganda leaflets.

Stub continued, "Matching Green, our base quarters, was fairly nice, at least compared to the ground forces. We had semi-permanent Nissen huts (better known as Quonset huts, a semicircular prefabricated structure of corrugated galvanized steel) with cots to sleep on. About 20 to 25 guys were assigned to each hut and separated by job description. In other words, engineers were together, radiomen, armorers, etc. The food was good, considering the situation, and we even had fresh eggs on occasion. We had a latrine and shower a short distance from the barracks. There also was a Non-Commissioned Officers' Club where we could get together, have a beer, gather around a piano, or just sit and talk.

Almost everyone had a bicycle for transportation. There was a small town, Bishop Stortford, that was close enough for us to ride to and there was a pub which served both mild and bitter beer. There was not much in the way of entertainment on the base but every week or so, we'd go to London for a couple of days. We'd catch a train in Chelmsford for a 30-minute ride into London where we quickly learned to appreciate the 'Tube' subway which was quick and easy transportation.

Occasionally, we'd hire a cab just to ride around and sight-see the many historical places. There were many places to go like USO shows, Red Cross clubs, and traditional pubs where you could enjoy a beer and throw darts. The dart games were very popular and the English took them very seriously. The beer, for the most part, was served at room temperature. There was a pub in Piccadilly Circus that served cold, pilsner beer, just like in the U.S. Except for gin, liquor was nowhere to be found. Once in a great while, someone on the street would peddle it but it was usually half-water and very expensive.

A popular place for servicemen was Covent Gardens, the Royal Opera House, a landmark turned into a dance hall holding hundreds of people and had music playing continuously. The bandstand was circular with a band on each side and it would turn a half circle and change bands without missing a beat. There were English girls there and I danced a few times but mostly just sat, watched, and listened to the music. There were many restaurants in London but difficult to find a good meal since, just as in the United States, meat and other types of food were rationed and it was just mostly fish that was available. The English men were somewhat resentful of the American soldiers because the pay of an average G.I. was considerably higher than the average worker there.

I was in London when the first buzz bomb hit. We didn't know what it was until later. It was very strange. We could see it coming in very low with a trail of fire following. I thought they were fighter planes at first. We knew as long as we could hear the engines, we didn't need to worry. When the engine cut out, though, it was only a matter of a few seconds until it hit the ground. The buzz bombs had no military value except for being very demoralizing. London was completely blacked-out at night except for the headlights of cars, mostly taxis with only a slit of light to see by."

The Germans introduced the *Fieseler* Fi 103 "flying bomb," a pilotless and disposable ballistic missile, to the world on June 13, 1944. Because their hope was the Fi 103 would avenge the Allied bombing raids on Germany, the Propaganda Ministry began calling the weapon the *Vergeltungswaffe Eins* (Vengeance Weapon 1), or "V-1" for short.

Powered by a "pulse jet" engine, the V-1 emitted a loud, rasping noise that could be heard from more than ten miles or sixteen kilometers away. This sound earned the V-1 the "Buzz Bomb." nickname. Germany launched an estimated 22,400 of the weapons, mostly from ground-based ramps, with nearly 2,000 also dropped from Heinkel He 111 bombers.

Pulse jet engines, or pulsejets, were a simple type of internal combustion engine with few or no moving parts. They were so-named because the combustion occured in pulses. They were able to run statically, which meant they did not have to have air forced into their inlets the way a standard jet engine does. The noise emitted can be likened to a motorcycle without a muffler.

Despite the fact that the American and British Air Forces possessed air superiority, the Luftwaffe was able to launch an essentially unstoppable weapon into England, Belgium, and France. There was simply no technology available to counter a cruise missile attack.

Conventional anti-aircraft guns were ineffective due to the bomb's high speed of 550 kilometers, or 350 miles per hour. Attempts to attack from the air using machine guns were unsuccessful because of the V-1's sheet steel structure. If a cannon shell detonated the warhead, the explosion could destroy the attacker. In a high-risk strategy, some airplanes even tried to nudge the V-1's off course by slamming into them. Thousands of barrage balloons were used in an attempt to destroy V-1's that struck tethering cables. The Germans fit the leading edges of the buzz bomb wings with cable cutters, however, to counter that practice. Fewer than 300 V-1s are estimated to have been brought down by balloons.

The product of a quantum leap of technology, the V-2 rocket was an even more ferocious weapon than the V-1. This advanced weapon landed without warning, taking just three minutes from a launch site in Holland, for instance, to reach its target in London. Forty-six feet or 14 meters high, it carried a full ton or 900 kg of explosives. The first attack on London came on September 8, 1944 and resulted in a crater 10 meters or 32 feet across, killing three people and injuring 22.

More than 1,300 V-2's were fired at England and, as Allied forces advanced toward Germany, hundreds more targeted Belgium and France. Several thousand people were killed by the missile but an even grimmer statistic was that some 20,000 slave laborers died constructing the weapons. They were drawn from the Buchenwald concentration camp and worked in an underground factory called Mittelwerk. They had little food, were deprived of sleep, and lived in less-than-sanitary conditions. Many were executed for attempting acts of sabotage.

Fueled by liquid ethanol and oxygen, the sophisticated V-2 rocket flew more than 80 km (50 miles) above the Earth at a trajectory of 190 km (120 miles) and with a range of up to 362 kilometers (225 miles.) The V-2 had an automatic guidance system which operated independently of controllers on the ground. Once the destination was programmed into the sophisticated on-board analog computer, the rocket's gyroscopes could continuously track the craft's position in three dimensions. When the V-2 went into the upper atmosphere, the air became so thin that the rudders were rendered ineffective. Movable vanes were added that connected to the guidance system deflecting the rocket exhaust to change course.

The Allies recognized that the V-2 was unlike anything that had been seen before. After the war, its architect, Werner von Braun, became a key figure in the development of American space-age rocketry. The Soviet Union took over the German V-2 factory and test range and got its share of the scientists, creating the Space Race that began a decade later. The Soviet R-7 rocket that launched the Sputnik satellite in 1957 was an upgraded V-2 as was the Redstone missile which carried Alan Shepard, America's first astronaut, into space in 1961.

Why Hitler chose to use the deadly V-1 and V-2 rockets on civilian rather than military targets is as inexplicable as was his decision not to support production on such innovations as assault rifles and jet aircraft, both of which had enormous success in limited operation but failed to impress him. For whatever reason, he seemed more intent on terrorizing Allied cities than in defeating the Allied military forces.

Chapter 7 – The 5 a.m. Death Call

Simone termed her initial prison confinement "Ten Days of Horror." Under huge, blinding lights, she was interrogated continuously by pairs of Gestapo agents in the dungeon known as "The Room." One of them stood behind her and another in front of her. They took turns asking her questions. If she failed to look at the interrogator, she was slapped in the face. Soon, Simone began to taste her own blood, her eyes blurred, and her head ached.

Using the dissociation technique taught to her by the Resistance, she daydreamed in an effort to calm herself and block the pain. She thought of her family and wondered what they were doing. She imagined she was going to a special social event and was trying to choose which of her favorite dresses to wear. Knowing she was doing her best to mentally detach herself from the situation, her torturers would continually shout her name to jolt her back to reality.

Simone kept waiting for them to stop but they didn't stop. The interrogation process continued day and night. Whenever she started to fall asleep, she was violently shaken until she awoke. When she begged for something to eat, they laughed as if the request was ridiculous. She was given only enough water to keep her alive.

They said the words, "Morse Code" over and over to see if they could get a reaction out of her. It really made no difference whether or not she knew Morse Code. They were just toying with her for their amusement. Like the others trapped in that hellacious prison, they wanted her to suffer as much as possible until she was killed. She wanted them to get it over but she also wanted them to leave her alone. They did neither. Her misery was just beginning.

They repeatedly demanded that she reveal the names of other members of the Underground, claiming they would release her in exchange for that information. She revealed nothing.

On her ninth day of captivity, Simone was taken out of "The Room" temporarily. The only female inmate among a prison full of men, she was forced along with the others to watch the torture of three of their fellow captives. The guards told them they would stop the punishment if the inmates divulged information about the Resistance. While screaming in pain, those being tortured begged the others not to break any confidences.

The Germans also threatened to shoot her mother unless Simone revealed the identity of other members of the Underground. In turn, they visited Marie-Ange telling her that Simone would be freed if she divulged the same information. None of those involved betrayed the French cause.

After the initial ten days of agony, it became clear to her captors that she wasn't going to reveal any information and so she was thrown into one of the standard prison cells. She immediately noticed that the dark, dank chamber floor appeared to be moving. She blinked, looked closer, and realized it wasn't the floor that was moving but the bugs on the floor.

The stink of feces and urine in the prison was unbearable. The only sounds were occasional cries of other prisoners. There was an ominous feeling of death in the air. The section of the prison where Simone was being kept was not a place where people came to be rehabilitated. Instead, Death Row was a final destination. A place where people came to be put through the worst suffering imaginable until their name came up for a final time.

Although there was hardly any available light, Simone tried to identify what was crawling on the floor. Some of the things she could identify and some she couldn't. She had never been so hungry in her life and didn't know when or if she was going to be fed next. Picking up a small worm, she closed her eyes and swallowed it without chewing. She was hoping she wouldn't actually taste it but she did. It was the most disgusting thing she had ever eaten. It was intolerable. She gagged and came close to vomiting. Then she put another in her mouth and gulped it down. She followed that with a third.

She thought of the delicious *hors d'oeuvres* and *petit fours* she used to relish and decided she was going to have to pretend she was eating those. She realized that surviving as long as possible would be as much a mental as a physical challenge. "They aren't going to defeat me. I'm going to outlast them," she announced out loud to no one in particular as she clenched her fists as if to challenge herself. She defiantly picked up a spider, pretending it was a crepe with strawberries on top, crushed it, and popped it into her mouth. If this was what she was going to have to do to survive, she was ready to do it. She had to subsist on the things from the floor as she would be given little to eat for the next several months. On those occasions she was given food, it typically was only a potato tossed at her or broth of unknown origin, sometimes filled with lice.

A number of times she was pulled from her cell so the Gestapo could have her listen to Morse Code transmissions which said her mother would be brought to the prison to face a firing squad and Simone would be forced to watch. She tried not to show any emotion but the guards looked at her and smiled. They knew full well she understood every word. The trauma prevented Simone from ever again being able to decode incoming messages.

Her father was held for questioning in another jail but released after a few weeks when the Germans concluded he had no knowledge of Simone's actions on behalf of the Resistance. The fact that he was a Provincial Supreme Court judge likely had something to do with the fact that no one in Simone's family was harmed.

As more and more troops were needed on the front lines, the prison guards were gradually being deployed and replaced by Dobermans and German Shepherds used as sentries. If there were noises in a cell, the dogs led the guards there and the prisoners were beaten. Sleeping was made more difficult because of the barking in the night followed by the screams of inmates. Simone was bothered for the rest of her life by the clicking sound of dog nails on the floor because it reminded her of the prison guard patrols.

The window of her cell was so high that she had to get up on tip-toes to look out. One day, she happened to spot her beloved sports car being taken away on a train, evidently to be given to someone as a gift. Her first reaction was to be angry and say to herself, "How dare they steal my car! What right do they have?" Then, she sighed in resignation, "What does it matter, anyhow? I have little use for it now." It was a bitter reminder of her former carefree life that seemed so far away.

Simone was allowed out of her cell once or twice a week for ten or fifteen minutes for "exercise." Although she was forbidden to speak to the other prisoners, at least when she was in the fresh air, she felt that she was part of the real world again. Outside, she liked to look up at the sun after the time it took for her eyes to adjust to the light and then, for the all-too-brief period that remained, smile and remember what life was like when she was still an innocent teenager back on the Riviera where her biggest worry was about not getting too sunburned. That warm, comforting feeling stayed with her for days to come until she was allowed those precious few minutes outside again. She later wrote in a journal she kept, "During this time, I have such nostalgia for my home, the sea, and of sweet times."

Simone and others learned to send silent written messages using square pieces of toilet paper attached to an ingenious pulley system made of thin wire and sewing thread that they stretched between cells outside the windows. She was able to jump up to the barred window and support herself with one hand while wrapping a note around the string with the other hand. At the same time, she had to listen carefully for the approach of the guards.

When someone is held in isolation, there's something reassuring about being able to communicate with others in any way possible. It's an affirmation that you're still human and there are other people with whom you can connect, even for a brief moment. It's worth taking the risk, even if it's just in writing, to exchange a simple greeting such as, "How are you?" or "Are you okay?"

One day, she was caught passing a toilet paper message and nervously awaited her punishment. Her assumption was that this would be considered a capital offense and she would be put to death immediately for disobeying the rules. After all, others had been executed for less than that. Instead, she was moved to a cramped bunker cell without a window and with a ceiling so low that she couldn't completely stand up.

The Germans soon threw a young girl who had been raped and battered into the cell. She smashed her head and body against the walls in front of Simone and died just hours later. Simone cradled her lifeless body in her arms and told her that everything was all right. "I knew it wasn't really all right but I didn't know what else to say," she admitted. "I will always regret that I never even learned her name. I've always had to refer to her only as 'The girl in my cell.'"

Prisoners continued to be tortured while the others were forced to line up and watch. On one of these occasions, Simone and a fellow inmate exchanged glances. It happened to be her boyfriend who, by coincidence, was being held in the same prison. One of the guards noticed that the two of them seemed to have a connection. Simone immediately bit her lower lip and remembered her uncle's words – "Then don't make any mistakes." She knew she had made a costly one.

It wasn't long before the boyfriend was hoisted to the ceiling and suspended from an overhead beam by meat hooks piercing his arms. As she was forced to stand and watch the blood spurt from his body, she was told she could save him by revealing the identity of other spies and members of the Resistance. The guards tried to provoke her chiding, "He's still alive. You can save him. Don't you care about him? If he dies, it will be your fault!" She refused to compromise anyone's identity, no matter what the cost might be. Simone watched his crucifixion until he took his final breath and was then returned to her bunker cell.

Signs on lamp posts in Nice to this day list the names of many of the martyrs who were killed in the prison.

Like the others on Death Row, Simone had to endure the agony of not knowing the date of her execution so she waited for her name to be announced at each "5 a.m. Death Call." She awakened every morning wondering if this would be her last. When she didn't hear her name, she breathed a sigh of relief. She knew she had at least one more day.

It seemed like so long ago since she stopped wondering how these people could be so cruel. She didn't think about that anymore, just accepting them for what they were. "During that time in prison, I never saw one German who was not rude and mean," she recalled with bitterness.

Her days behind bars became weeks and then months. She had no idea how long she had been incarcerated. The days were pretty much like the nights. The week-days were the same as the week-ends. There was nothing to look forward to. Her current life of despair was so far removed from her former life of luxury that she began to wonder if that former life ever existed at all.

Chapter 8 – "It was a Bloody Situation"

George reported matter-of-factly, "Some of our combat missions were pretty hairy and some were milk runs. I flew quite a few of them. On a few occasions, I lost people." Then, he flew the most important mission of his life.

French schoolboy Emile Sauras couldn't keep his eyes off the airplane-covered sky. He had never seen anything like it before. No one else had, either. Emile described it this way: "It's June 6, 1944, the day the Allies are embarking in Normandy. The advance of the Allies is very slow and the death toll is in big numbers. The principal of my High School, Lyceé of Rennes, instructs us to go home to our family. I return to Coësmes to the home of my parents. We are listening to the BBC London radio. The Allies have lost a lot of lives on the beaches of Normandy. The debarking of war equipment and food was very difficult but they succeed. Despite the resistance and determination of the Germans, particularly in Bretagne, the Allies advance."

The British and Americans began planning for the biggest amphibious invasion in history in 1942. In preparation for defense against it, Hitler gave Erwin Rommel responsibility for building the "Atlantic Wall," a 3,860-kilometer (2,400-mile) fortification of bunkers, landmines, and beach obstacles.

On November 3, 1943, Hitler issued Führer Directive No. 51 where he warned of "consequences of staggering proportions" if the Allies established a foothold in France. He instructed his army to launch a counter-attack to "throw the Allies back into the sea." Hitler boasted, "Once defeated, the enemy will never again try to invade."

The 9th Air Force was first tasked with providing air support to British and U.S. forces in North Africa. From there, its headquarters were moved to England. By D-Day, the 9th became the largest air force ever assembled under one command boasting 250,000 people and 3,500 aircraft. Among its 1,500 units were Bomber, Fighter, Troop Transport, Air Defense, Engineering and Service Commands.

Beginning in January of 1944, Supreme Allied Commander General Dwight Eisenhower directed a large-scale deception campaign to attempt to mislead the Germans about the intended target of the impending invasion. It was a spectacular success. A phantom army was created complete with cardboard cut-out tanks and military equipment, noise was piped over loudspeakers to simulate military base sounds, and nonsense radio transmissions were broadcast. Hitler became convinced that the Allies would land at Pas de Calais, the narrowest point between England and France.

The Normandy invasion bore the code name of "Operation Overlord." The "D" in "D-Day" stood simply for "Day" in the same way that "H" means "Hour." For security reasons and to keep the element of surprise, no particular date was assigned for its commencement. The sequence of events was planned as "Day 1 – O Hour," and then "Day 1 – 1 Hour," etc.

The original target date of June 5 was pushed back 24 hours due to bad weather. General Eisenhower told the troops that they were about to embark on a "Great Crusade, toward which we have striven these many months" and reassured them that "I have full confidence in your courage, devotion to duty, and skill in battle." He also reminded them that "The eyes of the world are upon you." The Allied participants recognized the magnitude as well as the difficulty of the task before them.

More than 5,000 ships and landing craft were deployed and 11,000 aircraft took to the skies. In preparation, there were naval bombardments, air strikes, and parachute and glider landings. Thousands of airborne troops landed behind enemy lines securing bridges and other strategic targets.

Army Air Forces Lt. Colonel Leslie Lennox described what it was like to partake in major combat missions: "Each group had a pattern for the airplanes to fly during climb to assembly altitude. The patterns for each group fit together like a jigsaw puzzle. Unfortunately, strong winds aloft would destroy the integrity of these patterns and there would be considerable over-running of each other's patterns.

Many of our take-offs were made before daylight during the winter of '44 and '45 when I was there so it was not uncommon to climb through several thousand feet of cloud overcast. Also, it was not uncommon to experience one or two near misses while climbing through the clouds, although you would never see the other airplane. You knew you had just had a near miss when suddenly the airplane would shake violently as it hit the prop wash (the disturbed mass of air pushed aft by the propeller) of another plane. It was a wonderful feeling to break out on top, so you could watch for other planes to keep from running into each other.

To add to the congestion we were creating, the Royal Air Force Lancasters, Halifaxes, and Wimpys would be returning from their night missions and fly through our formations. Needless to say, pilots had to keep their heads on a swivel and their eyes out of the cockpit.

When you consider the way our Air Traffic Control system operates today, and all of the facilities at their disposal to guide each individual airplane through the sky to ensure its safety, it's almost unbelievable that we were able to do what we did. To think of launching hundreds of airplanes in a small airspace, many times in total darkness, loaded with bombs, with complete radio silence, and no control from the ground, and do it successfully day after day, with young air crews with minimum experience, is absolutely mind-boggling."

Before they took to the skies on D-Day, the 391st Bomber Group had the following message from 9th Air Force Commander General Anderson read to them at 4:45 a.m. in a pre-dawn briefing: "The Allied Commanders knew the landing of troops on the European Continent depended upon the successful execution of the tasks assigned you. General Eisenhower, the Supreme Allied Commander, last week charged me personally with informing you that he and all commanders of ground troops are deeply grateful for what you have done and are fully aware that you have made possible the decision to land on the Continent. The words which would express my own pride in your accomplishments do not exist."

At this point, Group Commander Colonel Gerald E. Williams simply announced, "All right, men. This is it!"

Probably the proudest moment for the B-26 Marauder came on that momentous day when it was chosen by General Eisenhower to spearhead the invasion. Eight 9th Air Force groups of Marauders led the entire Allied air offensive to bomb shore installations ahead of the troop landings.

The 391st Bomber Group began dropping payload at 6:25 a.m. Just five minutes later, the landings commenced on five beaches along a 50-mile stretch of the Normandy Coast. They were code-named "Juno, Gold, Omaha, Utah, and Sword." A total of 156,000 American, Canadian, British, and Free French forces troops were deployed from bases along the southern English coast. At least 4,000 of them were lost the first day with the heaviest resistance coming at Omaha Beach, which alone accounted for half the total. Many more were wounded or missing in action.

George beamed with pride as he said, "I got to fly on D-Day. It was an exceptional thing to see. The orders were we had to fly regardless of altitude and the clouds were pretty low. If there was a problem with the aircraft, we were told to we had to stay in formation and not turn around or the Allies would have to shoot us down. They marked our wings with black and white lines. When you saw these grunts on the beaches under artillery fire struggling through the water and also watched our own ships bombarding the shore, it was a bloody situation. All of the pilots and air crew members wanted to fly as much as they possibly could in order to help these poor guys."

B-26 Marauder

"On D-Day, there were thousands of Allied ships of every possible description crossing the channel," added Stub. "There were ships as far as the eye could see. There were thousands of barrage balloons in the air. This was to prevent enemy aircraft from flying low. London had flown these balloons throughout the war. All Allied aircraft had special invasion markings on the wings – big twelve inch stripes, alternating black and white. It made the Allied planes easy to identify. Nevertheless, we avoided flying over the balloons."

"D-Day came. The Germans knew it was coming. We knew it was coming," claimed Jim Clark. "Nobody but Eisenhower and a few of his people knew when or where. The night before, they told us what they were fixing to do. The next morning, they briefed us again and the weather was real bad. We took off on instruments the morning of June 6 and managed to form up and head for Normandy and our targets which were the coastal gun firing on the invading ships. By the time we got there it was just daylight and we must have had a couple of thousand aircraft in the air. We were about 10,000 feet up and there were ships in either direction as far as I could see. I'm talking about ocean-type ships.

We were very fortunate and must have been one of the few groups that were able to see its target. There was loud cover but we got a gap and could see the guns firing. We dropped our bombs and stopped them. Just after that, we got into a cloud bank, iced up, and had to disperse formation. It was a bit of a mess until we reformed all returned to base. It wasn't really a tough mission, except for the bad weather."

George's 575th Squadron flew two missions on D-Day, both of them along the French coast. The first was to destroy a highway at Caen and the second was to target coastal defenses at Beneville. They bombed from 3,500 feet and both sorties were successful. The 391st flew 89 missions in all during D-Day. There were no losses of aircraft and just two wounded crew members.

Typical of the letters that U.S. soldiers sent home was this one from B-26 crew member Staff Sergeant James McLoughlin written after his second mission of the day: "This morning I had the biggest thrill of my life. After waiting for a year, it finally came and I had a birds-eye view from my turret of the greatest show on earth. It was bigger and greater than anything I could ever imagine. I just finished my 14-day furlough in Aberdeen and I got back just in time for "D" Day and "H" hour. I wouldn't want to miss this show for anything. It's a big one and we all know that we'll win."

The beaches were secured a week later with some 50,000 vehicles along with 100,000 tons of equipment and 326,000 troops put in place. Engineers from the 9th Air Force began building airstrips in Normandy within hours of the beach assaults. Its pilots led armored columns in the most effective use of air-ground co-operative warfare in history.

The exhausted German troops were hammered by the Allies. Leading up to D-Day, 35% of their soldiers had been wounded at least once. That number went up significantly on June 6 and in the days that followed. The Germans suffered 290,000 casualties in Normandy with 23,000 soldiers killed, 67,000 wounded, and 200,000 missing or taken POW. Of the 2,000 Panzer tanks that saw action, only 70 remained operable.

The French Resistance commited an estimated 1,000 acts of sabotage before, during, and immediately after the Normandy invasion. Every time a train track was dynamited, a communication network sabotaged, or military equipment damaged, a French village was subject to brutal retaliation. In Tulle, one hundred men were massacred three days after the Normandy invasion and 642 people in Oradour-sur-Glane, including 205 children, killed the following day. The men of Tulle were shot while the women and children were locked in a church and burned to death.

Larry Belcher, a navigator on one of the 391st B-26's, described this noteworthy event that took place in the hours following D-Day: "At the base of the Cherbourg peninsula sits Isigny-sur-Mer, atop the cliffs fronting Omaha Beach. While D-Day was important to generals, planners, and reporters, D+2 (June 8) was particularly important to the boys who were pinned down there. It was the day they were able to escape from a perilous situation.

The invasion was carried out by the Army, assisted by the Navy, but the Air Corps was also on maximum effort and all groups flew multiple missions during this period. For instance, our 391st Bomber Group, whose normal bombing altitude was 12,000 to 14,000 feet, flew three missions on D-Day at an altitude of 3,800 feet and two missions on D+1 at 2,800 feet to deny the enemy the ability to bring up reinforcements.

On D+2, the 391st was assigned the target of Isigny-sur-Mer. We had difficult weather and terrain conditions and friendly troop life-and-death considerations with which we had to contend. The bomb run could not be made straight in for fear that some of the bombs might fall short and land on our own troops. Nor could it be made from the back because bombs might fall long. The bomb run had to be made from along the peninsula's edge where visibility was so poor that the mission was flown at 1,800 feet.

Even at that altitude, the ground was barely visible and formation flying presented ominous possibilities of mid-air collisions. To counteract this, the formation was split into six flights of six planes each. Due to the low altitude and poor visibility, only one flight was able to locate and bomb the target but that was enough.

Thirty minutes after the target was bombed, the boys were able to climb the cliffs and capture the town. It was the first time any of the Allied troops were able to get off the beaches and it led to the capture of the Cherbourg peninsula and the establishment of a dependable supply route."

One of the tragedies involving members of the 391st occurred shortly thereafter. It's estimated that the odds of being killed were a frightening 71% for the first 30 flight missions. Smiley Colsch had flown 65 missions, had completed his tour, and clearly was bucking the odds. Like many pilots, however, Colsch wanted to stay until the war was over, figuring the job had not been finished. So he volunteered for what turns out to be another ill-fated second tour.

On his first mission, his B-26 somehow managed to get under the rest of the squadron's formation during a bombing run just as the "Bombs Away" signal was given by the plane flying above them. Three thousand-pound bombs were dropped and fell harmlessly by the plane. However, the fourth and final bomb hit one of the plane's engines and sheared it off. His disabled bomber spun out of control and crashed into another B-26. Of the twelve members of both flight crews, only one survived.

As happens with all wars, there were some enjoyable things to "blow off steam" or "get away from it all" that helped people maintain their sanity in the midst of the destruction and chaos surrounding them. Stub Miller described the flight crew's experience after D-Day: "Later in June, we were given a seven day leave for R&R. We were sent to a rest home in Lymington, England. When we arrived, we were issued civilian clothes and treated like royalty – breakfast in bed, good food, and each had a private bedroom. For recreation, we rode bicycles, went horseback riding, played ping-pong, pool and just relaxed and had a wonderful time. There were 12 of us there along with four or five Red Cross girls. It was a great vacation but then we had to return to duty."

What they went back to is something none of them expected - a harrowing mission aboard a plane with the unfortunate name of the "Miss Take." It nearly cost them their lives.

Chapter 9 – "Get Out of My Country!"

On June 9, 1944, three days after D-Day, there was a sudden British aerial bombing attack of a garage that stored engines and spare parts located next to the prison where Simone was being held. At that precise time, she happened to be out in the courtyard for her occasional few minutes of exercise. Some of the guards and workers became panic-stricken while others suffered injuries as part of the collateral damage. Relying on her nursing training, Simone was able to calm down the situation, comfort those who were just shaken by the experience, and treat those who had been hurt.

Simone rushed to the aid not only of French prisoners but also her former tormentors and torturers. With admiration, the prison Commandant watched how she toiled without regard for friend or foe, treating them all simply as people in need of help. He was so impressed that he decided to let her walk out of the prison to freedom, even writing a letter to her mother commending Simone for her selfless actions in the crisis.

Still not trusting the Germans, she worried that her release might be a ruse so the Gestapo could follow her and discover other members of the Resistance. She, of course, was willing to take the chance but remained cautious claiming, "They knew France soon would be invaded and wanted to wipe out the Resistance."

With her eyes full of tears, she admitted, "Of the 13 members of the Underground that were in my group arrested on March 13, 1944, I am the only one to have survived. One was sent to the Nordhausen death camp. Another was killed when he had gasoline injected into his blood stream. The rest were hung, shot, or died from torture."

As the prison gates were opened, Simone walked home slowly and painfully. She had been considerably weakened physically but her spirit was unshakable. Her parents and sisters were shocked to see her again, particularly in her haggard and emaciated condition. They hugged her and asked if she wanted something to eat. She broke down sobbing, "You don't know how long I've been waiting for someone to ask me that question. I never thought I'd hear it again." Then she ran to her mother and melted into her arms the way she used to do as a child. After the hug that seemed to last an eternity, Marie-Ange asked her daughter if she wanted to talk about what happened in prison. Simone told her she couldn't do that. In fact, she never described to her family the chilling details of those nightmarish months.

Simone could have spent time staying in bed to recuperate from her terrible ordeal. You wouldn't blame her for that. In fact, you wouldn't blame her for sitting out the rest of the war. But, that's not what she did.

When her mother showed her the letter she had received from the Commandant, Simone angrily tore it to pieces. The last thing she wanted would be to keep any sort of souvenir from one of the Nazis. She was anxious to get on to the next chapter of her life.

After being told the exciting news that the Allies had landed at Normandy just 72 hours earlier and the Germans were on the run, Simone didn't want to miss out on the action. She immediately donned men's clothing, grabbed a weapon from the Underground's stockpile, and took to the streets to fight alongside the other volunteers who were driving out the Germans. As she fired at them, she muttered under her breath words to the effect of, "Get out of my country! You don't belong here!" Simone notified both the SOE and the FFI that she was back in action and ready for her next assignment.

She soon received a heartfelt letter from a former prisoner named Francois that said,

"The news I heard yesterday of your liberation has given me great joy. I could not believe I'd be able to write to you today from Nice. We are almost in paradise here: no more prison bars, no more locked doors, no more screams. Nobody to charge toward us and nobody who speaks German. What a dream. And yet it became true. At least you also know this happiness. To say it all, if there was a charming young girl to have a correspondence with me, my happiness would be complete. I leave you now, hoping to see you soon."

She also got a poignant message from Paul, another member of the Resistance with whom she was imprisoned: "I am especially glad to have learned that you gained your freedom. You now know the pleasure to be at last out of the cage. This sudden freedom has filled us with wonder. It is true that the risk exists for us to go back to our work, but I hope that the events will go against the will of those who oppress us and shall fulfill our desires which are opposite of theirs.

I do regret I am unable to see you in order to thank you personally for your camaraderie which did so often help us to withstand what we did. But I hope I'll be able to do it soon. I don't think Charles and Greste will last for long. Yesterday we had the visit of Marcel's sister to whom I wrote to as soon as I arrived. Her devotion, to say the least, exceeds all one can imagine. I think that as soon as she received my letter she jumped in a cab without having dinner. Despite the troubles we are facing, she was smiling.

Words are missing to express what I feel. There still are good people on earth, aren't there? If you can, I would receive with great pleasure news from you telling how you only find joy after these months of suffering. What would I say more? Nothing important, I guess. But I could write a lot to shout my happiness and my relief before this wide-open window. In front of me, there are so many new things. Sky, trees, sun, and further, there is life. I can't help to see it as lovely. I will stop here. Although so many things are upside down, I hope you won't forget the friendly camaraderie which we had together during those terrible months."

A third letter came from a former inmate who professed his love for her declaring, "It's great to be free. For the first time in many years, I am happy. I tell you that without any shame and you must not laugh or even smile, little Simone. It hits me like a punch to my stomach, and you are the cause of that, adorable little pixie. I have always had a disdain for those who are in love and sentimental, and here I am like them. I have done the worst things. I am a bandit, it's true, but I am completely unable to do that now. One could have been and still being a man without any morals, but have lovely thoughts and nice gestures. Do you know, little Simone, that for a gesture that I'd like, I would give up and even destroy the most important things of my life?"

Truthfully, Simone didn't even recall the love-struck, would-be suitor. After receiving his letter, she decided to ask her sister Jacqueline to go and "check him out." He learned of this and was obviously offended writing back, "You can trust me, darling Simone. It is not nice to have used Jacqueline for spying on me this morning. It's a betrayal. I prefer it's not the case. But now you have a big advantage on me. Take notice that I don't care. What I know about you is your face and to look intensely in your eyes because it's through them that I love everything that is you. I cover you with thousands of sweet stars, just like my thoughts are for you."

Simone decided that she was not going to get together with anyone, particularly former prisoners, on a social basis. Many people would seek out and benefit from talking to others who had shared a common traumatic experience. She felt she had more important things to do, though. Besides that, she preferred to keep her feelings to herself and not speak about what she had experienced. In fact, she would rarely talk about it to anyone ever again. Her preference was to hold it inside, not appreciating the effect it would have on her.

Once more, her nursing training proved to be of benefit. In Nice, she was one of three women to care for some 300 wounded French citizens who were left behind by the retreating Germans.

She bid farewell to her family explaining she been given an assignment in Paris to support the Inter-Allied Mission as a liaison between the French Underground and Allied military forces. That didn't sound particularly dangerous to them so they were relieved. She didn't mention, though, that in her spare time, she would be engaging once again in combat operations on the streets.

She travelled alone by train from Nice, in the far southeastern corner of France and the only place she had ever lived, to Paris, one of the northernmost, a distance of 932 kilometers or 580 miles. There she would wear an International Red Cross uniform that gave her access to the Nazis so she could return to spying on them. In addition, she worked in the kitchen of a German general to collect intelligence to turn over to the Allies. After that experience, she didn't hesitate to tell anyone willing to listen about how she used to spit in the general's soup. She enjoyed demonstrating how she'd do it while punctuating her description with a "ptooyee" spitting sound at the end followed by a loud, derisive laugh.

While in Paris, she wrote for *La Français Libre* (The Free French), the underground newspaper started by Charles de Gaulle. According to historian Werner Rings, "These newspapers were distributed at the risk of people's lives, and possessed of far greater importance than anyone at first thought possible." He added, "Once equipped with an illegal news sheet, often handwritten and secretly passed from hand to hand, two or three like-minded friends would begin to form a group and recruit fellow fighters for the common cause. Born in the gloomy depths of the underground but expanding with tremendous speed, the clandestine press became, as it were, the soul of the Resistance."

While Simone passed secret messages back and forth regarding Resistance sabotage operations and activities, another heroic woman, Eileen Nearne, a Parisian born six months after her on March 15, 1921, did the same as liaison between London and Paris.

In a BBC Documentary in 1997, Eileen explained why she became a spy: "I had patriotic feelings and I knew I could do that kind of work since I was by nature a solitary person. That was essential to be able to adapt to that kind of life." She was only willing to do the interview if they agreed to let her wear a disguise and not have name revealed. When someone from Torquay, England, the town in which she was living, asked if it was her on television, Eileen dismissed the idea by saying, "No, you're mistaken."

Eileen managed to escape to Great Britain during the German Invasion of France in 1940. Assigned the code name of "ROSE," she parachuted back into occupied France to assist the Underground in the struggle for freedom. Her French upbringing proved invaluable and she was involved in many successful operations. Captured by the Gestapo in July of 1944, she was tortured but, like Simone, never divulged the names of any of her associates or revealed any other information that the Germans could find useful.

She described the Gestapo officers who interrogated her: "One of them rushed at me and slapped me as hard as he could around the head calling me a liar, a spy, a dirty bitch. And the other one said, 'We have ways of making people talk who don't want to.' They took me into a room where there was a bath and they held me under the water. You suffocate under the water, but you must stick to your story. I remembered that we'd been taught never to be afraid, never let them dominate you."

The last words they said to her were, "We are giving you the benefit of the doubt," which caused her heart to soar but then it quickly sank as they completed the sentence with, "but we are sending you to a concentration camp." "You'll have a good laugh there," one of the Nazis told her sarcastically. "It won't be like here. It will be your punishment for having worked against us." She was shipped to Ravensbrück in Germany in August of 1944 and later transferred to a forced labor camp in Silesia, on the German border, before escaping while being marched through a forest, finally meeting up with American soldiers in Leipzig.

Eileen never married nor had children. She didn't speak to anyone about what she did during World War II either before or after that BBC interview. In her later years, she was known in Torquay as an eccentric, elderly woman who didn't have much to do with other people and was surrounded only by her cats. No one knew she had been awarded the prestigious "Member of the British Empire" and the French *Croix de Guerre*. Sadly, there was no one to make arrangements for her funeral when she died in 2010.

Odile Nearne, Eileen's niece and only relative, was living in Verona, Italy when she later learned of her aunt's death and admitted, "She didn't want to talk about her past. She was a humble and modest person, and she didn't want the spotlight on her. But I also think that she had been so traumatized that reliving it would have stopped her from having a normal life, and she wanted to go on as best she could."

There's now a small blue plaque outside Eileen's flat in Torquay which Odile campaigned to have placed there. Knowing that she would prefer to stay "low profile" or, better yet, "no profile," her aunt's name was not used. The plaque says simply that there was a "war heroine" who did "courageous work" who once lived there.

Another notable woman, Marie-Medeleine Fourcade had a similar upbreaking as Simone's, born into an upper-class family on the French

Riviera. Living in Marseilles as the daughter of a steamship company executive, she was 11 years older than Simone. Before beginning her work for the Resistance, she made the difficult decision to send her two children to the safety of Switzerland.

She joined The Alliance Réseau, based in Vichy. Its nickname was "Noah's Ark" because Marie-Medeleine assigned members of the underground network the code names of animals. She took the name "HEDGEHOG" as her own.

The group focused on obtaining intelligence about the German military and transmitting it to Great Britain, helping shelter airmen who had been shot down, and distributing shortwave radios to Resistance members. Assuming leadership of the Alliance network after the arrest of its former leader, Georges Loustaunau-Lacau, she became the only French woman heading a Resistance organization.

In August of 1941, the British sent her a wireless operator to assist her. The operator turned out to be a double agent and Marie-Medeleine, along with several others, were arrested by the Gestapo. She managed to escape, however, and was forced into hiding. In July of 1943, British Intelligence felt it was too dangerous for her to remain in France so she was smuggled to England to run a network from a house in Chelsea.

After D-Day, Marie-Madeleine returned to France but was spotted and again captured by the Gestapo. Similar to Simone, she was starved but the ensuing weight loss had an unexpected benefit – it enabled her to squeeze through the bars of her prison cell window and, once again, escape. She joined the Maquis and worked with the SOE. She personally went to Alsace to give American General George Patton information about the location and strength of German troops in that region. The intelligence she provided proved invaluable to the Allied cause.

Despite what she experienced, Simone never doubted that she made the right decision to fight for her country. She spoke for herself, as well as the estimated 15 to 20% of the members of the Resistance who were female, declaring, "I regret nothing. There was something exciting about the danger of what I did during the war. I believe the woman sitting home waiting had a harder job because she had so much time to think of what could happen to her family."

Chapter 10 - The Final Flight of the "Miss Take"

On July 8, 1944, approximately a month after D-Day and Simone's release from prison, a Marauder, serial number 42-95821, from the 391st Bomber Group, 9th Air Force took off from Matching Green. Promoted to Lieutenant Colonel just two weeks earlier, George Stalnaker was at the controls of the "Miss Take," given the code number of "08-0" for this mission, and leading a squadron consisting of 18 aircraft, three groups of six, flying in a 'V' formation.

A B-26B, the "Miss Take" had two 2,000 horsepower Pratt & Whitney 18-cylinder R-2800-43 engines. The wing span of this latest version of the Marauder had been increased from 65 feet to 71 feet with two additional 50 caliber guns added in the tail position. The area of the vertical tail surface was expanded and armament raised to include one fixed and one flexible gun in the nose, four "package guns" on the sides of the forward fuselage, two in the dorsal turret, two flexible "waist" guns, one tunnel gun, and two tail guns. The crew was now normally seven rather than five.

As Squadron Commander and "Box Lead" instructing the other planes when to drop their bombs, George would be expected to have additional crew members, such as a navigator, bombardier, and extra radio gunner. The "Miss Take" carried eight airmen on this critical sortie.

The regular flight crew was seasoned and battle-tested, with every member having received at least one Air Medal. The Air Medal was instituted on May 11th 1942 to recognize air crew members "Who while serving in any capacity of the Army of the United States, distinguishes himself by meritorious achievement while participating in an aerial flight." Bombardier Captain Edgar G. Williams had eight, George seven, navigator 1LT Francis J. Murphy seven, Tail Gunner/Armorer SSG Stanley W. Miller seven, Co-pilot 2LT Eugene R. Squier four, and Radio Operator/Gunner 1LT James B. Clark seven.

The eldest at 27 years old, George had flown 35 missions in his seven months of service. The 26-year-old Squier, a dental technician from San Francisco, had 36 missions in two years and two months of service. A former accountant from Sacramento, CA, Murphy, also 26 years old, had 43 missions in two years and five months. The twenty-five-year-old Clark, 43 missions in three years and six months. Williams, from Glens Falls, NY, a twenty-six-year old former accountant, had two years and seven months with 46 missions. With 49 missions, Stub Miller, 22 years old at this point, had served for 18 months.

Engineer/Gunner T/SGT Richard B. Smith performed admirably after being pressed into service when regular Radioman Tom Larson was hospitalized after being hit by shrapnel on a previous flight. A 23-year-old former general mechanic from Natrona, PA, Smith had previously flown 55 missions in eight months.

There was one other member of the crew, a SSG waist gunner who was a last-minute replacement due to an illness. George later indicated that he preferred that he not be identified by name. Unlike the rest of the crew, he had virtually no experience under fire. He did not perform to expectations, as George later explains.

The "Miss Take" mission was to destroy the railway bridge on the Noire River in Nantes in Northwest France. It was the last remaining bridge available to the Germans for sending reinforcements in trucks and tanks up from the southern part of France to the Normandy area where there was still heavy fighting.

Unlike buildings, bridges are tall and narrow and can be difficult targets to hit. A perfect cluster of bombs could be dropped right on the target and yet the bridge can still be left standing. The resultant explosions could simply damage a bit of superstructure or maybe make a hole in the flooring. Many bridges are solid while others are a web of bracing. Some have thick supports that collapse when a bomb strikes but others are built so that a bomb can slip between those supports and fall harmlessly into the water. When double bridges are partly destroyed, the other half can sometimes still be crossed. The bombs need to fall in the right places and explode at the right time for the mission to succeed.

"We were called in very early in the morning for our pre-briefing," recounted George. "It was somewhere around three or four a.m. They went out and scrubbed the mission because the weather was so bad. Our route was supposed to take us from the east to the west so we wouldn't be flying into the sun but they couldn't get decent enough weather. They made us sit around all day. If we hadn't flown that mission, it was going to be our six-week turn to go to London on leave. It was getting to be so late in the afternoon that I put on my pinks and greens and put money in my pocket."

The fabrics used for officer uniforms, purchased by their wearers, were of better quality than those used for government-issued enlisted uniforms. Officer's coats were made from a high-lustrous 19 oz. wool dyed in a dark shade of Olive Drab #51, called "green," or sometimes "chocolate." Trousers were dyed in a shade of Olive Drab #54, generally known as "pink." The contrast between the two colors was

George and his flight crew standing in front of the "Miss Take"

usually referred to as "pinks and greens" and made for easy identification when they were   with a group of enlisted soldiers.

George continued, "So, I said to myself, 'Heck, we're never going to fly this mission.' By golly, about four or five o'clock, they called us down and I saw they have given the port of Saint-Nazaire as the IP (initial point) flying up the Noire River to Nantes. It would be coming out of the west and flying to the east.

The map was just as red as it could be, which meant heavy flak. I can remember standing there as the leader and I looked at the map and I said, 'What stupid son of a bitch ever gave us that route?' I felt this tap on my shoulder and there were these stars gleaming at me. General Herbert Thatcher was standing there and responded, 'I did.' I said to myself, 'Oh, boy, I've really done it now.' But he was nice. He said, 'Don't you worry about the flak, George. The fighters are going to take it all out.' I remember a year later I saw him and I kidded him by remarking, 'Boy, the fighters really took out all that flak, didn't they?'

I said to myself that it was too late anyway to go. But we suited up and got in the airplanes. I thought that we still weren't going to go because it was so doggone late. But, about 7 or 7:30 in the evening on the 8th of July, we went. I didn't even tighten my parachute straps. I was still wearing my pinks and greens and not my heavy underclothing which my straps had been adjusted for. That was to my dismay later.

By golly, we got the green light from the tower to start the engines and so we did. We taxied up to the take-off point and got the next green light to go down the runway and take off. I was still surprised that we had done that. We got down to Saint-Nazaire and it was very close to 9 o'clock. We were at about 10,000 feet on some of our previous missions. We had been as low as 500 feet and gotten pieces of bombs in our engines from other planes in the lead and also picked up a lot of machine gun fire so whatever the cloud cover allowed, that's what we did.

We started that bomb run and it must have lasted about three or four minutes. It seemed like an eternity. We saw the fighters go down to get the flak. We saw it coming up in the distance. There were six particular bursts that seemed to be trying to get us. Every 20 seconds or so, my navigator could see flashing on the ground. It was getting closer and closer. Pretty soon you could hear it clang off the armored seats and it would hit the windshield and side windows making big holes in them. My turret gunner called and told me that the right engine was either on fire or smoking very badly. We were losing power out of that engine and we must have been taking some hits out of the left engine because

93

we couldn't hold altitude." At this point, the engines were down to 35% of full power.

George added, "Then turret gunner Jim Clark said he moved out of the turret because it had just been smashed. I know many may think that it wasn't as rough as I'm describing it but it actually was. I was terrified. My navigator Frank Murphy kept crossing himself while saying the 'Hail Mary' over and over again. Just hearing flak bang against the plane over and over again I thought that it was just going to go right through my face. I said if I don't take my feet off the rudder pedals I'm going to turn off this target.

I called my bombardier and said 'If we get hit, you don't have a prayer. I can't hold altitude. I can only hold it down to 500 feet a minute so that doesn't make our chances of hitting anything very good and we were leading these airplanes.' I told him he could come out of there if he wanted to. He said, 'If you can give me 30 more seconds at this 500-feet-a-minute descent, I think I can hit it.' The flak was such that it would just go bang and you'd fly right into the smoke as it went off. I knew with one or two more hits we were going to go down."

Bombardier Ed Williams said 'Bombs Away' and he hadn't said anything more than the 'A' of 'Away' when he shot back there up into the radio compartment. Our speed was down to just 140 miles/hour. We hit that bridge right on with our 2,000 pounders. Ed was a gutsy guy. I turned up in about as steep a bank as you could ever get."

Left wing man Tommy Tucker was able to drop right into formation and not get hit. George then feathered the right engine as the plane went into that bank. Feathering involves reducing drag by twisting a propeller engine parallel to the wind, similar to putting your hand out parallel to the ground while riding in a fast-moving car to minimize the resistance.

"By the time we got straightened out again the rest of the airplanes had gone on past us," continued George. "We were sitting there as a single engine and flying up toward Normandy. I asked Ed to figure out if we could get to Normandy Beach. They had a runway there since this was about a month after D-day. I asked him how much altitude we would have and Gene Squier was in the radio compartment talking to Ed. He had been shot up in a mission before not with me but with somebody else. Really shot up. His flak suit had great big holes in it. I heard Gene Squier say, 'Tell him we can't make it and we can jump and get out of this fucking war.' He was just kidding but Ed came in and said truthfully at this rate of descent we'll be 20,000 feet under the ground when we get to Normandy.

I had a gunner and I don't want to use his name but he was not my usual waist gunner and he was the macho type who was always beating his chest and was a big 'I am' type. He kept screeching things like, 'Oh, you can get us back' and 'You've got to get us home' and 'Please get us back.' (George says this while imitating the waist gunner in a whiny voice.) Everybody else was very calm.

Stub Miller, one of the most courageous guys I've ever run into, called from the turret and said, 'Sir, I'm tossing out the machine guns and belts of ammunition to try to lighten the aircraft. If you need me to jump to lighten the airplane, I volunteer to jump.' I told him to stand by and I might have to ask him to. This other gunner really hollered and yelled, 'My God, no, no, no.' Finally, I told Stub that I'm going to ask him to jump and so he did. To me, Stub Miller was one of the real heroes of the entire war."

"I certainly didn't know George the way that my husband did," admitted Stub's wife Bess. "Stub thought so much of him. They both trusted and admired each other. They got along perfectly. George would write to me and tell me how much he appreciated him and always depended on him. Stub used to say that he'd jump out of a plane if that's what George asked him to do. On that final mission, it turned out that's exactly what he DID ask him to do."

"It was just a couple of minutes later that I saw we weren't going to make it," admitted George. "We were between Rennes and Nantes at that time. We figured if we got too far north we'd be getting into the fighting area and we'd likely get captured. If we jumped too close to Nantes, they'd probably be pretty mad at us for bombing and we wouldn't get very good treatment. So, looking at the map I said it's time for us to go now and they did. They all jumped.

The co-pilot, 2LT Gene Squier, and I and this waist gunner were left in the airplane. I said to the waist gunner that I'm going to count to 10 and if you're still there I'm jumping because I'm going to be damned if I'm going to get killed going in with this airplane because you're still in it. So, I counted to 10 and called his name out several times. He didn't call back so I had to presume he had jumped. Gene went back and jumped."

George then trimmed the airplane. When a pilot had to pull the control stick all the way back on a climb, this device kept the pitch steady so there would be less strain on the pilot and improve control of the aircraft. He ran back to the bomb bay, straddled the compartment, held his legs together, and jumped. The final crew member to do so, George dropped out at 9 p.m. at a height of 6,000 feet with the plane 17 kilometers (about 10½ miles) northwest of Chateaubriant.

Stub recounted his version of the events: "We started flying two missions a day. We were glad to do it. We knew we were doing something special then. A month and two days after D-Day, I was with our Squadron Commander Lt. Col. George W. Stalnaker and we flew a mission to central France. It was over water all the way to avoid flak. We were to fly up the Loire River to Nantes and bomb the railroad bridge there.

At briefing, the Intelligence people always told us what to do and we always did what they told us. It seemed to me like they were usually wrong. They told us to fly in formation up the mouth of the river and take a nice, long 10-minute bombing run. They said there is a flak position up the river, but it won't be manned. They said to fly straight and level right up to the target, bomb it, and head north for home. They were sure right except for one thing. That flak position WAS manned and they shot the hell out of us. Ordinarily we would take a one-minute bomb run. As we headed for the target, we were taking evasive action. By the time we got there, we had one engine knocked out and the other one hit.

Since I occupied the top turret position, it was my duty to inform the pilot as to what was happening behind us. Sometimes the airplanes behind the lead plane could be in a heavy concentration of flak and the pilot couldn't see behind, so it was my job to relay the information to him so we could take evasive action until we reached our target. The lead plane was the only one with a bombsight and after we reached the target area, we had to fly straight and level so the bombardier could adjust the bombsight. This involved a period of from one to two minutes.

We were leading the group and I think we had good results as we bombed and turned north on a single engine that was not operating at full tilt. I began to think we were in trouble when I saw other B-26's from our group flying on altitude and going right on past. I thought, 'Oh, boy, we've had it.' I was standing behind George and noticed our rate of descent was 500 feet a minute. We were at 10,000 feet when we left the target and we went down to 5,000 feet. George handled it real nice.

The replacement gunner didn't want to jump. George told him that he could ride this thing by himself because we were all fixing to jump out so he had better go now. The rest of us lined up like paratroopers. We opened the bomb doors and there was no panic, there was no rush, we just stepped out. All nice and easy."

Some say the replacement gunner was taken prisoner by the Germans while others say he just disappeared into the countryside. To this day, no one knows the truth. Official military records still list him as "Missing in Action."

"On three or four missions before July 8 we had hits on one or other engine, which had made it necessary to come back on a single engine," noted Stub. "This may not sound like a big deal but this was the same airplane that, at one time, would hardly be able to fly on two engines."

The "Miss Take" could barely stay in the air. The 'stall speed' of a B-26 was 135 mph so the plane had to go 'downhill' to maintain sufficient speed. They were able to stay airborne but not fly fast enough to stay with the rest of the Group. By dropping out of formation, it made them a prime target for enemy fighters. So, to give themselves a better chance of survival, they chose to bail out in an orderly fashion and get as far as possible behind enemy lines.

A P-47 Thunderbolt Fighter followed George all the way down. When the pilot saw George jump as the last man out, he knew that he was the bomber's pilot. He circled and, when he did, the prop wash collapsed George's parachute. He tried to signal him to move away by waving. The pilot thought George was waving at him so he'd wave back. He continued to circle around and each time George would have to spread out his chute as it kept collapsing.

Each time George's parachute deflated, the single-pilot, single-engine P-47 would be busy circling around and then spot him again with his chute fully deployed. If it had been a larger plane, a navigator or co-pilot would certainly have seen the chute close and then lurch upon re-opening.

You might think that George would have been annoyed with the P-47 pilot. That wasn't the case, though. He confessed, "I kind of admired him because he was all by himself and was there trying to protect me. If any German fighter had come along, he wouldn't have had much of a chance."

One of the largest and heaviest fighter aircraft in the war, the P-47 was ruggedly constructed and well-armed with eight .50-caliber machine guns, four per wing. However, it had a loaded weight of 17,500 pounds. That made it effective for diving but gave it a poor rate of climb and lack of maneuverability. Little wonder it was dubbed the "Jug" and many compared it to a flying bathtub. So, George knew that the plane would have been an easy target.

According to Stub, "Our starboard engine was hit during the bomb run and was burning. Had we tried to put the fire out, it would have affected our speed and altitude, affecting the accuracy of the bombsight. We continued on for a very nervous two minutes but we hit

97

our target and destroyed the bridge. As soon as our bombs were away, we dropped out of formation and feathered our engine. Since our portside engine wasn't developing full power either, we started dropping altitude very rapidly. George and his advisors in front of the plane calculated that we couldn't make it back to friendly territory so it was decided we should abandon ship and parachute to the ground some distance behind enemy lines. We threw everything we could overboard to lighten the load so we could stay in the air as long as we could and finally it was decided we must evacuate.

I was in the back section. Our waist gunner was in near panic so George asked me to pave the way and jump first. I took a deep breath, lived my whole life over again, and then jumped head-first out of the waist window. I was so relieved to be clean of the plane that I actually had to think to reach up and pull the ripcord. Thank God, everything worked as it was supposed to. I just hung there in the air, thinking how quiet it was and wondering what was awaiting me on the ground. I remember thinking that, one way or another, the war was over for me."

From their various vantage points, the crew members watched the Miss Take stall, spin out of control, and burst into flames upon impact with the ground. An eyewitness later described the event: "I saw the men parachute from the sky like birds and then only an enormous ball of fire when their plane exploded." The spectacular crash, which killed a horse and two cows, was witnessed by many of the French people in the area. Unfortunately, it was also witnessed by many of the Germans.

George recalled, "I was not much more than 500 ft. from hitting the ground and I heard these voices saying, *Vive L'Amérique*! or 'Long Live America!' I looked down and there were a bunch of peasants in this field. There was a doggone barbed wire fence with a big stake sticking out of the corner of the fence. I kept heading right for it. I just couldn't steer that parachute away from there. I said to myself that it was a matter of landing correctly with legs slightly apart or saving my masculinity and keeping my legs together. So, I put my legs together and I said a prayer. It wasn't meant to be profane but I said, 'Dear Jesus, you can't let me get this far and let this happen to me.'

I fell right on the pole and the barbed wire fence. I got scratched up on my legs somewhat but, thank goodness, I survived it. As soon as I landed, all these peasants gathered around me. Like a damn fool, I gave them all my cigarettes because I was so glad to be safe."

The "Miss Take" crew almost made a deadly "mistake." The parachute target they picked had no indicators on the map that it was actually a Gestapo Headquarters. Fortunately, all but one of them missed the target. Stub Miller was unlucky enough, however, to wind up dangerously close to the enemy. The crew came through the parachute landing in relatively good shape. Murphy had a sprained ankle, Smith hit his head on the ground, Williams injured his shoulder and elbow, Clark sprained both his ankles and wrenched his right knee, and George only had those scratches. Squier and Miller were injury-free.

Stub explained, "I never saw the airplane or any of the other crew during my descent. Because we had been traveling at a speed of about 160 mph with our chutes and would land miles from each other, I never really expected that we would be able to get together once on the ground. At about 9 p.m., I landed in a field about 300 yards away from some farmhouses but not far from the Gestapo HQ. My parachute was hanging in a tree. After pulling the chute out of the tree and disposing of it, I made my way over toward the farmhouses where a group of people were congregated. Fortunately for me, they were friendly toward Americans and within a few minutes I was in French civilian clothing. I had learned a few words of the French language but not nearly enough to communicate with them.

On every mission, we were issued an 'escape kit' which consisted of several items essential for our well-being – a map of the country over which we were flying, some adrenalin tablets for energy, tablets for water purification to provide drinking water, and a small amount of money. In our case, it was $20 worth of French money. I always carried two full packs of cigarettes on each mission just in case we didn't get back so I would have enough to last a couple of days. There were several adults and children in this group and I pulled out my cigarettes and offered them to these people. Everyone, including the children, took one so that took care of one pack.

It was not long before bedtime when I landed. These people took me in and provided me with a bed. There were two beds side by side. I was in one and a young girl about 16 years of age in the other. The following morning, there were about 15 or 16 people at the breakfast table. Our coffee cups were about half full and they were passing a container of a clear white liquid around and adding it to their coffee. I didn't know what it was, couldn't ask, so I just followed what they did. I thought it might be liquid sugar so I used a lot of it. I was thinking that I could use the energy. It turned out to be Calvados (140 proof apple brandy from the southern Normandy region) and it just about curled my hair!"

After breakfast, the locals disassembled two or three broken bicycles and used the parts to put together a functioning one for Stub who used $10 to pay them for their efforts. He also had them write a note in French saying that he was an American and that he needed food and help. Then they took him about a mile away to a highway, headed him south toward Spain, a neutral country, and hoping he could find his way from there to England.

"I was on my own," continued Stub. "It was a nice, warm, sunny day and I was enjoying my trip. It was prudent to avoid large towns so after traveling for two of three hours, I went over a small hill and saw a big city in front of me. I later learned that it was Chateaubriant. I decided to turn off on the first road I came to and go around the town. It was a very narrow road, about 15 feet wide, with two-story houses on each side. After about 100 yards, I looked up and got my first glimpse of the enemy. There were about 200 German soldiers doing a close-order drill in the middle of the road.

A German officer got out of the car and started talking to someone in the second floor window. I was trapped. I couldn't go in either direction. I jumped off my bicycle and started pumping air into the tires. I pumped for several minutes and was afraid I would be conspicuous so I decided to take my chances and walk by the German officer. I walked shoulder to shoulder by him pushing my bike and he didn't even look at me. I was even wearing my Air Corps flight jacket but otherwise was dressed in French clothing. I thought for sure that 'This is it' but he evidently thought I was French.

Once I was out of sight, I discarded my flight jacket. I figured it was better to be cold than be a Prisoner of War. After regaining my composure, I proceeded traveling south, only to encounter a whole regiment of Germans going north, probably up to the Normandy coast. There were many trucks carrying men and artillery. I stood, shaking in my boots, as 75 to 100 pieces of artillery passed by. They, too, took me for a Frenchman and paid no attention to me."

Stub selected two farmhouses that appeared the most run-down, assuming they would be occupied by people who were not German sympathizers. The family in the first gave him something to eat but offered no help otherwise. Early in the afternoon, he stopped at the second where there were several adults and some teenage boys who seemed to be excited about something. Two of the boys took him quickly away from the house to a wooded area where they told him to stay until they returned. After about an hour, they returned and had a priest with them. Stub started talking to him very limited French but he answered in perfect English. Stub was so surprised that he said, "Oh, you speak American" and the priest responded, "No, I don't speak American but I do speak English."

He told Stub there were some airmen hiding in the woods back up north from where he had just been that morning. He didn't know if they were American or not but said they were waiting for the French Underground to help them. Stub decided to try to locate the others. He had traveled about 40 miles that day and was tired but these two boys agreed to help him find his way back to these people. They each had a bike and with one on each side of him, they took his arms and proceeded to take him back north.

They traveled 10 or 15 miles when the boys stopped and pointed to some houses grouped together about a quarter of a mile away. They explained that these houses contained German sympathizers but one particular family would help Stub. They felt they couldn't take him any closer and tried to express the importance of selecting the right house. Not understanding French, he was very unsure of their directions but wound up selected the right one and they willingly took him into their home. He hadn't had anything to drink all day and was very thirsty so he asked them for some water. They thought he wanted to wash so they brought a pan of water. Stub snickered, "I drank right from the pan, realized the mistake I had made, and then washed in it."

According to George, "I saw the other chutes of my crew some distance away as I came down. I landed in a field near quite a big farm where a group of people were standing, laughing, and talking. One man came up to me at once and took my chute, harness, and Mae West." The latter is an inflatable life jacket for emergency use by airplane pilots in flights over water. The origin of the name is pretty obvious. Later, George gave him his escape kit as well as it became evident that he wasn't going to need it.

After co-pilot Gene Squier bailed out of the aircraft and got down to about 1,000 feet, he saw the French running through the fields pointing at his chute. He side-slipped the parachute, which involves tugging on the line to fall sideways through the air in a downward direction, to avoid the woods and landed hard in a small field. After hiding his chute in a gully, he shoved his Mae West and helmet into a hedge.

Gene said, "When I came to the road, a Frenchman stopped me to shake hands. He wanted me to go with him but I was suspicious thinking that it seemed too easy so I went on his way. I later learned that the man would have given me the help he needed. I was soon blocked by a thick hedgerow and as I hesitated, I heard shouting on the far side. Fearing that these were German voices, I turned east until I reached a wheat field in which I hid. I spent the night here in the open after I had cleaned out my wallet and sewn my compass and hacksaw into my jacket."

"The only thing they ever told us about how to operate a parachute was to pull the rip-cord," admitted Jim Clark. "As I stepped out of that airplane, I worried that I would hit some part of it as I went out. What I didn't realize was that I was going the same speed as the airplane. I couldn't do anything but go straight down until the air hit me. Anyway, I went out feet first. It seemed to me like when I got to 20 or 30 feet below the airplane, I pulled that end, the chute opened real easy, and I never did turn over or anything. I just hung there and watched the airplane all the way to the ground.

It went into a big 180 degree turn downwards. At the end of the turn, it went straight down. When it hit, it blew up like hell with all the 100 octane gas. There was me hanging there in the sky and the weather was beautiful. It was nice. I was just enjoying that parachute jump and thinking, 'Well heck, I'm never going to get down the rate I am going.' It seemed like I was going to hang there forever.

Of course, I was a mile high when I jumped. When I got down below 500 feet, I could see I was zooming along pretty fast. Sure enough, there was a great big old tree and I hit it right in the middle. Just before I hit, the air dumped out of my parachute and I got to coming down really fast. I broke a limb off that tree as big as a leg with my knee. Then I hit with my feet. I landed on my butt and it really shook me up.

The first thing I did was jump up and my ankles just collapsed. They were both badly sprained and my right knee was damaged so I fell right back down. I couldn't stand up so I just got on my knees and pulled my parachute out of the tree and then took my Mae West off. I had landed in a real nice sandy place where it was easy to dig. So I just dug me a hole and buried the Mae West and parachute. I started to crawl, looking for a good place to hide. I crawled about 50 yards and found a big thorn thicket and wriggled about 20 feet into that. Intelligence had told us that if we hide as near as we could to where we landed, and stay hidden for 24 hours, the Germans would quit looking for us so that is what I intended to do.

There in the thorn bush I decided it was time for me to smoke a Lucky Strike so I reached down into my pocket and got one out. I reached into another pocket for my Zippo lighter to light it, but I lost that Zippo on the way down. So I just sat there and chewed on that Lucky Strike for hours. I got some kind of lonesome in that thorn bush but was determined to stay there for 24 hours before I did anything.

After dark, I heard someone chomping around out there and I thought, 'Oh hell, the Germans are looking for me.' I didn't dare hardly breathe. Pretty soon, a dog started barking round there and I thought, 'Heck, they have gone and got the bloodhounds after me, they've got me for sure.' This dog found me alright. He just crawled right in to about two feet of me and just sat there barking. Then here comes a man and he crawled up in that thorn bush and pulls me out. Well, of course, I was thinking it was the Gestapo or something but then pretty soon I knew he wasn't German. I could tell by his actions that he was friendly and knew he must be French, although I couldn't speak French and he couldn't speak English. But, he was real nice.

I later found out his name was Joseph Bodard. When he pulled me out, he found I couldn't walk. Despite the fact that he was a little guy weighing about 140 lbs. and I weighed 180 lbs., he put me on his back and carried me until he gave out. Next, he took his coat off and laid it down and motioned for me to sit on that coat until he came back for it. Well, I wasn't going anywhere. I didn't know where to go and couldn't walk anyway, so I sat and waited. He wasn't gone long and came back with a red-headed Irishman by the name of Frank Murphy, the bombardier on our plane. I was certainly glad to see him.

They carried me back to Joe's house and hid us in the hay loft of the barn. Wouldn't you think that would be the first place anyone would look? Well anyway, this is where they hid us. I think every Frenchman within 50 miles must have seen us parachute. If they didn't see, then somebody told them and they all came up that night to see us in the hay loft of that barn. It was like we were film stars.

The next morning, old Joe came to the hay loft and with signals and signs, got the idea over to us that he couldn't keep us there anymore and we would have to go. Well, we presumed he was kicking us out and we would have to go and fend for ourselves. Intelligence had told us that the way to get out of France was to go to Spain, 700 to 800 miles south. So, they decided we all had to get out of the hay loft. Frank Murphy had my feet and I guess Ed Williams had my other end and they were going to carry me to Spain. I told them there was no way they could ever get me to Spain that way. I told them they should leave me there and let the Germans get me. They should see if they could make it on their own. They said, 'Hell no, we're going to go and we're all going to stay together.'

We weren't really abandoned like we thought we were. Our French friends took us to a wheat field not far from the place, put us under an apple tree, and brought us some of the best food I have ever tasted in my life. It wasn't anything fancy, just home-baked French bread, real big warm loaves. They cut them open and put about half a pound of home-made butter in the middle and brought us several bottles of red wine. We drank that wine and ate that bread and it was real good. We stayed there in the wheat field like it seemed about three days. It rained and we didn't have coats. We just stayed there and got wet. It was kind of uncomfortable but it was summer and wasn't too bad.

They decided they would move us into the forest which was about 10 miles across country from there. They said to walk straight but I couldn't walk, anyway. Joseph Bodard had figured out a way to get me there and he had a little apple-cart-looking thing with some hard rubber tire wheels on it. What it amounted to was a kind of trailer that he tied on behind his bicycle. He took me on the road and we took off and he is pulling. I was sitting in this wooden box tied on behind his bicycle and we headed right out to this forest by the road.

It was an old rough, dirt road with a little village at the bottom of the road and there were a few Germans in this village. We attempted this trip before sundown. The village is at the foot of a hill and we started down. He's pulling me in his trailer and every time we hit a bump it bounced a foot or two. I thought, 'Gee, I'm going to fall out when it bounces.' We got down this hill and he nearly did quit pedaling. I'm telling you, I'll bet he was doing 50 miles an hour when we went through that village. Every time we hit a bump, I thought he was going to throw me just plum out. We fairly flew through that village and kept going. I saw Germans standing around there but they didn't pay any attention to us. They just thought we were a couple of crazy Frenchmen.

We went right on through that village and into the forest and set up another camp there. They didn't have much food themselves but everybody in the whole countryside decided they would feed us. They brought us some real good food and we ate what we could and tried to tell them we didn't need that much but there were too many different people bringing us food. We ate all we could and appreciated it all.

Ed Williams, Frank Murphy, and I went into the forest together and Lt. Col. Stalnaker joined us. That was really good because he had taken French in college and could speak a little of it, not too well, but it was certainly better than we could do. They found Stanley Miller wandering around, trying to walk to Spain, and brought him to us.

After a while they decided we should be French civilians so we got rid of everything we had that was made in the United States including pocket knives, wrist watches, underwear, everything. We stripped to the skin and put on old clothes that were really worn out. Tattered old clothes were the best they had, I guess, and that's when we became French civilians."

Chapter 11 - "We are Veritable Brothers."

Upon hearing the news that George and his crew were MIA, Colonel Gerald Williams immediately gave command of the 575th Squadron to LTC Ernest N. Ljunggren who, up to that point, had been Operations Officer for the 391st Bomber Group HQ.

According to Stub Miller, "My brother Ray was a pilot of an L-5, a small single engine plane and was stationed somewhere in the southwest area of England. He flew over to visit me several times, bringing 10 or 12 cartons of cigarettes. I had accumulated about 50 cartons along with cookies and candy I had received from home. When word reached the base that we had been shot down, I later learned the fellows in my barracks made a bee-line for my goodies. We were only able to buy six packs of cigarettes a week so they were precious. The guys never bothered anyone's personal belongings, but just took the perishables.

Ray was flying at tree top levels and on June 18, he flew into some high tension electrical wires and was killed. Then I was shot down and listed as MIA. I was terribly concerned about my folks." Stub's parents had lost one son and now had another that was missing. Unfortunately, he and the other members of the Miss Take would be out of contact with the outside world for more than a month.

Back home, Bess recalled, "One day I was at my job as a Head Telephone Operator and my boss came over to me saying there was a problem and he had to take me home. My uncle had a stroke, was still in the hospital, and I thought something might have happened to him. My whole family was there, including my sister. They had a telegram but I couldn't bring myself to read it. They told me Stub was Missing in Action. I was crying but my dad told me that he would probably be all right. I felt better after that. I always believed what my dad told me. I just knew I'd have to wait. I continued to write to Stub every day. He and I had always done that. I wasn't going to stop now."

From the ground, Emile Sauras, observed, "It's Saturday, July 8. I see hundreds of planes circling in the sky. Their mission is to bomb the German factories for one and the other is the destruction of the Port of Nantes. At the beginning of the afternoon, I am looking at the planes passing over when suddenly I see the shooting of a bomber which dives toward the ground. One of their airplane motors has been shot out. A column of black smoke comes from the plane. There are aviators jumping with parachutes. I am looking at the last, very certainly the pilot, who is going toward the factory that makes shingles in Plessis in a village that I know very well that we call 'La Cité.' The plane disappears behind a tree and explodes in a big ball of fire.

Eight km from there, the radio station of 'Rennes Bretagne' is occupied by the Germans. I know that the soldiers are very concerned about the advance of the Allied forces and will try everything possible to capture those who just jumped from the plane in flames. They will search all the town of Coësmes. So, I take my bicycle and head in the direction of the area where the last parachute came down. When I get there, I find the pilot who is very calm and is gathering in his parachute in the middle of curious villagers who regard him with sympathy. They don't know if the Germans saw the parachutes and whether they will be there in a short amount of time. I approach the pilot and tell him we must go quickly. He understands me right away and follows me."

George echoed, "After I hit the ground, this one boy, Emile Sauras, kept tugging at my Mae West and I finally got the idea that he wanted me to follow him. He kept saying *Allez Vites* which I knew meant he wanted me to go with him. I had taken some French at West Point so I could understand a little of it and speak it in a very fractured way. He led me away. I found out later that about five minutes after that, the Germans had gotten there. Fortunately, they headed in the opposite direction of the way Emile had taken me.

He took me to his father's stone hut where I hid in an attic that night. He and his family fed me and in the morning they took my uniform and gave me peasant clothes. They wanted my West Point ring. They said the Germans would recognize it. I said, 'I went through four years to get that thing and I can't give it up.' So, they sewed it into the cuff of the pants."

For downed pilots, it was a risk either way to stay in military uniform or change into French civilian clothes. Being caught by the Germans in uniform could mean either being shot or captured and sent to a Prisoner of War camp. Wearing civilian clothes and then being captured, however, would likely mean being executed as a spy. For the French, it was made clear what their fate would be in helping Allied soldiers in printed warning notices posted on the walls of many buildings and signed by German General Otto von Stülpnager: "All males who come to the aid, either directly or indirectly, of the crews of enemy aircraft coming down in parachutes, or having made a forced landing, helps in their escape, hides them, or comes to their aid in any fashion, will be shot on the spot. Women who render the same help will be sent to concentration camps in Germany."

Emile continued, "We are going down through several fields and we get close to a river called 'Du Plessis.' I invite the American pilot, whom I found very likable, to follow me by walking in the water so the German dogs will not be able to trace our steps. We follow the river current for at least 200 meters and arrive at my parent's house. We pass by the garden and walk into the kitchen to the very stunned looks of my parents.

Maman understands right away that the situation is grave. Always generous, she invites my new friend to join in the family dinner. My papa is very calm and shows the Lt. Colonel where he is going to spend the night. It is a very big room with two country beds and big comforters. A trap door accessed by a wooden step stool leads to the basement which is just below. He shows him the door of the basement which then gives access to the courtyard and garden that we came through earlier.

At the back of the yard, my brother François and I dig a crude hiding place. We explain to George that in case of danger he must come out without noise and hide himself in the temporary hole. Night falls and Maman has prepared a very good meal that George appreciates. He eats quite well. His composure really stuns me. Then he lies down on one of the big beds and falls asleep very quickly as if he was in his own home.

Papa prepares his double-barreled hunting gun with some bullets that are on the table. He also takes out the 6 millimeter carbine rifle which was on top of our armoire. What would we do if the Germans come? He says, 'Who cares?' That reassures us! So we keep guard all night. As soon as a car slows down on the road, our hearts start racing. All through the night, unrelentingly, the German soldiers continue their search."

"They put me down in the basement and I slept there that night," continued George. "The next morning they took me out way, way early. It was cold with fog with dew all over. They gave me some hard-boiled eggs and a bottle of cider. They took me out to the middle of this wheat field. I sat there all day long and I could hear the sirens going round and round. There were cars going up and down the road. The Germans had seen the fact that I was a Lt. Colonel on the chute and were naturally trying to find me. It had my name, rank, and ASN (Army Serial Number) on it. It was a nervous day, I can tell you."

According to Emile, "Early the next morning, Sunday July 9, we wake up our guest who sleeps without worrying. A quick wash, a large lunch, and we start talking about the situation. Maman prepares a suit for George. It is Papa's wedding suit. It is a very nice suit. George tries on the jacket and it fits him quite well. The pants are a little short but not too noticeable. The black shoes and the little Basque hat make him look like a good middle-class Frenchman.

During the night, my father and I talk a lot. We decide to hide George in the wheat field which is on the other side of the road to avoid a German patrol that is always a possibility. Maman prepares a very nice meal and blanket for my friend under an apple tree in the wheat field so he will not be visible to a German plane.

Just then, somebody knocks on the door. He is a friend of my father. He is the Forest Ranger and his name is Cadoret. He looks uneasy and hesitates to start talking. Then suddenly he asks my father, 'Is it true that Emile picked up an American? I have heard this.' My father says yes. 'Ah! That's very good,' responds Cadoret, 'because there are four Americans hidden in my storage barn and I don't know what to do with them!'

I tell the Forest Ranger that I will come in the afternoon to identify the others and he leaves reassured. We are certain of him. We know he will not talk. I go see George and tell him the story. He gives me the names of his crew members. I ask him to let me borrow his beautiful West Point ring. It will be my passport. I put George under his apple tree asking him to be very quiet.

As for me, every Sunday I meet with friends in the little town of Coësmes at the Hotel Perrin so that's what I do the next day, July 9. I am relieved that they speak a lot about the plane crash but do not ask me any questions. In talking with them, I learn that George's parachute was taken to City Hall and that the Germans went to look for him in the opposite direction than the one we took. The secretary at City Hall happens to be my old teacher."

George went on to say, "The search seemed to be getting pretty hot so on Sunday, they decided to get me out of there. They said to come on because we're going to find your companions. They took me close to where we fell. They told me to call for my friends. I said the Germans will hear it. They said again to call for my friends. I called out their names. If this were a movie, you'd never imagine doing anything so stupid."

Emile related, "On Monday, July 10, after a quick meal and warning from my parents to be very careful, I go to the forest to find George's friends. Cadoret is waiting for me in front of the hunting pavilion and brings me to the end of his courtyard. He knocks two times at the door of the barn. It opens and I see four men there. I sense how scared they are. To put them at ease and have them trust me, I show them George's ring. At first, they are stunned. They think George was killed. I have a hard time trying to explain to them that their boss is my friend and is alive and well and hidden at my house. Finally, I see their faces getting brighter. The radio man wipes away some tears and smiles. I ask them their names. They are Edgar Williams, Frank Murphy, Richard Smith, and Stanley Miller. I promise them that I'll come back soon with their Lt. Colonel. They give me some warm handshakes before I leave. I am very happy that I was able to reassure them.

I do not know who he is, but that evening a young man from the Resistance comes to tell me that he had the order to take George to the hunting pavilion and to wait there for new orders to transfer very near with the other parachutists. The next day passes without any incident. The Germans seem to have abandoned their search. It is also true that they are losing ground, retreating, and things are not going to well for them. I go see my friend George in the wheat field and he comes back with me to sleep at my house.

Wednesday, July 12 is a beautiful day. The sky is blue and the sun shines. George eats a very big breakfast. I explain to him that we are going to leave to meet with his four friends. We are all very emotional. Papa gets his old watch and winds it with a special little key. He looks at George with much emotion and gives to him that family heirloom that he loves so much. Right away, George gets his chronometer and gives it to my father. The emotion is very intense. George embraces Papa and Maman in his arms with a lot of affection. Everyone is trying not to cry and we must leave.

George takes Maman's bicycle and pedals looking back several times. My parents stay on the side of the street waving at us until we disappear. We pedal our bikes slowly without talking to each other. Our hearts are very heavy. After riding about four km on the road, we take a little side forest path. The hunting cabin is about 100 meters further. Cadoret is waiting for us and there is a joyful reunion of the five men who congratulate each other and recount their adventures.

According to George, "My waist gunner didn't show up and my co-pilot Gene Squier didn't show up and Jim Clark, the turret gunner, didn't show up. But the rest of them did. That was the four other guys and myself. I can't tell you how glad I was to see them."

"I don't understand a thing they are telling each other because it's all in English but I can certainly feel how happy they are," noted Emile. "I leave them so that they can have their great joy together. George and I embrace. I know already that I will never forget him. I return to my house with both bicycles. I am a little sad.

At the beginning of the afternoon, a member of the Resistance who was at Coësmes comes and asks me to come to his village at 8 p.m.

so I can help him and his comrades transfer another parachutist who fell hard twisting both his ankles and was wounded in the heel of one of his feet. He cannot walk normally. We are supposed to meet in front of the cemetery at the entrance. The evening comes but the night is not dark enough. The moon is too bright in the sky and this doesn't please me at all. I arrive a little early and hear some strange squeaky metal noises. It's my friends and they are bringing Jim Clark in a little trailer carried by three strong young men. My job is to lead them by 100 meters and to turn around quickly and advise them if there is any danger.

The time seems to me to be terribly long. Happily, we arrive at the large storage barn at the entrance of the forest path. That is by the path that George and his four friends came with the guard. They had about 3 kilometers to walk. We find them hiding in the bushes and staying silent while awaiting the arrival of the car which will take them to a safe hiding place. We will only find out at the end of the German occupation that it was in the small village of Poline.

Very soon a car comes with no lights on. It advances a little way down the small path trail. Its headlights blink twice and then it turns around so as to be able to depart in a hurry. In that car there are two people from the Resistance – Captain Ráton and his friend Jochault. They get out of the car and wave at us to approach. I take Jim Clark on my back. He is heavy but I am young and solid. I don't really understand how two French men and six Americans can fit inside such a tiny little car!

We say goodbye not knowing if we will ever see each other again. I return home, sad but proud of what I have accomplished."

Emile and the members of the flight crew stay in touch for the rest of their lives. George will always have special affection for the young boy who risked his life to save him from the Germans. In turn, Emile commented years later, "George is a marvelous man. He will always be *mon meilleur* ami (my best friend). We are veritable brothers."

"After we all got together and went to hide in the forest, my turret gunner turned up two days later riding a bicycle, said George. "He had started for Spain but had been sent back by French helpers and advised to contact us. The same Frenchmen continued to help us while we were in the forest. They brought us food and blankets and all the civilian clothes we needed. These men were not Resistance but knew various people in the vicinity who were. The Underground in this region was strong and well-organized.

We were sent by car, guarded by two Resistance members, to a town about six kilometers away. All along the road, their people were stationed, waiting to throw up road blocks if the Germans should pursue the car. We had been asked for identification papers and without seeming to interrogate us, they asked a great many technical questions about planes, equipment, etc. until they had satisfied themselves about us. Security in this group seemed to be excellent.

They got us together and we went to Joseph Bodard's place. He was hiding two imposing-looking Senagalese soldiers who were wearing the blue and red French uniforms and stood at one end of the barn. They stared at us and we stared at them. There was no communication between us. Joseph and some other guys tried to carry us up in the hills. Jim had banged up his knee pretty bad and couldn't walk. So I carried him on my back and put him in a wheel barrow. We all got up into this wooded hill. We stayed there about two or three days.

Someone had found Stub Miller and guided him to the others. He had fallen close to a town called Châteaubriant which turned out to be a Gestapo headquarters. He had on his leather flight jacket and some people had given him a bike. He inadvertently got into this town and stopped behind a big Mercedes touring car. He saw these two German officers coming down the steps of this building so he bent over and pretended he was working on the bike. If you stop and think, he had the Air Forces insignia on his left shoulder and had the coveralls of an American air crew member. It's just one of those things that they never paid any attention to him. They got in the car and drove away. He turned around and got his fanny out of there as fast as he could.

I remember when we were staying in the woods and we had snails crawling all over our faces. Everybody was quite calm. I don't know why. We never really worried. Maybe we were just too stupid to worry while we were behind the lines. We were looking at our escape and evasion maps and trying to figure out how to get to Spain. That was the way you were supposed to go. Go down to the Pyrenees, get into Spain, and you could get back up into England that way.

We knew we had knocked out that last bridge, though, and we were trying to figure out what we were going to do. There were six of us now. We never did get with Gene Squier who got out later. It turned out he was picked up by this same guy who was hiding the Senegalese and he stayed hidden for the whole 30 days we were behind the lines."

2LT Squier described his stay with Joseph Bodard this way: "After spending my first night hiding in the wheat field, I decided in the morning to travel about 10 miles before coming to an isolated farmhouse. Here I was taken in immediately. The farmer, Joseph Bodard, gave me his best suit and put me up for the night. The next day I set out again. A half-mile down the road, I was startled when an old couple asked me if I was an American aviator. I told them that I was. They fed and sheltered me and made it clear that they had contacts.

At dawn, they hustled me into their chicken coop and told me they feared that one of their neighbors was a German collaborator. I was kept here for six days. I used the chocolate, milk, matches, compass, and Horlicks (a powdered malted milk drink) from my aids box. They all proved to be good and useful. A man came to see me and we were very suspicious of one another. He had our crew list but we finally convinced one another that neither was a stool pigeon.

He took me to his home and I found out that he had hidden six of my crew with him and had passed them on. I was told to follow immediately but something went wrong and I stayed here for three weeks. While I was there, I was approached by a French officer who wanted me to join the Maquis, the French Resistance fighters. He was to return in three days to take me but he never showed up again.

A rumor got about that the Americans were near Rennes. We started out for the lines several times but were always stopped on the way by other Frenchmen who said the time was not yet ripe. Finally, the Americans took Rennes but by-passed our town which was 40 km to the south. When the townspeople raised the tricolor flag, I said the time had really come for me to leave. The town held a small festival in my honor and then American military vehicles began to roll, though. I tried to stop one but they were going too fast and ignored me in my civilian clothes.

The next day, as we were about to leave, a Frenchman ran in and said there were eleven Germans looking for an American officer to whom they could surrender. I had a hard time convincing them that I was an American officer and they would not surrender their arms until they were sure of that as they were fearful of French reprisals. We took them to City Hall and locked them up before leaving. In Rennes, the snipers were still active and the only Americans I could find were drunk so my friend took me to his home there.

The next morning, we contacted an American Colonel. My friend asked if he could take me back to the village for a big Allied demonstration. The Colonel gave me his permission and put a reconnaissance car at our disposal. We drove back to the farmer who had given me my civilian clothes and I returned them in exchange for my uniform. We went into the village where I was received by the mayor and there was a big celebration. The next day, I returned to the Colonel. His headquarters were now set up and he had me passed on immediately to the U.K."

When asked if he had any suggestions for others in the future who would be trapped behind enemy lines, Gene gave this advice: "Be sure your G.I. shoes are well-broken-in."

Simone, on the other hand, was amused by the fact that when Americans parachuted behind enemy lines, the Underground dressed them in French clothing and tried to pass them off as peasants. She noted, "They usually have good shoes and are in good health. Those are always two sure signs that they aren't French in this day and age." So, unlike Gene, her advice would have been, "Get rid of those G.I. shoes as fast as you can if you don't want the enemy to be able to identify you. Better to have a few blisters than be captured or killed."

According to George, "The waist gunner never showed up. Nobody knows what happened to him, except these French Underground people said to us years later that he had married a French girl, was farming in the area, and he never turned himself back into the American forces when they passed through that area. So, that was no skin off my nose. I was glad he didn't get killed but I didn't have much use for the guy. I'd rather not mention any more about him.

We were up in this hill and two French guys came up. One was a Lt. Antoine and the other a Lt. Vítor. Both real courageous guys. They asked us if they helped us would we fight if we get jumped by the Germans. They told us if they were going to help us, they could get executed. I was the only one who could speak any French at all so I explained it and all the guys said, 'Sure, sure.' They said that if we wouldn't fight, they wouldn't turn us in, but they wouldn't help us either. They gave us some pistols and some Sten guns, which are kind of like tommy guns, and some grenades. They put us into a little Volkswagen Beetle type of car. Two of them were in the front seat with me. I was in the middle. The other five guys were in the back so you can imagine how crowded it was.

It was twilight and we came down out of the hills into a town and then came to a screeching halt. Right in front of us was a big column of Conestoga wagons just like the old western wagons from the movies. There was a German M.P. with his hand held up. He told us to halt. He looked like he was about ten feet tall. There was an officer on a horse observing the wagon train going by. We sat there and the engine was idling. We looked out at some of the houses and you could see some of the people watching. They knew who we were. Of course, the Krauts (a derogatory term for Germans referring to their traditional food of sauerkraut) didn't know who we were."

According to Jim, "I was sitting in the back of the car and had a cardboard box full of hand grenades, a .45 pistol, and everybody else had an automatic rifle. You could be arrested for just riding in an automobile in France if you weren't German and so we were all nervous. I thought that the Germans had the most modern weapons in the world. I guess they must have lost them in Russia, or something, because it looked like they had some antiques. This was a horse-drawn artillery column. I thought they would arrest us any minute now.' But I guess they would have had to come after us on horses since they didn't have any trucks or anything."

George went on to say, "The French always told each other that we were Americans and there was no secret about that. They were rubbing their hands and seemed very concerned. The German M.P. starts to walk toward the car. I thought to myself, 'Boy, we've really had it now. This is going to be it.' I figured if there was going to be any shooting we might as well try to protect ourselves. Everyone got their weapons ready. I remember I was sitting with mine pointed up and looking up. The M.P. suddenly said, *Allez* for 'Go.'

The driver just floor-boarded it and let the clutch out. The M.P. jumped back and we headed toward that German officer on the horse. The horse reared up. I remember I was looking up at him with my pistol drawn and he was looking down at us with his pistol drawn. It only lasted a hundredth of a second. It was just one of those moments when you knew you were enemies. Thank God, I didn't shoot and he didn't shoot. If I had shot, they probably would have slaughtered a lot of French people in the village.

We kept heading for one of the wagons. We went right under the nose of one of the horses and out the other side. There was another M.P. on the other side. He held up his hand for us to stop. We kept on going. Then he just disappeared like someone had yanked him back. We kept going down the road and then we saw villagers pulling logs and timber across the road to prevent any kind of pursuit of us. By golly, they had this thing well-organized."

Chapter 12 - The Knights from the Sky

"We were taken next to the house of a well-to-do merchant," said George. "His wife was rather scared to have us there at first but we were well taken care of. We hid in a barn at night and were not allowed to speak loudly or go out as there were collaborators next door. We drove and drove and it must have been very close to midnight when we got out of town. We had to get out of the car and we walked for quite a ways. They said we couldn't go into town because the Germans would see us and we'd be stopped and questioned. So we'd have to get out and sneak through these trees. Finally, we came to this stone barn. It was real dark and we didn't know where we were."

The barn belonged to the mayor of the town and his family. The Olivos had two girls and two boys - Marinette was 18 years old, Tata 11, Marcel 12, and Emile 10. The flight crew was bedded in the haystack inside the barn, given a bucket for their functional needs, and provided with food. The Olivos owned a shop where they sold food. It was more of a take-out convenience store than a sit-down restaurant. They told the flyers the German soldiers would come there on a regular basis to get provisions and they, therefore, had to be very quiet because the house was right next to the barn.

George went on to say, "We stayed there for about 15 days. I admired that family. Maman was terrified. We didn't realize it at the time but the barn was right on the main road and through the town that's where the German troops would pass by. They had some pretty large troop movements but we did try to stay as quiet as we could.

I would play cards with Papa all afternoon and try to make conversation. One day they brought us some cookies. Papa didn't come in and I said, 'Boy can I use a nap.' So, I lay down in the haystack and went to sleep. Ed Williams ate my cookies. I woke up and asked Ed what happened to my cookies. He said he ate them so I swung at him. We rolled in the haystack a little bit. Then we got over it.

I guess the most remarkable thing was we'd look out the window and see these German planes flying by at tree-top altitude and we could hear tanks on the road. We ran out of cigarettes and a bunch of us were heavy smokers. One day they came in and said we can't get you any more cigarettes. They were giving us these Gauloise cigarettes that were tearing our throats out but it was all we had." The French-made cigarettes to which George referred are short, wide, unfiltered, and made with strong, dark tobaccos from Turkey and Syria. They produce a strong, cigar-like aroma.

"We started getting down on our hands and knees in the barn and digging out all the butts that we had stomped out, just getting a shred of tobacco here and a shred there," continued George. "We'd roll it up in newspaper and get a big flaming puff out of it and that's all we had to do. We were all addicts, I guess."

Two Underground Lieutenants came to the barn and queried George as to where the toilets were on the B-17 and the B-26 to prove that they weren't enemy agents. They asked him to write seven copies of a report about weapons the flight crew had been given, what had happened after the landing, who had helped them, etc. They told him the other two crew members were safe but never gave any more definitive news. They were also told they might be flown to England shortly.

Stub remembered, "The Olivo's young son, I would guess about 10 years old, had a 'French to English' dictionary. We spent the evening talking back and forth with the help of the dictionary. The next morning, the man brought out a horse and two-wheel wagon loaded with straw and hid me under it. In this fashion, I was taken to my rendezvous. By nightfall we had reached our destination and he delivered me to a wooded area where some of my crew were hiding.

It seemed very confusing but eventually the six of us got together in these woods. We remained there for a few days, which seemed like ages, and they moved us again. This was the French Underground at work. They obtained a car for some of our travel. This was a feat in itself, as only Germans had cars. After dark, we walked out of the woods and were picked up by the car. It was a very dark night and we traveled without lights. After traveling some distance, we stopped outside the small village of Poligné and proceeded on foot. We walked our way through brush until we came to a barn which was our home for several days. The barn was about the size of a one and a half car garage. The Olivos had spread straw on the ground for us to sleep on and there was a picnic-type table for us to eat on."

"That big picnic table in the middle of the barn floor had a table cloth on it and they had a four course dinner ready for us. That was my first sample of real good French cooking and it was delicious," added Jim.

Stub continued, "The barn was located about two feet from the main road through town and the Germans were on it so we had to talk in a whisper. There was a small window on the side not facing the road so we could look out and let some light in. We spent our days playing cards and planning our escape. I had a pocket knife which I used to carve and whittle just to keep busy.

We learned the father of our host family, the Olivos, had been very reluctant to keep us there. That is understandable because if they had been caught, the Germans would have killed the entire family. Besides the father and mother, the family consisted of the four children. Marinette proved to be a tireless worker. She prepared food and brought it to us, gave us water for washing, and cleaned up and emptied our latrine. She performed these duties three times a day. One day she came into the barn wearing a pair of fancy wooden shoes. I admired them and she said if I would leave her the money, she would mail a pair to me after the war. So I gave her my last $10."

Augusta Olivo, nicknamed "Tata," gave the following account of the events: "It was the fourth year of the war. I was eleven years old. Six Americans parachuted into my parent's farmhouse in Poligné, France in July of 1944. Since D-Day, we felt the Germans had lost hope to win this war. The French Resistance was conducting many operations against them. My parents and my older sister Marinette, who was 18 at the time, listened to the English radio (London BBC) and followed the progress of the Allied troops, American or English, in Normandy.

One evening, several members of the Resistance came to ask my parents to hide six American parachutists. They contacted my parents because they knew they strongly supported the Allies and also because my parents had a retail shop in our little village. It would be easier for them to feed a few more people.

My dad and Marinette accepted them immediately with a certain enthusiasm. Maman was more conscious of the danger that the situation would bring to the whole family. She also realized the difficulty of feeding six more people without anyone noticing. As a result, she was more hesitant about diving into such an adventure. She knew the Germans were nervous and would not hesitate to execute opponents and those who helped the Resistance. The three youngest children (Marcel, Emile, and I) being oblivious to the danger, thought we were living a fairy tale. Six American aviators in our barn after four years of German occupation? Incredible!

One evening at dusk, six of the eight crew members of the plane that had been shot down in the Guerche de Bretagne forest, which is several tens of kilometers away from Poligné, arrived at our place. They were nothing like the 'Knights from the Sky' that we had dreamed about. They dressed like local farmers and their clothes were only approximately suited to their size. George Stalnaker was the only one who was very chic. He was wearing a wedding suit!

Our parents told us in no uncertain terms to keep things quiet. Our lives were at stake and potentially those of all the village

117

inhabitants. We promised and said nothing. It did not prevent us from spending long moments in the barn with our new friends. George spoke French but the others did not understand a word we were saying. We could not understand their attempts to communicate, either. To overcome this, we spoke in sign language and smiles. We also played a lot of cards.

Stub Miller carved wooden staffs and gave one to me with my name engraved on it. Needless to say, I was extremely proud of it! There was one problem that was bothering my poor mother. They smoked! Furthermore, they smoked 'Camels,' a brand that was unknown in France. I don't know how they managed to have so much of it but its aroma was definitely filling the road that was running along the barn. Maman was not sleeping well at all and was spending endless time listening for suspicious noises from her room's window. Marinette knew a few English words and was spending a lot of time with the crew members. She brought them food three times a day and was also looking after the sick and injured.

Jim Clark had a sprained ankle and had a sore throat that needed constant attention. A bottle of 'Negrita' rum that we had kept since the beginning of the war became the prescribed drug in the absence of antibiotics, unavailable in France at this time. It certainly tasted better, anyhow, and Jim, drinking abundantly from this wonderful prescription, got well!"

Jim later confessed: "I was smoking that French black tobacco and we were rolling our own cigarettes. It was really strong. I got to coughing pretty bad from smoking too much. The old mama of the family decided I was sick so she put a hot plaster on my chest and ordered me to lie down and stay in bed. I told her I wasn't sick but she wouldn't pay any heed to me. We couldn't talk too well together anyway. Since part of the treatment was hot rum every 90 minutes, I got to liking that pretty good. So I decided to just let her treat me until she thought I was well, which she did for about three days."

Tata went on to say, "Maman still worried, trying to conceal that something was going on in the barn. She kept on operating her store, even if her regular customers would wander into the garden – right below the barn's window. Her other problem was finding food. Other shopkeepers in the area like the baker and butcher started to wonder about all the quantities being procured and were surprised by the sudden appetite of the Olivo family. Marinette, as active as ever, was dealing with the household chores like washing the dishes, doing routine maintenance, etc. She also communicated the latest news heard on the radio reporting on the advances of the Allied troops.

We had a moment of great stress when we learned that German soldiers were looking for a French man that had insulted one of their own in a neighborhood café. The members of the Resistance came to warn my parents that there was a risk that the Germans could visit all of the houses in the village during their investigation. Our American friends were also warned and my brother Marcel remembers seeing George loading bullets in his pistol, ready to defend all of us. A few days before he had showed me, the little girl, two pistols that had thoroughly impressed me. The weapons were hidden under the hay that he used as a mattress when sleeping. Fortunately, the Germans did not show up.

After 15 days passed by, including the one with the recent alert, our friends started to get restless and George, with the approval of the Resistance, told my parents that they wanted to leave. He was also concerned about our safety. So members of the Resistance came and took the crew in a Citroën car. The destination was kept secret from us so we could not tell anything even if we were arrested and interrogated."

"We stayed in that barn for a couple of weeks and it was like being in a jail cell, just four walls, no windows, no nothing," explained Jim. "They were lovely people and they treated us wonderfully and fed us the best food I ever ate - four course meals, wine, and everything. You can't get too much of a good thing, though, when you want to be doing something else. We were shacked up in this one room and ready to fight one another when finally they took us out of there and to another place. All this was arranged by the French Underground and it always amazed me how well they organized it."

Oldest daughter Marinette remembered the experience this way: "On Wednesday, July 12, 1944 around 11:30 p.m., six fliers accompanied by the two 'Resistants' arrived at our home. For extra precautions, the car that brought them from Coësmes to Poligne had stopped on the *tertre* (mound of earth) away from our place. I have always wondered how six big men ever could have fit into that car! They walked down the hill, with the exception of Jim Clark, who had twisted both his ankles. He managed to ride the bicycle of one of the members of the Resistance. They used a tiny path through the garden in the back of the houses lining the main street and finally reached the barn. We had prepared a meal for them. For dessert, I had baked a cake. It was an 'American cake' from a recipe in my cookbook and I had topped it off with a small American flag I had drawn with crayons.

I tried to speak English but the English that had brought me good grades in school in themes and translations was impossible for our Americans to understand and I could not understand them either.

Luckily, Lt. Colonel Stalnaker spoke French a little. He became very useful in the days that followed. An easy friendship soon developed between our guests and my family. My parents now had six big boys who called them 'Papa and Maman.' As for us children, we had found some great buddies with whom we talked or played cards.

Stub Miller, who liked to work with wood, carved a stick made of oak that we still have today. Colonel Stalnaker tried to take advantage of this sojourn to improve his French. I remember that he wanted me to help him with the use of the subjunctive in French.

When the fliers came to us, I had been surprised to see the way they were dressed. I had expected to see them in uniform but they were dressed like debonair country folks. The Colonel was wearing the ancient wedding suit of a long-gone ancestor! Some of the clothes, donated by local farmers, were in rags. Pants had to be made. Mr. Loret, a tailor from Rennes, who had left the city with his family as so many did to avoid the bombardments, took care of the sewing and fitting of the old clothes. Alterations to their civilian clothes had to be made along the way.

When our 'boys' first came, after sleeping in the open in the wet woods, they were not in too good shape. Jim Clark not only had twisted his ankles but he had caught a bad cold. Taking care of him without adequate medicine was not easy. Salt water baths for his feet and sweet hot milk, laced with rum, soon helped him recover. In the meantime, he was a danger to all. He coughed quite a bit and only the wall of the barn separated him from the frequently-used narrow sidewalk. Germans passed by constantly and could very well have heard him.

To feed six extra mouths in the days of food rationing was not easy. We had to think of plausible reasons for the extra meat and vegetables we needed. I would take the food to the barn in a basket covered by a towel and would bring the dirty dishes back to the house under the same cover. Antoine and Victor often came to see how the fliers were getting along and to keep them posted on their progress in trying to find a way to send them back to England. But, as the days passed, that possibility seemed more and more remote. We gave the fliers a small radio with earphones so they could listen to the BBC and follow the progress of the war in Normandy. The Resistance also managed to find tobacco for their American friends.

My brothers and sisters often visited the Americans. They managed to jump out of a hidden window in the garden and reach the barn, unseen by the growing population of the village. Refugees from Rennes, Paris, and Rouen, having escaped from their endangered cities, crowded our little village.

120

Through a keyhole in the barn, our friends could see the comings and goings into the café but the days were long as they waited. Waited for what? The days passed. When would they be able to leave? A solution had to be found. The Germans were everywhere. One night, in the café, a drunk man called a German a *salé boche*. ("salé" means "dirty" and "boche" is a term for "head" implying that Germans are obstinate or head-strong). To call a German names could bring about very serious consequences. Many French people found that out during the occupation!

The very next morning, the Germans came to the café. They asked in their usual threatening manner where the man was who had dared insult a solder of the Third Reich! They were furious and threatened to search the café and the entire village. My brother and I, hidden behind a hedge, were witness to all of this. Our anxiety was extreme. What was going to happen? We had warned our friends, the Americans, of the incident. If need be, they could have hidden in a trench which had been dug next to the barn and covered themselves with branches.

Danger was real until Mr. Loret, the tailor from Rennes walked in. He was an active member of the Underground. In his home in Rennes, he had a printing press hidden in his attic. He printed many false papers and food coupons during the Occupation. His home was searched four times by the Germans but the press, well-hidden under the roof, was never found. He took an active part with couriers transmitting messages from the occupied zone to the free zone.

Mr. Loret had helped dress the fliers in their civilian clothes. Now he helped them avoid a potential catastrophe. We saw him talk to the German officers and managed to persuade them that the man who had insulted the German was drunk at the time, a little crazy, and anyway came from a neighboring village. He also added that the people in the café were hoping for a German victory. Although the first statements were true, the last one certainly wasn't.

Later we learned that the drunk man's brother, also a refugee in our village, was a very active member of the Resistance and was being hunted by the Gestapo. And so the Germans went back to Rennes. What a close call! Only after it was all over did our Americans know of their great danger.

On July 24, Victor and Antoine were able to find a new hiding place in Saint-Ganton for the Americans. We parted with tears. We were sad to see those boys leave. They had become our friends. What would their immediate future bring? They left us their names and addresses and I promised that, after the war, I would write to them.

They left by the same narrow path. A car was waiting to take them to their hiding place. Our old barn is still there to this day, keeping many memories within its walls."

Chapter 13 – Silver Streak & Turtle Neck

"After about 15 days in the Olivo's barn, some of the fellows began to get impatient and thought we should leave and go on our own," said Stub. "But we had been lectured as to what we should do in this situation and had been told that once the Underground helped us, even though we grew impatient, to stick with them. If you ever left them, they wouldn't help you again. It was only a few more days when we were advised to leave the barn after dark one night. About a mile down the road, we sat and waited until a car came to pick us up. It was an old 1936 Chrysler. The back seat had been removed and the trunk propped open. Lt. Colonel Stalnaker sat in front with two guides. The other five of us lay on our stomachs looking out the rear. We were given automatic rifles, .45 caliber automatic pistols, and hand grenades in case we were pursued.

Taking narrow country roads, we traveled at 60 mph with no headlights. We sped through a couple of German checkpoints without even slowing down. It was at a 90-degree intersection and they had us completely blocked. This was a very large group with many trucks, artillery guns, horse-drawn guns, and German soldiers. One was in the middle of the intersection directing traffic. We waited and watched our chance to break through the intersection and sped away. Because we had a car, they probably thought we were Germans so they didn't chase us. We breathed a sigh of relief and proceeded on our way. After a very long ride, we arrived at the town of Pipriac. We were handed over to an elderly lady who had a small house and we stayed with her for the next few days.

There was a hill behind the house and after dark the six of us and six or eight Frenchmen would all go up to the top. We'd sit on the ground in a circle. A bottle of cognac would be passed around and each person would take a drink. Rather than offend them, I would put the bottle to my lips but not drink from it. It was a real treat to be outside in the fresh air."

According to George, "We said good-bye to the Olivo family. Members of the Underground asked us to climb out through the window quietly and sneak over to a drop-off place by the road. We walked a fair distance from the Olivo's barn. We had to go through the town. I remember we were lying on top of this earth parapet. We could look down and see the steel helmets of the German soldiers moving down this road. A Chrysler Airflow with kind of a swooping back pulled up. They put us in that car and there were no lights on. We went down the road and I mean fast. Anyone who has driven in France knows they

123

always go fast. When they come to an intersection, they just beep the horn and keep going. We'd do that and we'd stop and there would be another Underground guy waiting for us.

Then we had to stop and go in the other direction. They told us they were running into German blockades. They were trying to get us up to the city of Rennes where the British would fly in with DC-3's, what we called Goony Birds, surreptitiously and drop off supplies, pick up agents, and stuff like that. They were trying to get us up there so we could be put aboard so we could be flown back to England. Every place we went there was a German outfit blocking it. So, they were still trying to locate us. They probably knew that the British were doing these flights. I can only surmise. But, nevertheless, we never could get out of there.

They finally drove us to a little town and got us out of the car. They gave us some bags of food, cigarettes, and things and we were carrying those on our back walking through this very primitive type of little town. They started singing songs like *'La Marseillaise'* and we started to sing the *'Mademoiselle from Armentieres.'* Again, I felt this is absolutely stupid for us to be doing things like this. But, by golly, if the French Underground guys do this, I guess we can. We went to some kind of a little pub and sat and had some drinks. This one guy, Emile Pinot was his name, told how he had been in the French Army and had lost his hand and no one would help him. He said there were times when he had helped wounded Germans and he was quite bitter.

They took us to this peasant hut. A little old lady in a long black peasant gown was there. She must have been in her 70's. They set up a machine gun in her living room that could sweep the field. It turns out her home was actually a headquarters for saboteurs. The Germans had cut off the electricity in Nantes a few days before and 5,000 tons of food in a refrigerated plant had been destroyed. This was at a time when many French people were starving.

We stayed at the woman's home for several days. She would go out in the fields and work all day with a hand sickle and then come in and apologize to us for having meals that were late. We kept apologizing to her that we were there inconveniencing her. She couldn't have been nicer. The French Underground came to see us almost every day. We always had a radio. They would throw wires over the main wire and that would give us electricity.

At night they would take us out to a little hill and we'd have a very little fire. We'd be in the center portion of the circle and the townspeople would be on the outside. This is up in Brittany where there are hardy people. I remember offering the bottle of wine to this girl behind me. She said, "*Non!*' real loud and, boy, I turned back around in a flash. I didn't want to get any of those guys mad at us.

One day the lady wanted to show us off so she took us across the street. There was a long table and a whole bunch of the town's citizens were there. She had myself and the crew up at the head of the table just standing. Everybody had tea cups. She had a jelly glass and she gave me one. There were these bottles of colorless fluid. She filled mine clear up to the top and hers clear up to the top. She then put a teaspoon in everybody else's cup. Just a teaspoon. Then to me she said, 'Rendre le fond sec!' or 'Make the bottom dry!' That means 'Bottoms up.' I said 'Whew, boy. The honor of America is at stake.' So I went chug-a-lug. I remember all these French people were leaning forward. It was 'Calvados.' If you've ever tasted 'Calvados,' it will rip your head off. It's re-done cider to where the proof is high as a kite. So I started to chug-a-lug that thing and I could feel the tears coming to my eyes.

She kept rubbing her stomach saying, *Bon pour l'estomac.* which meant 'Good for the stomach.' I had to stand there and smile because if I had done anything else the honor of America would have been shattered. Everyone else drank their little teaspoon full and then she put some coffee in the cups and we drank that up. That was the end of that."

The Underground stole some bicycles for each of the members of the flight crew. They found peasant clothes, tennis shoes, berets, French identification cards, etc. George's I.D. said he was a roofer by trade. They told the crew that if the Germans ever stopped them, to just say the word 'Breton' and just keep saying that because it's a unique language, similar to Welch. A lot of people in Normandy only speak the Breton language. They felt the Germans might be able to understand French but they couldn't understand that language. The hope was that if they said that, they wouldn't ask any more questions. Fortunately, they were never asked.

There was one razor blade for the six crew members. They were told they had to shave because the French typically either grew a beard or were clean-shaven. Nothing in between. The Resistance also told them that when they smoked, they had to hang cigarettes off their lips and not take them out of their mouths with their hands because they could identify that as American gesture. Similarly, there were stories of Americans behind enemy lines who were caught by the Germans because of the way they used a knife and fork in a café or restaurant. Europeans will typically eat two-handed, keeping a knife in one hand and a fork in the other, while an American will eat in a more awkward, one-handed way by switching to the dominant hand to use the fork after cutting food with a knife.

125

"Because I was the commander, I was the last one to shave and I remember how it felt like I was pulling my beard out with tweezers because we hadn't shaved now for quite some time. The bicycle I had didn't have any tires so they wrapped rags around the wheels. We took off for the town of Vitré which is about 25 miles from there. I don't think I've ever been as tired in my life as I was then. They gave us two guides. We called one of them 'Silver Streak' because he could really ride a bicycle and the other guy 'Turtle Neck' because that's the kind of sweater he was wearing."

"These two Frenchmen lived in a town that had just been liberated by the Americans." added Jim. "They decided it would be their patriotic duty to get on their bicycles and cycle through the German lines, go into the French interior, and find people like us that needed to be brought back. So they came and found us and brought us some bicycles which they stole. These machines were pretty well worn out but they brought them to us, we got on them, and took off down the highway. Silver Streak and Turtle Neck had real good bicycles and ours weren't.

The way we did it was there would be one Frenchman in front, and 50 yards behind would be two Americans and 50 yards behind that two more Americans, etc. The other Frenchman would be bringing up the rear. He had a patching kit and bicycle pump. Anyone who had a flat, Silver Streak would fix it. He'd take the tire off, patch it, put it back on, and pump it up and then have to catch up with the others. I don't see how he made it but he did. He was one hell of a man!"

George continued, "We went down a hill and I fell way behind because I had those rag tires. Going uphill, I just had to get off and push the thing. We ate well but our weight had dropped down and we didn't have that much staying power, at least I didn't.

As we got closer to Vitré, we ran into a bunch of German troops on the road. They didn't pay any attention to us and we tried to ignore them. You'd have the feeling that 'USA' was written right across your chest. They didn't bother us, though. Some were regular French Army troops who for the most part were the most decent of the enemy soldiers in that war. We went into town and they took us to this beautiful house. It was owned by an officer of the Bank of France who had cleared out and allowed us to stay there at least a week. The Germans were retreating in heavy force then. We would lie on the second floor balcony of the house and watch them do their retreating.

One time, a P-47 came down and strafed the troops. They were very disciplined. They had no panic. They would get off the road, shoot at the airplane, and they had their tanks covered with camouflage. Across the street, kitty-corner there was a bench. If the French were sitting on the bench, no German would sit on it. If there were no French, then the Germans would sit down. They were really quite disciplined. We noted that. Also, we noted that they were using ambulances to carry their girlfriends. At night time, the officers would cat around with these girls in those ambulances.

You'd see it in the newsreels how they'd give the 'Heil Hitler!' salute. You'd see an officer with his troops walking up toward another officer with his troops. They'd bang their heels together and give that salute." The salute was easily recognized by Americans because it was the same as the official gesture, called the "Bellamy Salute," that accompanied the American Pledge of Allegiance until President Roosevelt ordered the change to the now-familiar hand-over-heart in December of 1942.

At Nazi rallies, thousands of Germans would give the salute while shouting the rallying cry of "*Seig Heil*" or "*Hail Victory.*" If it was reminiscent of the cheering at American football, it was with good reason. Former Harvard student Ernst "Putzi" Hanfstaengl, a member of Hitler's inner circle, wrote marches for the Nazis, including one that took the cheer *"Harvard! Harvard! Harvard! Rah! Rah! Rah!"* and turned it into the infamous *"Sieg Heil! Sieg Heil!"* song.

Putzi was so impressed by the rousing spirit at American sporting events that he passed the marches on to Hitler, who sought to emulate the frenetic atmosphere, complete with the chanting. Putzi said he played some of the football marches from his Harvard days on the piano and had Hitler "shouting with enthusiasm." He claimed Hitler pranced around the room like a drum major saying, "That is it, Hanfstaengl. That is what we need for the movement, marvelous."

"We also saw truckloads of American Prisoners of War going by," sighed George in resignation. "We just wished we could do something about it. There wasn't a thing you could do. The French people came to see us every day. There was one girl who was working for the Gestapo but she was actually part of the French Underground. She was the girlfriend of the Assistant Chief of Police who was also with the Underground. She figured here are some Americans and they're strange stuff. I remember when we'd light a cigarette and put it in our mouths, she'd light a match and look into our eyes very winsomely. We'd look into her eyes. The Asst. Chief of Police would come over, grab her, bend her over, and give her a big kiss. He was just putting his mark on her to let us know that she was his girlfriend. This went on for a few days.

Once they said, 'Have we got a treat for you.' They sat us around the dining room table. It was tripe. One of the guys wrinkled his nose and I said, 'Hey, these people have knocked themselves out for us. They made this stuff for us and we're going to eat it.' We all ate it but I don't think I've ever been so revolted in my life. It was really something I'd never do again.

One day the owner of the house took us out in the front yard, which had a drop-off. They asked us not to say anything. They went out and patted the Germans on the head while they had us there. They just wanted to show they had guts. I had to admire them for it.

One night they came in and they said, 'The Americans are coming. The Americans are coming. They're going to get here tonight.' They ripped open these cushions. They took out French, American, British, and Russian flags. They had scotch, bourbon, and champagne. We all got really 'shmuckered.' We sang songs again. We sang the *'Star Spangled Banner'* and they sang encores of *'La Marseillaise'* and the *'Mademoiselle from Armentieres.'*

It got pretty late at night. The Americans hadn't shown up. By that time, nobody cared. The French guys all went home. Our French guides went next door where they were staying. We all just flopped down and went to sleep. The next morning Jim Clark went into the bathroom. He was half seated on the toilet with his pants pulled down and this German soldier stuck his head through the window. He pulled his pants up and came out and said to us, 'The Krauts are right out there.' We peeked out through the curtains and there were a whole bunch of Germans sitting on the front porch. They didn't come in. The only thing I can figure is that they were waiting for someone of authority to tell them what to do. They had heard the party the night before and some suspicions were aroused.

"Oh, hell, there's no way I was going to get caught with my pants down," joked Jim. "I'd hear about that the rest of my life. So, I pulled them up and made good speed out of there."

"I went around the back and called to Silver Streak and Turtle Neck as quietly as I could that the Boche is out front," continued George. "They said to stand fast. It seemed like an eternity but it couldn't have been any more than five minutes. The Krauts did start banging on the front door. Everyone got out in the back yard. Silver Streak and Turtle Neck came back in. They said you go out two by two. There will be a French policeman on a bicycle. I want one of your guys to get on a bicycle and follow him. If he looks left or right, you follow in that direction. Hang cigarettes from your lips which, as I said, is hard for an American to do and we'll walk down the street.

We went out two by two and walked through the town where all these Kraut soldiers were. We brushed shoulders with them. None of them turned to look at us or bothered us. Finally, we got down to a ditch outside of this highway. There were these German columns with their tanks and their guns going by. Every time there was a break in one of the columns, one or two of us would run across the road and jump into the ditch on the other side until we all got across."

"It's good we got out of there," admitted Jim. "The Chief of the Underground, who was also the Chief of Police, found out they were fixing to raid this house we had been in for about three days. So, we just up and walked out the door around 8 a.m. We went down the street and walked out of town with the Germans everywhere. We just walked right through them, looked them in the eye, and they took no heed."

According to George, "We met two Frenchmen here who had come through the lines from Bayeux. They offered to take us north. We expected the pro-Nazi Vichy police to come after us soon as news of our presence had gotten around and so we accepted the offer. On July 31, we left and walked most of the way to Vitré where we were given false identity papers. The Police Commissioner there found a place to stay in a large empty house belonging to the Cashier of the Banque de France.

While we were there during the next four days, a Division of German troops passed through the town. They looked pretty fit and their equipment was O.K. still but they seemed despondent and not well-organized. One could feel that they expected defeat, except perhaps for the NCO's and junior officers. We saw other mixed parties of German paratroopers, tank men, etc. going south in groups of 20 or so. There were about 50 light tanks and lots of ambulances, some of them Paris buses with Red Cross flags tied over them.

There was a girl here who worked for the Gestapo but really gave all the information she got to the Resistance. She told us that Rennes was being evacuated and that the Germans planned to leave Vitré the next day. On the morning of August 3, the bank cashier came and said we ought to leave. The Germans were going but were taking hostages with them and were searching the town. He did not know where the U.S. troops were. So we cleared out with the two French guides and some Resistance people walking out of town in groups of three to avoid attracting too much attention."

"We left on bicycles that the Underground had stolen and hidden in an old windmill," remembered Stub. "We divided up into four groups of two each and traveled three or four hundred yards apart. I was riding with a guide named Jean Marion at the head of the group. There were many people on their way out of town so it was difficult to keep track of each other. Jean would give me instructions as to what direction to go and then he would ride back to check on the others. I was so unsure of his French instructions and he would be gone sometimes for 30 to 40 minutes that I could only hope and pray that I was making the right decisions. I guess I did because we arrived in Vitré late that afternoon. Once we got there, a bank president moved out of his house to let us hide for a few days."

"It was the finest home in town," noted Jim. "They even had supper ready for us. The banker got up and said, 'My home is your home.' Then he just moved his family out and went to a hotel or something and just left the whole home there with all the clothes, valuables, and whatever. The Americans had broken through and the Germans were on bicycles, ox carts, anything they could find to get the hell out of there. It seemed like the whole damn German Army was retreating. I was real surprised to see their trucks. They were just old commercial trucks with no four-wheel drive or nothing. Just plain old trucks, except that was about the only military-type truck they had left."

George added, "The house was near the downtown area and was located at a 'Y' intersection. We could look out the window and watch the Germans retreating from the battle zone. Some were walking, some riding in cars or trucks, very disorganized. Some Germans became suspicious of us and we were told by our guide that we must leave immediately. It was 9 a.m. and as we left by the rear door, they were coming in the front.

As with many French towns, Vitré had a wall built around it for protection with only a couple of gates to enter or exit. There was a large crowd of people in town this day, both French and German and we left in four groups of two. We had walked about 50 yards apart when we had to pass two German Military Police to get out. As we passed, they were talking to each other and pointing at us. I thought, 'This is it.'

For some unknown reason, we walked around the block and had to pass them the second time. This time they started to walk toward us and I knew this time, for sure, we would be captured and taken as prisoners. They walked in front of us and just passed by. We must have really looked French but we felt so conspicuous. We traveled on foot cross country to avoid the roads. It was a very difficult means of travel because the terrain is very rough in France.

A guide that they had given us, along with Silver Streak and Turtle Neck, and the six of us snuck up into some fields with thick growth. You can't push through it. They didn't want us to cut right through. Wisely so, because that would have made us really visible to anybody from the road. So, we would stoop down and walk around each field. We did that all morning long."

"The guide was 67 years old," added Jim. "He lived in the neighborhood and knew all there was to know about the area. Silver Streak and Turtle Neck didn't know the country like this old man. The last part of the journey was on foot. When we were riding bicycles, I was the strongest rider of the bunch, except for the two Frenchmen. When it came to walking, though, I was the failure. I had on a pair of sandals that were inches too short for me. My heels hung off the back of those things and I had blisters as big as half dollars. I sure didn't do well walking. Our old guide just walked me into the ground.

As we would sometimes stop to rest, our guide would walk off and talk to farmers along the way, seeking information. Finally, late that afternoon he said, 'I have been told there are some American tanks on the highway.' I realized then that what we were doing was cutting through trails in the forest parallel to the highway headed toward the beach-head. The old man went out to the highway himself, leaving us in the forest. When he came back, he said, 'I saw American tanks. Let's go there.' So that's what we did. Sure enough, we got out on the highway and saw some dust in the distance."

George recalled excitedly, "I said, 'I bet that's the Americans.' Then, here came these American tanks. Sherman tanks. A whole column of them heading in the opposite direction. We started yelling and hollering at them. In the lead tank, we heard one of the guys turn to the other and say, 'By God, listen to those frogs try to talk English.'" That's a term used when talking disparagingly about the French, referring to the frog's legs that are supposedly part of their gourmet diet. It's ironic because there were widespread food shortages throughout France. Gourmet food had not been available to them for a number of years.

According to Jim, "We thought we had been rescued. But, they didn't stop. They kept right on going. We were out there in these dirty French clothes that we had been wearing for a month and we hadn't had a bath. We didn't smell too good. They thought we were a bunch like French bums or hobos. I guess that's what we looked like. We were jumping up and down trying to get them to stop."

George said, "We saw an American Captain in a jeep and kept waving for him to stop. He finally stopped. But then, he wouldn't believe that we were Americans. Ed turns to me and says, 'What do you think of this Captain's actions, Colonel?' The Captain asks, 'Colonel?' I say, 'You're damn right I am and it's time for you to pay attention to us!'

I cut my trouser cuff open and got my West Point ring. I told him we don't have our dog tags and all we have is our French I.D. cards.

131

But, by God, I've got my West Point ring. You know the chances of someone other than an American having one of those is very slim. He looked it over and my name was on the inside along with my date of graduation." A West Point graduate himself, the Captain examined the ring, realized George was telling the truth, snapped to attention, and saluted him.

"So, he got a Personnel Carrier and put us aboard it," continued George. "We asked our French guide if he'd be willing to take these guys down and show him where the German positions are. He said he would. The Captain wisely latched onto that and they were able to take the town of Vitré without firing a shot. They gave credit to a guide who showed them where the positions were. That was our guide."

Stub recalled, "At about 9 p.m., after eight or nine hours of walking and covering about 25 miles, we encountered an American tank unit. They were traveling about 20 to 25 mph so we waved and yelled and they waved back but didn't stop. Finally, as the last tank was passing, an officer gave the order to stop. We had no identification to show them and we had a hard time proving to them that we were Americans. Lt. Colonel George had his West Point ring sewed into his pant cuff so he pulled it out and showed it to the officer who finally believed him.

We sat and talked and smoked their cigarettes for a while. It was 11 or 12 p.m. when they gave us a truck and a driver. About an hour later, we arrived at Headquarters. Here, we had to really provide our identities. We were interrogated individually and were asked questions that only Americans would know. It was 5 a.m. before they finished. They had no beds so we lay down on the ground and slept until 7 a.m. We could hardly walk the next morning as we were sore and stiff. This place was a staging area and thousands of German prisoners were being held here. There were no restraints. They were just grouped together in a field. I had the feeling they were content to be captured and weren't going to try to escape."

Jim remembered, "We were on the ground with G.I.'s and the tank people, in between American and German lines and the K-rations weren't bad at all."

The "Field Ration, Type K" or "K-ration" was produced originally by the Quartermaster Command's Subsistence Branch at the request of the USAAF (the U.S. Army Air Forces.) They were intended for use by paratroopers in short-term emergencies but then their use spread throughout the Army. In the field, soldiers would subsist on them for days or weeks at a time. By 1944, over 100 million K-rations were produced.

There were universal complaints from soldiers about K-rations, particularly the processed "mystery meat" or "spam" they contained. For Jim to say they "weren't bad at all" is considered high praise. Today, of course, the word "spam" is used to describe disliked and unwanted e-mail.

According to George, "The Personnel Carrier took us up to Division HQ of the 4th Armored division. We were introduced to this Major General. We were sitting in a middle of a field where they were bivouacked. I remember this French Liaison Officer came over and told us he was very sorry but they didn't allow French civilians to be within this bivouac area. We had to tell him we were Americans. The General sent an orderly over. He had this mobile home which he used for his HQ. He asked us if we wanted to watch the attack on Rennes. We said yes. It was evening. They got folding chairs for all of us and we sat there. The orderly served us scotch. We watched these poor G.I.'s attack Rennes."

The next day the flight crew was taken to General George Patton's 3rd Army HQ where a big tarpaulin was put on the ground. The soldiers had the fliers stand in the middle of it and take off all their clothes. They, however, refused get rid of their berets because they wanted to take them home as souvenirs. The crew hadn't had a bath for 30 days. They were sleeping in hay most of the time and so were buggy with lice. They were sprayed down with chemicals and water. After that, the soldiers got sticks and folded the tarp up, poured gasoline on it, and burned it. They used sticks because they wouldn't dare touch it. They gave the flight crew G.I. clothing and even managed to rustle up some silver leaves for George to wear. They didn't, however, have official hats or shoes for them. George, in fact, was still wearing tennis shoes. So, it was a hodge-podge of semi-official military clothing but at least the crew was clean.

"We were issued some mis-matched military clothing but not complete uniforms. It was a real treat to finally shower and get into clean clothes," admitted Stub.

"I never saw such a nervous bunch of officers," laughed George. "Colonels, Majors, and Captains all running around saying, 'Don't let General Patton see you. Don't let General Patton see you.' I asked them why. They said, 'Because you're not in proper uniform. The General is a stickler for people being in proper uniform.' I said, 'My God, we've been behind German lines for a month. I don't think he'd expect us to be in proper uniform.' It turned out we never did see him. They were glad to get us out of there, though.

133

They put us in another Personnel Carrier and brought us to Granville up in northern France. If you ever want to have something to show you how terrible war is, we passed by miles of German tanks that were just heel to toe with bodies hanging out of them. It smelled horrible. It was horrible to see it. Then we passed the St. Mary's L'Église cemetery. There were American bodies just stacked up like cord wood in cloth bags. There were G.I.s checking the dog tags and placing the bodies in graves. Not in a disrespectful way. But, they'd put the dog tags on a stake so that later on they could put crosses and names on. When you saw how high these stacks of bodies were, it was a terribly sad situation. War can have some funny things happen in it but certainly I don't think anybody who has ever fought in one is pro-war."

The crew was taken to Granville. While waiting for transportation from there, they were sitting and relaxing on a small stone wall. Red-headed bombardier Frank Murphy could pass for a German but, in truth, didn't look like a typical Frenchman. A G.I. came up to him and was trying to talk broken French. He said in a stumbling way, "Pardonnez-mois, monsieur, where is the whore house?" Murphy let him struggle all the way through the sentence and then quickly responded, "Search me, Bud, I'm new here myself."

They spent three days debriefing with the CIC (Counter-Intelligence Corps), which eventually became part of the CIA (Central Intelligence Agency).

"They flew us back out to London and put us in this special place for interrogation," added George. "We were told we couldn't go back to combat, especially in the area where we were. While we were up there, in walked our co-pilot – 2LT Eugene Squier. He told us how he had been hidden by Joseph Bodard for all that time and some Germans had even surrendered to him. He had no weapons, no nothing, and was in peasant clothes. But, they told the Germans that this was an American officer and so they surrendered to him."

Stub recalled, "We were sent to Cherbourg, France. It had been liberated but there were still snipers in the area. We spent a couple of days here before being sent back to our base in England. First, we were put on a C-47 and taken to a small town in southern England. Col. George called our base and they sent a plane down to pick us up and take us back. The entire base turned out to greet us. What a happy reunion!!! We all went to the briefing room, the scotch was brought out, and we had a big party!!!"

"After a couple of days with the 391st, we were sent to London where we completed our paperwork to return to the States," said Jim. "While in London, we were put through more interrogation by SHAEF

(Supreme Headquarters Allied Expeditionary Forces.)   After being reunited with Gene Squier, our crew was complete except for that substitute waist gunner, who we never heard from and we presumed was taken as a Prisoner of War."

"It was great going back up to our outfit," chimed in George. "I was interrogated by USTAF (The United States Strategic Air Forces) and told I was going to be put into HQ after going back to the States for R&R. We had a wonderful reunion with all of the troops, still wearing our berets which we kept as souvenirs. Then, we were ready to fly back to the States. We couldn't wait. That broke us all up. We had been away for a long time."

Stalnaker's crew is reunited with the 391st Bomber Group

Chapter 14 - The Top Floor

George and the flight crew returned home in C-54 cargo plane that had no seats. There were several nets and quilts aboard so they jury-rigged beds and slept most of the way. They were the only passengers on the plane.

On their way overseas, they had flown the southern route but on this flight they flew the shorter northern route. They left London early in the morning and went to Edinburgh and spent the night there. Flying out early in the next morning, their first stop was Reykjavic, Iceland. They were on the ground just long enough to refuel and get something to eat. Then, they were off again. They followed the same procedure in Greenland and Newfoundland. At the end of two days and two nights, they landed in New York. It was late evening when they arrived but that didn't stop them from celebrating with bacon, eggs, and cold beer. They were finally back home.

"One of the first things I tried to do when I got back to the States was get Silver Stars for both Stub Miller and Ed Williams but Colonel Williams told me that only one would be awarded for the crew and it would have to go to the aircraft commander, who was me," said George.

He, therefore, was presented with the Silver Star and cited for gallantry in action. The citation read, "During the bombing run, Lt. Colonel Stalnaker's plane was hit by flak which critically damaged the right engine. Although his plane was losing altitude rapidly, he displayed unusual fortitude and skill, determined to lead his formation over the target. He ignored his personal safety and continued the bombing run. After releasing his bombs on the target, he peeled away from the formation, but remained at the controls of his doomed aircraft until all his crew had jumped to safety. Only then did Colonel Stalnaker himself abandon his ship, which stalled and crashed in flames."

"Six weeks after the crew was reported MIA, I had an emergency appendectomy." recounted Bess Miller. "I was still in the hospital and doctor was in the middle of taking my stitches out. Suddenly, my sister Phyllis opened the door and poked her head in. She asked if she could come in. The doctor knew right away it was important so he told her she could. Then she gave me the telegram that said Stub was alive. I was hysterical. I had just hoped and prayed that he'd be okay. I got another telegram saying he was being sent to a Redistribution Center in Miami. I didn't understand what that was and it didn't matter to me. Stub was coming home. I was so thrilled. So happy. I could hardly stand it. When he got back, there was a pile of my letters waiting for him."

Known as "The most beautiful boot camp in America" during World War II, Miami Beach housed close to 500,000 troops at some 300 hotels and apartment buildings for the Army Air Forces Technical Training Command. Hotel dining rooms were converted to mess halls, movie theaters became testing centers, golf courses turned into marching grounds for troops, hotel pools were used to teach lifesaving, and the beaches became places for physical training. By war's end, 25% of all officers and 20% of enlisted men in the Army Air Forces received training there. The Women's Army Corps Communications Detachment, famous for deciphering messages and breaking enemy codes, was also stationed there.

Many vowed to return to South Florida if they survived the war. Large numbers of them did just that in creating an economic boom of people buying houses with G.I. Loans, families vacationing there, and retirees wanting to take advantage of the climate.

Another group of hotels and buildings served as an Army Redistribution Station for soldiers returning from battle. These men were reunited with their families, debriefed about their wartime experiences, and given rest and relaxation before being released or reassigned.

According to Stub, "After I bid my comrades goodbye and boarded a train for Chicago, I was met by Bess and I had a 30-day furlough before heading for the Redistribution Center in Miami Beach. The government had taken over all the hotels along the beach and was using them for housing the troops back from overseas duty.

Bess and I had a real nice room at the Coral Reef Hotel overlooking the ocean. It was a great place for a vacation. Another hotel down the beach was used for a mess hall and it was equal to a gourmet restaurant. The food was fabulous. You had all you wanted to eat and drink and the wives were allowed to eat with us. I had much free time and only had to report for physical examinations, mental attitude checks, and aptitude tests."

After two weeks of R&R, they sent Stub by troop train to a convalescent hospital in St. Petersburg. The six-story luxury hotel, the Don César, was a 20-minute bus ride from the downtown area. Bess took public transportation over to St. Pete from Miami and arrived a couple of days before they were allowed to communicate. She tried to contact Stub right away but he was never given the messages.

Stub admitted, "I was assigned to a psychiatrist named Major Ford and after just a couple of appointments, he decided I needed some extra attention. I was really worse than I thought. Without telling me what to expect, he scheduled me for special treatment. Just after lunch on a Tuesday, I reported to the clinic, was handed a pair of pajamas, and instructed to get into them and get into bed.

Then I was given a shot in the arm and that was the last thing I remember until I awoke and heard the fellow in the other bed talking to someone. One of them made a comment about this being Sunday and I said to them, 'You guys are crazy. This is Wednesday.' Then a minute or two later I heard church bells ringing. As soon as I could get up, I went to a telephone to call Bess. I asked her what day it was and she told me it was Sunday and wanted to know where I had been all week. I said, 'Are you sure this is Sunday?' I had been asleep for five days!

They found what was bothering me most was my only brother Ray being killed three weeks before I went MIA. I had no one to share this grief with so I was slow to heal. Major Ford learned what was bothering me so our conversations would gradually work around to this. He kept hounding me until I would blow my cool and then he'd give me a pass to go into town and spend three days with Bess. Then I'd go back for another session and go through the same thing again. Finally, at the end of eight weeks, I could talk about it and not be disturbed."

"There were seven floors of that Psychiatric Hospital in St. Pete" recalled Bess. "The higher up you were, the worst shape you were in. Stub got up to the top floor. He had so much trouble talking about what happened to his brother and about his being shot down over France. He'd wake up from a nightmare in the middle of the night screaming, 'Watch out. Watch out.' It was awful seeing him go through that. Fortunately, he got over it. It just took some time."

From St. Pete, Stub was sent back to Miami Beach for another two weeks of R&R, permanently grounded, and restricted to duty within the continental limits of the United States. He was then sent to Chanute Field, Illinois where he enrolled in a school for advanced airplane engine repair. After three months, he completed the course and was assigned as Shift Supervisor in the afternoon from 12 to 6 p.m. He had 30 instructors under him, each with nine or ten students, for a total of about 300 people. The range in rank was from Major down to E-5 buck Sergeant.

"There were new classes every week," said Stub. "I had a very good relationship with the instructors and students and enjoyed my job."

For the most part, Stub was symptom-free from that point. George, too, had the problem of waking from a nightmare in a panic, calling out for the flight crew to "Watch Out!" It's an affliction for which he never sought help and was never able to overcome. Unlike Stub, George never let anyone know of his condition and didn't receive treatment.

The other crew members were affected in various ways. For example, Raymond Smith, the son of Technical Sgt. Richard, reported that his father was not ever able to talk about being shot down and spending time behind enemy lines. He said, "Each time Dad would start to tell us his story, he would cry and not finish. He was a good and humble man."

It was called "Shell Shock" in World War I and "Battle Fatigue" or "Combat Fatigue" in World War II. Today, it's known as "PTSD" (Post-Traumatic Stress Disorder.) The terrible truth about war is that not all soldiers who lose their lives die in battle. It's not like they're unable to let go of the past. It's that the past is unable to let go of them.

Telling everyone that he felt fine, George stayed with his parents in Des Moines after returning from England on leave and while preparing for his next assignment. Luther and Margaret were shocked to receive the first telegram about his being Missing in Action and then delighted to receive the second saying he evaded capture and would be returning to the United States. Naturally, they breathed a huge sigh of relief when they could hug their son in person upon his return home.

Downplaying the danger he was in during his month behind enemy lines, George explained to them how he got his Purple Heart saying, "When I bailed out, I landed on a barbed wire fence." He laughed while Margaret gasped. "It wasn't anything. It's almost silly for me to wear the ribbon. I got a cut over one eye once when I wasn't in combat that was worse and I didn't get a Purple Heart for that."

He showed his parents some of his other ribbons touching the ETO (European Theater of Operations) ribbon he called the "Spam" bar and his bronze star he called "Yellow Fever." He showed them what he termed a silver embroidered "Caterpillar" which signified his having parachuted out of his plane during combat and a silver winged "Boot" that he said he received for having returned safety from behind enemy lines.

George turned serious as he described to them the mutual respect the branches of the armed forces have for each other in wartime: "In non-combat, it's more of a rivalry but in combat, the co-ordination is beautiful. I have seen wounded infantrymen and Air Force personnel who are complete strangers in hospitals thank each other for their efforts. It's very special."

While staying with his parents, George was able to enjoy a reunion with his younger brother Howard. After graduating from Drake University, Howard enlisted in the U.S. Navy on March 5, 1941, becoming a torpedo bomber pilot. A Lieutenant Commander, he served in the Pacific Theater of Operations, earning two Distinguished Flying Crosses.

He was aboard the light aircraft carrier USS Princeton during the largest naval engagement in history, the Battle of Leyte Gulf, which took place on October 23 through 26 of 1944 in the Philippines. Almost unimaginable in scope, the sea was crowded with 282 American, Australian, and Japanese ships.

Shortly before 10 a.m. on October 24, Howard was in the process of attaching the fuel nozzle in preparing his aircraft for launch. It was one of the nine Grumman TBF Avenger naval torpedo bombers on board the Independence-class light aircraft carrier. The heaviest single-engine craft of World War II, the TBF didn't exactly have a classic sleek profile, causing it to be referred to as the "turkey" and "pregnant beast." It, significantly, did have the first compound angle wing-folding mechanism in order to maximize storage space on an aircraft carrier.

Suddenly, a disaster occured as a single engine Japanese Yokosuka D4Y Suisei (meaning "Comet" and nicknamed a "Judy" by the Allies) dive bomber dropped a single bomb which happened to fall precisely between the elevators, through the flight deck, and into the hangar of the Princeton before exploding. A fire broke out which caused further gasoline-aided explosions.

Howard received the order to shut down immediately. "I thought I was going to fly. I guess I'm going to fight fires," he concluded.

The USS Irwin destroyer and USS Birmingham cruiser came alongside to assist but wound up colliding with the Princeton in the rough seas. At 3:24 p.m., a huge explosion aboard the Princeton caused considerable damage to the Birmingham. Although the Irwin was also damaged, it launched boats throughout the night and the following day to rescue as many of the aircraft carrier's crew as possible. A final explosion destroyed the Princeton's forward section sending debris as high as 2,000 feet in the air prior to the ship's sinking at 5:50 p.m.

Luther and Margaret Stalnaker found out about the tragedy the way most Americans did in those days – by hearing it on radio broadcasts and reading about it in the newspapers.

It turned out that, after working in vain to try to help save the ship, Howard was in the water overnight until finally being rescued by the Irwin. There were 108 casualties in all with 1,361 crewmembers rescued.

"My grandparents had just about gotten over the shock of George being shot down and MIA that summer when they learned about my dad's ship being sunk. Communication being what it was then, it took about a week for them to find out that he had been rescued and was all

141

right," said Howard's son Jim who followed family tradition of distinguished military service as a Marine Colonel during Operation Enduring Freedom in Afghanistan and led a squadron of F-18's during the Gulf War. He went on to command the largest Aircraft Group in Marine Corps history from 2005 to 2007 and completed 751 carrier landings, more than any other pilot. His nickname of "Balls" Stalnaker was well-earned.

An overwhelming defeat for the Japanese, the Battle of Leytle Gulf represented the end of the Imperial Fleet. The Japanese lost four aircraft carriers, three battleships, 10 cruisers, and 11 destroyers. In addition to the Princeton, American losses were two aircraft carriers and three destroyers.

Upon being discharged, Howard took a long train ride home from Seattle to Des Moines. He reportedly spent some time drinking at the train's bar car on the trip. George volunteered to drive to the station to pick him up and was greeted with these first words: "Where can we get a drink around here?" He and George had not seen each other since the start of the war and got caught up on things at a Des Moines hotel bar. Evidently, they had quite of bit of catching up to do. Upon seeing the condition her two sons were in as they staggered to the front door, Margaret proceeded to faint. Luther, always calm and understanding, walked them both up and down the street until they were sober and presentable.

The second anniversary of the 391st was highlighted by a dinner on January 21, 1945 at the Red Cross Aero Club. Group Commander Gerald Williams read the following message from 9th Air Force Commander General Anderson: "It makes me proud to consider the second anniversary of your group's activities, your achievements in the first year of combat. Your group entered combat just seven months ago in the most difficult and stubbornly contested theater in the world. In the short space of a few months, your bombing skill rates you among the leaders of the division and the fact that you have maintained that record with remarkable consistency, despite weather, losses and enemy opposition, reflects the deepest devotion to duty.

In more than 200 missions that you have flown, a larger proportion of aircraft have succeeded in completing the attack than in any other group in the division. In combat with German aircraft, you have displayed heroism and have won for yourselves well-earned battle honors. As this division takes stock of itself and prepares to make its utmost effort in landing the blow which, together with our ground forces heroic fighting, will break our enemy for good, I take deep pride in knowing what skill and strength you will bring to bear against him. I send you my congratulations and my gratitude."

Colonel Williams then announced to a rousing cheer that the 391st had received a Distinguished Unit Citation for its exemplary work during the brutal month-long Battle of the Bulge which began on December 16, 1944 and helped turn the German counteroffensive in the Ardennes into a defeat. The attack began with a massive Nazi assault of over 200,000 troops and 1,000 tanks. This still stands as the deadliest battle in history for American troops with more than 80,000 casualties.

The heaviest losses sustained by the 391st in a single operation occured on the morning of December 23, 1944, in a Battle of the Bulge assault on the railroad viaduct at Ahrweiler, Germany. Upon completion of a second bombing run, the formation was attacked by an estimated fifty to seventy-five FW-19U's and ME-109's. Sixteen aircraft were missing in action and almost all of the returning planes badly damaged. Despite this, all available aircraft flew the afternoon of the same day in a mission that destroyed a communications center and three main highways in Neuerberg, Germany which supported the enemy's ground forces.

In the early months of 1945, the Group continued to paralyze the transportation and communication systems of Germany. During March alone, 37 missions were undertaken to attack railroad bridges, marshaling yards, highway intersections and bridges over roads, troop concentrations, ammunition and fuel dumps, and industrial areas.

General Anderson challenged the 9th Air Force to continue to strike the enemy hard by urging, "The 9th has always had high standards. It is to your everlasting credit that not once have you failed to meet the standards. As a result your record is equal to any — surpassed by none. The Hun knows it to his sorrow. Your heroism, your quiet endurance of cold, mud and rain, can only be hinted at here. The full story can be written only when victory is won. Let us go forward determined to maintain our standards, to let nothing mar our great record, to smash the enemy until he quits."

Chapter 15 - The Liberation of Paris

Named American Ambassador to France by the Continental Congress on October 26, 1776, Benjamin Franklin became a fixture in Paris society. With the signing of the Treaty of Alliance on February 6, 1778, France officially recognized the United States as an independent country, leading to a war with Great Britain. The Americans were happy to gain the support of a powerful military force. The French were more than willing to fight with the Americans to help them gain their independence from Great Britain, their arch-rivals. That was the beginning of a special relationship between the two countries.

Thomas Jefferson, the author of the Declaration of Independence, followed Franklin as Ambassador. While in Paris on July 14, 1789, he provided Americans with first-hand accounts of the beginning of the French Revolution as armed citizens stormed and captured the Bastille Prison.

A French aristocrat, The Marquis de Lafayette forged a close relationship with General George Washington and was his top-ranking officer during the American Revolutionary War. Lafayette's gift of the key to the Bastille Prison is still on display at Washington's home in Mount Vernon, VA. It symbolizes the struggle for freedom that was the French dream and went on to become the American dream, as well.

The nations teamed as Allies again in the War of 1812. The ship Isere brought the Statue of Liberty, officially named "Liberty Enlightening the World" to America as a gift from the people of France on June 17, 1885. The enormous copper statue, measuring 46 meters (151 feet 1 inch) from base to torch and 93 meters (305 feet 1 inch) from ground to torch, was designed by sculptor Frédéric Auguste Bartholdi and built by Gustave Eiffel. Known as the "Father of the Statue of Liberty," Parisian Edouard de Laboulaye proposed that the French people finance and build a monument for the United States with the proviso that the pedestal be built by America. He wanted France to learn from America's "struggles, defeats, and triumphs."

As President of the French Anti-Slavery Society, Laboulaye believed that the passage of the 13th Amendment in 1865 abolishing slavery was a milestone worth celebrating. He felt "the common law of free peoples" guaranteed that everyone had an inalienable, sacred right to freedom.

There are broken chains at the bottom of the statue representing escape from tyranny and servitude. The torch the great lady holds is a symbol of enlightenment. The statue features a sonnet by American poet Emma Lazarus written in 1883 to help raise funds for the statue. It wound up repurposing the statue as a symbol of hope and welcome to immigrants arriving to Ellis Island from abroad. The poem's timeless words include the following:

"Give me your tired, your poor,
Your huddled masses yearning to breathe free,
The wretched refuse of your teeming shore.
Send these, the homeless, tempest-tost to me,
I lift my lamp beside the golden door!"

Paris became the Post-Renaissance center of fashion, culture, music, and art. The City of Lights attracted famous American ex-patriots such as Ernest Hemingway, F. Scott Fitzgerald, Gertrude Stein, and T.S. Eliot. Andrew Bird's lyrics of *"How ya gonna keep 'em down on the farm after they've seen Paree?"*, Cole Porter's *"I love Paris in the springtime"*, and George Gershwin's *"An American in Paris"* musical epitomized the evocative image of the city. The Eiffel Tower, Champs Élysées, Place de la Concorde, Louvre, and Seine River are among the countless tourist attractions that Americans and others around the world flock to see.

In an unlikely occurrence in Paris in the spring of 1944, American Captain William Overstreet, Jr. of the 357th Fighter Group, 363rd Squadron chased a German fighter plane through the Eiffel Tower. Piloting a P-51 Mustang, nicknamed "The Berlin Express," he was involved in a dogfight with a German Messerschmitt Bf 109G. When the German plane tried to escape by flying underneath the base arch, the appropriately-named Overstreet followed. Thousands of Parisians witnessed this drama unfold and cheered as the American plane hit the Messerschmitt with machine gun fire. Many reported that the spirits of the French were buoyed by the spectacle, leading to a number of acts of defiance and sabotage against the Germans and helping to fuel the spirit of the Resistance.

Overstreet was later quoted as saying that his exploits were "No big deal." He claimed, "There's actually more space under that tower than you think. Of course, I didn't know that until I did it. I had no time for math or geometry, simply thinking that if the Messerschmitt could go through that gap so could the Mustang." The base arch is actually about 12 stories high and the width roughly the same as a football field so it wasn't a tight squeeze for either pilot.

A daredevil, Overstreet was known for doing loop-the-loops over and under the Golden Gate Bridge in San Francisco. Once when flying over Nazi-occupied territory, his plane was hit by anti-aircraft flak which cut his oxygen supply leaving him semi-conscious, yet he was still able to fly the P-51 to safety.

Several weeks after his Eiffel Tower adventure, he and his group flew eight D-Day missions to support the Allied landings. On his discharge from the service, this daredevil returned to the United States to become something a little less exciting - an accountant.

The Allies continued to march toward Paris after D-Day, facing significant German resistance along the way. By the end of June of 1944, a total of 850,000 troops and 150,000 vehicles had disembarked in Normandy. They took the port of Cherbourg and kept advancing toward the Seine River and Paris, which had been under the control of the Nazis since the Compiegne Armistice of June 22, 1940.

While waiting for liberation by the Allied forces, a horrific event took place on August 5 and 6 of 1944 as the people in the town of Port-de-Roche. One of the survivors, Marcel Philippe, recounted this story at a ceremony in Langon that was later attended by George and several members of his flight crew during a reunion trip to France: "German SS troops were shooting in the darkness, in all directions it seemed. An officer ordered the shooting to stop, perhaps thinking that I was the leader of the group and wanted to take me alive. I took advantage of those few seconds of calm to run to the loft of a barn at the Banthomy farm. Reaching through the overhead trap, I kicked the ladder backwards just as a German officer was about to climb in after me. I lost my balance and fell in such a way that big bundles of hay fell on top of me and covered me completely.

The SS put the ladder back in place and climbed into the loft. Several times, I felt the soldiers walk over my body. I could hardly breathe and thought that surely they would start shooting into the hay. 'That's it. I've had it,' I thought. But it seems that the Germans thought that the 'terrorist' had escaped through the other barn door leading to the horse stable.

Long minutes passed. I tried to get a little air but did not move an inch. It was at that time that I was able to see and hear when I finally got up and looked through the two holes that are still there today in the wall of the loft. Shooting had started again. The Germans caught Jean LeBreton, twenty years old, and Jules LeFraiche, twenty-nine years old. These young men were members of my group.

Through the holes, I could see the road leading to the village, as well as the front of one of the houses being used as a hiding place for the Underground. Fifty meters from the house was a pile of barnyard manure. The SS made four young men, including Jean and Jules, climb on it. A wall hid this horrible scene from my line of sight but I heard it all. I heard screams. It was only later that I would learn all the details.

I saw a cart loaded with straw on its way to the village. Celestin Poulain, twenty-six years old, accompanied by Germans, led the horse. What I did not know at the time was that the bodies of my friends were under the straw.

The sinister parade went toward the cemetery where German soldiers forced Celestin to dig a grave in which they threw the bodies of the four men. Then, preparing themselves for the following event, the SS made Celestin dig another grave, parallel to the first one.

From my watching position, I saw Celestin come back from the village, leading his empty cart. Fifteen minutes later, I saw him come out, surrounded by four Germans who made him walk down the few steps to the nearby garden. An officer followed. He removed his gun from its holster and fired one shot from his revolver. Celestin Poulain joined the other men he had been forced to bury. They made him dig his own grave.

I had known many close calls because of my participation in the Saint-Marcel Underground. I stayed hidden all day and only on Monday, the 7th at 4 a.m. did I escape to Port-de-Roche between two German patrols. I found refuge in a prearranged location. For three days and three nights, I had not slept. I fell asleep like a log and I don't know how much later I woke up. I heard a woman's voice, Jeanette Gaudichon, relating the recent drama and mentioning my name as one of six men shot by the SS. You can imagine everyone's surprise when they found me among them.

That very day, the German outfit of 4,000 men left Langon to continue fighting in the St. Nazaire region. I helped remove land mines for the rest of the war."

In a subsequent ceremony in which George, Jim Clark, Stub Miller, and Ed Williams participated, a monument was dedicated to those martyrs killed at Port-de-Roche. The plaque on it read:

"We chose the hardest stone, the quartz of our land, for it is in the image of their courage. It will defy the centuries, bringing to future generations their painful meaning. We erected these stones and grouped them as a 'V' for 'Victory' for whom these men were the artisans and the victims. Their names on the center stone will testify to their sacrifice for freedom till the end of time."

According to an article published by the "Ouest-France" (West France) newspaper, located in Rennes, "There are times in the life of a man or woman that cannot be expressed, so full of painful emotion they may be. Yesterday in the memory of those shot to death on August 6,

1944, hundreds of people, no doubt, shared those feelings. This was an occasion for a whole village, a whole country, to remember once more, those who were killed so savagely.

The presence of the former American fliers and their wives added a human dimension to this moving ceremony. This Sunday will long be remembered in the little village. Four Americans came back where they fell from their 'flying machine' forty years before. Silently, they testified to the precious gift they brought – FREEDOM. The fliers' visit to this part of France is more than a courtesy call. It is an homage to those Combattants de L'ombre (Underground Fighters) who risked their lives, harassing the Nazis constantly, and helping numbers of Allied soldiers from being taken prisoners."

In truth, General Eisenhower's military priority was not the liberation of Paris but rather reaching Berlin before the Soviets. He had a dilemma because he learned that Hitler had given the order to destroy Paris should the Allies approach. He didn't want the historic and culturally-important city to come to a tragic end. However, he knew a long war of attrition in Paris, such as that fought by the Russians in the Battles of Leningrad and Stalingrad, would significantly tax the Allies' available manpower, resources, and material.

In a scene reminiscent of the stage musical *Les Miserables*, the citizens erected barricades on the streets of Paris to impede the progress of Nazi tanks, trucks, and other mechanized vehicles. According to Maurice Kriegel-Valrimont, a member of the three-man Military Action Committee set up by the National Resistance Council and the leader of the insurrection, "The people were like ants - tens of thousands of them. In 36 hours, there were 600 or more barricades. Some of them were real masterpieces, built by craftsmen and strong enough to stop a tank. Others would have just collapsed, but the Germans did not know which was which." He concluded, "Fear had changed sides, and now the initiative did too. The Germans were the ones on the defensive, and they fell back on a handful of strongpoints."

The Resistance was even able to wiretap the phones of Abwehr headquarters in Paris. The result was that much of the time, they had advance knowledge of the German's plans.

Resistance leader Jean Moulin deserved substantial credit for his work in unifying the various citizen's groups that led to their converging on the capital on August 19, 1944, openly attacking German forces with rifles and grenades while rounding up collaborators for execution. By August 22, some 1,500 members of the Underground and civilians had given their lives. The city, though, was finally ready to be liberated.

Forcing Eisenhower's hand, General Philippe Leclerc led the French 2nd Armored Division in an uprising on the night of August 24 as General George Patton approached Paris with the U.S. Third Army. The attack had the support of General Charles de Gaulle. The next morning, the main units of the U.S. 2nd Armored Division and 4th Armored Division entered the city.

Dietrich von Choltitz, the German Garrison Commander and the Military Governor of the capital, surrendered to the French at the Hôtel Meurice, the provisional headquarters of the Government of the French Republic, despite angry and repeated orders from Hitler that Paris "must not fall into the enemy's hand except lying in complete debris." Charles de Gaulle arrived triumphantly to take control of the city and hundreds of thousands of French citizens took to the streets to celebrate. On August 27, de Gaulle called for the disbanding of all para-military groups and encouraged them to join the new Free French Army under his control.

Kriegel-Valrimont proclaimed, "It was worth it all for this! Paris is free, the enemy is our prisoner, the war is going to be won!"

On D-Day, the Resistance was believed to have about 100,000 members. As momentum grew with the Allies marching across France toward Germany, the organization swelled to approximately 400,000 fighters by October. After de Gaulle's call to consolidate all Resistance forces, the rebuilt French Army quickly became the fourth largest in the European Theater of Operations, growing to 1.2 million soldiers.

Seldom has any city experienced more sheer exultation and jubilation than Paris after the liberation. "To say it was unforgettable is meaningless," effused Kriegel-Valrimont. It was phenomenal. Everyone should have a day like that once in their lifetime."

The Americans were welcomed as glorious conquerors. They were celebrated just as much as the heroic members of the French Underground who paraded on the streets. Shouts of *Vive l'Amérique*! were as common as *Vive De Gaulle*! and *Vive La France*! General Eisenhower later claimed, "We shouldn't blame them for being a bit hysterical."

In a letter to his family, historian Arthur Schlesinger, Jr. wrote this account of the scene in Paris: "The boulevards were jammed with noisy, happy, cheerful crowds. I have never seen so many people. The Opera was illuminated and bedecked with flags and made a very stunning picture. We got there just as bands were playing the various national anthems. It was very moving to stand in that crowded square while thousands of people sang *La Marseillaise*.

From the steps of the Madeleine you could see the flood-lit fountains playing in the Place de La Concorde and in the background the Chamber of Deputies, also under lights. We started walking. For the first time the crowd got a bit rough. The Rue Royale was packed, not only with people but with cars, trucks, and the crowd got a bit panicky and pushed wildly, jamming people against the automobiles and buildings. It soon appeared futile to try to reach the Place de la Concorde, so we hopped on a U.S. jeep, along with about eighty French people, and finally shook loose from the log-jam to career around Paris madly for a while."

After being stationed in England temporarily, George received orders to report to the United States Strategic Air Forces Intelligence Staff stationed in Paris. As wartime assignments go, that's an enviable one. Who wouldn't want to be stationed there, especially in the afterglow of the city's liberation? He had no idea that he would soon meet a special woman who was going to change his life.

Larry J. Kolb in his 2004 book, *Overworld: The Life and Times of a Reluctant Spy,* related the story of how his father, Colonel Jack Kolb, and George began a close friendship after George arrived in Paris: "There he was," George told him, "the baby-faced bruiser from Georgia. He happened to be from G-2 and therefore not the sort to be trusted. But I trusted him anyway. And, by the way, your father was one hell of a boxer. You should've seen him!"

"My record was fifty-two and one," Jack chimed in proudly. "And the one was when I got disqualified for punching the referee!" Jack swung at the referee because he was trying to stop him from punching his opponent after a clinch. Despite that indiscretion, he was good enough to become the Army's Heavyweight Boxing Champion.

George used to tease Jack saying, "Only a boxer would have a nose like yours." Larry defended his father's nose this way: "Maybe it was a little smooshed but it's wasn't misshapen or anything. It was symmetrical. It wasn't so bad."

The two friends told Larry about the night they were in a restaurant filled with homesick American soldiers. There was a record player but all the songs they had were in French. One of the GI's had heard Jack singing and offered to buy him dinner if he would sing his favorite song and so he did. Then another offered to buy George dinner if Jack would sing another song, so he did. Pretty soon, Jack and George couldn't eat or drink another thing and GI's were lining up to pay to hear their favorites. The most-requested songs that night were "Goodnight Irene," "The Tennessee Waltz," and "Ghost Riders in the Sky."

Jack would, in turn, often rely on George's talent as what he termed a "grammarian." With English as one of his majors in college, George was adept at composition and so Jack would ask for help crafting military intelligence messages, especially those that required precise language. According to George's son Jerry, this was a lifelong pursuit: "My dad was really well-versed in the use of proper English. He would correct our grammar often, whether we wanted him to or not."

In the super-charged, celebratory atmosphere enveloping Paris, George and Simone met at a party on a cold night in January at the home of a friend of the de Cruzel family, Liliane Chabere. George was in his full military dress uniform so Simone didn't have to ask the usual conversation starter – "What do you do?" He asked her that question, though. She responded with, "I'm a nurse for the International Red Cross." He sensed there was more to the story than that and was confident she'd share it with him when she was ready.

The attraction between them was immediate. They were rarely apart after that first night. Simone wrote in a tiny journal, "It's Tuesday, January 30, 1945. I am crazy happy. I just met someone very special. George explained his fantastic story when his plane was in flames and how he escaped from behind the German lines in Brittany. He is wonderful." It didn't take long for Simone to trust George enough to tell him her complete story. He stared into her bright blue eyes as she described her war experiences. As she did, his jaw dropped and he repeated phrases such as, "You did WHAT?" and "Are you KIDDING me?" George was spellbound. He found Simone stunning in every sense of the word.

According to son Jerry, "When my dad talked about his romance with my mom, he'd always say how beautiful and fun she was. He loved her very much and was very proud of her. They would sometimes laugh about her pronunciation of American words."

"My mother was swept off her feet," said daughter Claire (Stalnaker) Hayden. "My dad was a dashing, cocky, hell-bent-for-leather kind of guy. When they met at a dinner party, so mundane after their daring wartime exploits, fireworks went off!"

On Valentine's Day, she got what she called an "adorable letter" from George along with orchids. Simone began to introduce him to her family and friends. "I always talk about my darling Colonel. Everybody loves him," boasted Simone. Their connection deepened. It wasn't long before she wrote, "He's got everything going for him. He's handsome and smart with a big heart. George is the most adorable treasure the earth has ever seen. I am so in love."

151

On March 20, Simone reported that "George offers me a wonderful golden watch. I feel more and more happy." They walked hand-in-hand along the Seine and the Champs Élysée. They frequented outdoor cafés, toured the museums, and visited art galleries. There's no better city than Paris in which to be young and in love. They learned each other's language in many ways – not just English and French.

George and Simone began to talk in terms of their having a future together. It's strange because not long before neither one thought they would have any kind of future at all.

In Berlin, meanwhile, the American, British, and French forces were set to enter the city where they would meet up with Soviet troops moving in from the east. Fifty-five feet beneath the Chancellery in Berlin, in a refurbished air raid shelter, Adolf Hitler retreated to his Führerbunker, an 18-room self-contained complex with its own water and electrical supply.

In a macabre scene the early morning of April 29, 1945, the 56-year-old Hitler and the 33-year-old Eva Braun were married in the bunker study room to the sound of exploding shells and shaking walls. The Allied bombing offensive that began in 1943 produced an estimated 500,000 German civilian casualties and left much of its capital city of Berlin in ruins. Germany was hit with so many bombs during the war, in fact, that some 5,500 of them are still being discovered and diffused every year. It's such a common occurrence that it's not even reported by the local news media unless there is an explosion, traffic disruption, or major evacuation.

A minor official of the Propaganda Ministry, Walter Wagner, officiated at the ceremony in the early hours. Wearing a black silk dress, Eva started to sign the marriage document using her maiden name but stopped, crossing out the "B" and writing "Eva Hitler, born Braun." The wedding register was witnessed by Propaganda Minister Joseph Goebbels and head of the *Parteikanzlei* (Nazi Party Chancellery) Martin Bormann. The couple celebrated by having breakfast with champagne. When they first met, she was just a 17-year-old working as an assistant for his personal photographer and had been his mistress since.

Hitler dictated the following Last Will and Testament to his secretary, Traudl Junge: "As I did not consider that I could take responsibility, during the years of struggle, of contracting a marriage, I have now decided, before the closing of my earthly career, to take as my wife that girl who, after many years of faithful friendship, entered, of her own free will, the practically besieged town in order to share her destiny

152

with me. At her own desire she goes as my wife with me into death. It will compensate us for what we both lost through my work."

He ended the document with, "I myself and my wife - in order to escape the disgrace of deposition or capitulation - choose death. It is our wish to be burnt immediately on the spot where I have carried out the greatest part of my daily work in the course of a twelve years' service to my people." He signed it with, "Given in Berlin, 29th April 1945, 4:00 a.m."

Later that day, Hitler tested out the cyanide poison that *Reichsführer* of the *Schutzstaffel* Heinrich Himmler had given him on his beloved German Shepherd dog Blondi who lay dead on the carpet after being injected. Hitler was previously quoted as saying, "Miss Braun is, besides my dog Blondi, the only one I can absolutely count on."

At 3:30 p.m. on April 30, the newlyweds bit into thin glass vials of cyanide and Hitler proceeded to shoot himself in the head with a 7.65 mm Walther pistol.

In his book, *"I was Hitler's Chauffeur,"* translated into English in 2010, Erich Kampka described how Hitler's personal adjutant Otto Günsche asked him to get 200 litres of petrol explaining, "The Chief is dead." Kampka described it as "a dreadful shock" and asked, "How could that happen?" Günsche raised his right arm, held his hand like a pistol, pointed to his mouth, and mimicked a shooting motion.

Kampka told of how he entered Hitler's suite and saw him sitting in an almost upright position on a blood-soaked sofa. Eva was lying beside him but had not used the revolver at her side, preferring just to take the poison. There was a bullet hole in Hitler's right temple and blood trickled down his check. His pistol lay on the floor where he dropped it.

The bodies were carried up the twenty steps to the bunker exit and placed on the ground outside. According to Kampka, "Dr. Goebbels took a box of matches from his pocket and handed it to me. I set light to the rag and, once it was afire, lobbed it towards the petrol-soaked corpses. As we watched, in seconds a bright flame flared up, gurgling and hissing, accompanied by billowing black smoke. This dark pall of smoke against the background of the burning Reich capital made a grisly sight." The remains were buried in a shallow grave in a garden.

After overseeing Hitler's cremation, Propaganda Minister Joseph Goebbels went back into the bunker, gave his wife and six children capsules of cyanide poison, and shot himself.

Shortly thereafter, Radio Hamburg made the official announcement that "Our Führer Adolf Hitler died for Germany in his command post in the Reich Chancellery this afternoon, fighting to his last breath against Bolshevism." Several weeks later, Heinrich Himmler, the Reich leader of the Gestapo, also took his own life.

Buoyed by the news of Hitler's death and knowing the war in Europe would likely be over within days, George took Simone on a B-26 Marauder trip from Nice to Paris on May 1. Her reaction was, "What a rendezvous with my darling! We had clear weather until Marseille but hit a snow storm in Lyons. George lets me pilot a bit. It's like I'm living a dream."

Chapter 16 – "Can You Imagine a Happier Scene?"

One of the most commonly asked questions about World War II is, "Weren't there Germans who objected to the Nazi dogma?" The answer is yes. There certainly were those who were horrified by the actions of the German government but remained silent. Today's counterpart would be a country such as North Korea with no open political dialogue. Those who disagreed with government policies and actions were silenced using various means, including being put to death "for security reasons." Most dissenters didn't dare express their feelings, let alone take action.

There were, however, notable exceptions in Germany. Sophie Scholl, along with her brother Hans and their mutual friend Chroph Probst, were political activists who helped form the White Rose, a non-violent resistance group that defied the Nazis by creating and distributing leaflets at the University of Munich. They called for the German people to resist the influence of the Nazis. They wrote: "Hitler is leading the German people into the abyss. Blindly they follow their seducers into ruin," along with "For Hitler and his followers, no punishment is commensurate with their crimes," and "Are we to be forever a nation which is hated and rejected by all mankind?" The trio also painted "Freedom" and "Down with Hitler" on buildings in Munich as well as crossing out swastikas.

Their messages began to find their way throughout the country, including Berlin. The three dissidents were hunted down, captured by the Gestapo, and executed for treason on February 22, 1943. Defiant to the end and suffering a broken leg along with other injuries from her "interrogation," the 21-year-old Sophie's last words were, "What does my death matter, if through us thousands of people are awakened and stirred to action?" Unfortunately, not enough Germans were, in fact, "awakened and stirred to action."

Ironically, one who was turned out to be Albert Goering, very much unlike his older brother Hermann, Commander of the Luftwaffe, President of the Reichstag, and Prime Minister of Prussia. Albert risked his life a number of times to save innocent people. He moved to Austria after the Nazis rose to power and often spoke out against them. When the country was annexed by Germany in 1938, Hermann kept the Gestapo away from Albert despite the fact that he distributed exit visas to Jewish residents and political dissidents. He influenced Hermann to order the release of many prisoners of concentration camps for humanitarian reasons. Arrested a number of times for "subversive" activities, a death warrant was issued for him in 1944. Again, his connections were able to ensure his freedom.

Imprisoned for two years after the war because of his family name, he was eventually released but found himself unemployable and lived in poverty. He was looked after by those he helped.

As an indicator of the number of Germans who had contempt for Hitler, there were at least 40 known attempts on his life, beginning as early as 1921 when shots were fired at him from a crowd in Berlin and then both in Thuringia and Leipzig in 1923. None of the shooters hit their target. Heinrich Grunow fired at a car in 1935 and killed the man in the back seat. Assuming it was the Führer, Grunow then shot himself. By a quirk of fate, Hitler was driving the car and his chauffeur was sitting in the back seat at the time.

In 1937, a soldier planted a bomb under a stage. He went to the toilet, however, and got locked in so was unable to detonate the explosive when Hitler stood up to speak.

Johann Georg Elser put a bomb in one of the pillars at the Beer Hall in Munich where Hitler was due to speak in 1939. It was timed to go off at 9:30 p.m. but at 9:12, he suddenly ended his speech and abruptly departed. Eight people were killed and sixty-five others wounded, including Eva Braun's father.

Major General Henning Von Treskow and Field Marshal Gunthere von Klug hatched another plot in 1943 to plant explosives disguised as bottles of Cognac on Hitler's plane. The cold of an unheated locker where two bottles were placed, however, prevented the detonation of the bombs as the acid was frozen in the detonator cap. Eight days later, Von Gertsdorff carried a bomb with him and planned to explode it when he was greeted by Hitler during a weapons inspection in Berlin. For some reason, Hitler walked right past him.

In 1944, Colonel Claus Count von Stauffenberg carried a bomb in his briefcase during a planned meeting at Wolf's Lair in Wolfsschanze. He placed it under a table and left saying he had an urgent telephone call to make. The bomb exploded but Hitler was only slightly wounded.

How Hitler managed to survive all of the assassination attempts is one of history's strangest mysteries. You might say he lived a charmed life, but "charm" is not a fit word to describe someone who is likely the most despised person in history. It's ironic that after all the failed assassination attempts, Hitler would take his own life in the end.

On the other hand, German generals came and went with dizzying speed during World War II. The job did not have much of a life expectancy. Germany lost 136 of them during the war, which averaged out to one every other week. Hitler personally ordered the execution of

84 of them, for one reason or another. It's likely there were those who hesitated a bit when they were offered a promotion to general because there was a sudden opening. They were reluctant to ask, "What happened to the person who previously held this position?"

Another commonly asked question is "Were ALL Germans inhumane to those who were captured or imprisoned?" The answer is no. Although Simone's experience was all-too-common, the man known as the "Master Interrogator" worked for the Luftwaffe and was the exact opposite. If George or other members of his flight crew had been captured by the Nazis, it's likely they would have been questioned by Hans Scharff, a man who interrogated airmen from the American Eighth and Ninth Air Forces. He used kindness and friendly conversation to extract information. Showing compassion and respect, he got many of them to drop their guard and divulge information they claimed afterwards they never told him.

After the war, Scharff emigrated from Germany to the United States, getting former prisoners to sponsor his entry and eventual citizenship. In 1948, he began giving lectures to the Air Force on interrogation techniques. The military later incorporated his methods into its curriculum in interrogation schools.

His successful techniques have since been studied and contrasted to abusive treatment. It's been found that typically a greater volume of information and more accurate information can be obtained using the "good cop" rather than the "bad cop" approach.

A man of many talents, Scharff married an American and found success in an unlikely new career as a mosaic artist. One of his works is on the 15-foot arched walls of Cinderella's Castle at Disney World's Magic Kingdom in Orlando, Florida. Not many people are aware of the fact that the beautiful "Story of Cinderella" mosaic was, in fact, created by the Nazi's Master Interrogator.

Knowing that plans needed to be formulated for postwar Europe, the so-called "Big Three" attended The Yalta Conference which took place in a Russian resort town in the Crimea from February 4 through 11 in 1945. U.S. President Franklin D. Roosevelt and British Prime Minister Winston Churchill were able to convince Soviet Premier Joseph Stalin to enter the war against Japan. Stalin kept his commitment by declaring war on August 9th and sending more than a million troops into Japanese-occupied Manchuria. The Russian manpower that was so critical to the fight in Europe now aided the Allies on the Pacific front.

A politician named Josif Djugashvili abandoned his given name and began using the pseudonym "Stalin" in 1913. It translates to "Man of Steel." A prerequisite for becoming a ruthless dictator seems to be possession of high self-esteem.

Strange as it sounds, Stalin attended a seminary in Tblisi to study for the priesthood in the Georgian Orthodox Church. It's there that he secretly began to read Karl Marx's "Communist Manifesto" and become involved in the revolutionary movement against the Czar of Russia. Expelled from the seminary, he joined the Marxist Social Democratic movement, the Bolsheviks, led by Vladimir Lenin. He engaged in criminal activities, including bank robberies, to help fund the Bolshevik Party. Arrested multiple times, he was exiled to Siberia and imprisoned.

After his release, he outmaneuvered a number of others to seize control of the party when Lenin died in 1924. Once in power, he ruled by terror, having potential enemies executed or sent to the Gulag system of forced labor camps. He expanded the powers of the secret police and encouraged citizens to spy on one another. Stalin became Dictator of the USSR, (Union of Soviet Socialist Republics) in 1929.

He launched a series of five-year plans intended to transform the country from an agrarian society to an industrial superpower. His plan centered on government control of the economy and included eliminating privatization of agriculture in favor of government-owned and operated farms.

In the mid to late 1930s, Stalin instituted the Great Purge, a series of murderous campaigns designed to rid Soviet society of those he considered a threat. It is estimated that he was responsible for the deaths of as many as 20 million people during his brutal rule.

Just as Hitler did in Germany and Mussolini in Italy, Stalin built a cult of personality around himself. Soviet history books were rewritten to give him a more prominent role in the revolution, cities were renamed in his honor, and he became the subject of numerous legends about other aspects of his life. He was the subject of flattering artwork, literature and media coverage.

Stalin's alignment with the other Allied nations during World War II is an unlikely one. The best explanation for it is the old proverb "The enemy of my enemy is my friend." Without the Soviet Union on the Allied side, the Germans could have concentrated on the Western Front and the outcome of World War II could have been very different. Stalin served as dictator for a remarkably long period of time, ending with his death in 1953 when Nikita Khrushchev, his successor, instituted a de-Stalinization process which discredited him.

On April 12, 1945, a calamity occured that had a devastating effect on the American psyche. The previous month, hospital tests had indicated President Roosevelt was suffering from coronary artery disease, congestive heart failure, and atherosclerosis. He was feeling weak and his complexion had noticeably changed to ashen gray.

Accordingly, the President traveled to the "Little White House" in Warm Springs, Georgia for two weeks of relaxation. He had first visited the health spa twenty-one years earlier. After being diagnosed with polio, he tried numerous therapies for his paralyzed lower body and liked the Warm Springs resort, known for its healing mineral waters, so much that he bought it. He later established the National Association for Infantile Paralysis, later re-named the March of Dimes, which funded research leading to Jonas Salk's polio vaccine.

FDR concealed his disease as much as possible for political reasons. He actually became accustomed to disguising his affliction long before he became President. In private, he'd use a wheelchair and walk with the help of iron braces fitted to his legs. In public, though, he'd invariably be seated. He even installed hand controls in his car so he could be seen driving. The public never noticed, or wanted to notice, that it was a carefully orchestrated stage show. There was an unspoken understanding with the press that photographs revealing FDR's paralysis were not to be taken. Leaders at the time were expected to show strength without vulnerability.

Around 1 p.m., while sitting for a portrait, FDR suddenly collapsed, complaining of a painful ache in the back of his head. A doctor was summoned who immediately recognized the symptoms of a cerebral hemorrhage and gave the President an adrenaline shot in an attempt to revive him. The 32nd President was pronounced dead, however, at 3:30 p.m.

His wife Eleanor had delivered a speech that afternoon and was listening to a piano performance when she was suddenly summoned to the White House. She later described the ride as one of dread, somehow knowing that her husband had died. Once she arrived, aides gave her the news. Their daughter Anna arrived and both changed into black dresses. Eleanor then phoned their four sons, all of whom were on active duty with the military.

At 5:30 pm, she greeted Vice President Harry Truman, who had not yet been told the news. Eleanor said simply, "Harry, the President is dead." He asked if there was anything he could do for her. She replied, "Is there anything we can do for YOU? For you are the one in trouble now." Truman took the oath of office later that day.

The new President had a tough act to follow. FDR also left him with the difficult decision of whether or not to use the atomic bomb, after learning of its existence. As Vice President, he had never been told about the Manhattan Project.

The only President to be elected to four terms, Roosevelt led the country through the Great Depression and World War II, two of the most difficult times in American history. A whole generation had grown up knowing no other President. His social programs redefined the role of government, put American leadership on the world stage during World War II, and made an indelible mark on world history.

The Third Reich that Hitler boasted would last 1,000 years turned out to last only twelve. According to Simone, "The German creeps are losing. They surrender one after another. On May 7, the Armistice is signed in Reims. Go Allies!"

Located about 80 miles east of Paris and 55 miles east of the Compiegne Forest where Germany surrendered in World War I, Reims was the same city where the French yielded to Germany on June 21, 1940. Without Hitler and his complete rule of the military, the Germans weren't sure at first who could authorize a surrender. Chief of Staff to the Fuëhrer Karl Doenitz finally granted authority to Chief of the Wermacht General Gustav Jodl to sign the official document ending the War in Europe, effective the following day.

The ceremony in the red-brick schoolhouse being used as Supreme Allied Headquarters was brief, beginning at 2:45 p.m. and lasting only five minutes. Under Jodl's signature were those of Lt. Gen. Walter Bedell Smith, General Eisenhower's Chief of Staff; General Ivan Suslaparov, head of the Russian mission to France; and General Francois Sevez of France.

Jodl announced, "With this signature the German people and the German armed forces are for better or worse delivered into the victors' hands. In this war, which has lasted more than five years, both have achieved and suffered more than perhaps any other people in the world. In this hour I can only express the hope that the victor will treat them with generosity."

Suslaparov led the Russian officers into General Eisenhower's office and shook his hand proclaiming, "This is a great moment for all of us." Eisenhower replied, "You said it!"

George and Simone walked through the streets of Paris witnessing the euphoria of people all around them celebrating the Allied victory.

160

They listened to church bells ringing and watched the dancing in the streets.

The couple felt they didn't have time to waste. It's as if they had to make up for the time that had already been lost to them. In the middle of the jubilation, she turned to him saying, "The war is finally over! Can you imagine a happier scene?" "Actually, I can," he answered. He reached into his pocket and pulled out an engagement ring asking, "Simone, *veux-tu m'épouser?*" which translates as, "Will you marry me?" It's a phrase he practiced saying all day. He wanted to make sure he got it exactly right. She responded, "Of course, I will!" They kissed and embraced. A crowd of cheering people formed a circle around George and Simone. While holding hands, they danced around the couple shouting good wishes.

Simone wrote in her journal, "The same day that the war ends, George offers me an engagement ring. How beautiful it is. After a long search he found a splendid diamond. It's very pure and 2½ carats. He is an angel. No words are sufficient for such an event. I must write a book for all the emotions I am feeling. It's for the victory. Unconditional German surrender! George and I are going to be married!"

All this was tempered by the grim news that was quickly surfacing as descriptions of Nazi death camps dominated the headlines. Simone reacted to the grisly stories told by the survivors from places such as Buchenwald, Dachau, and Nordhausen by admitting, "Nothing is sure concerning the friends and families of my former prison inmates. I think about them all the time. Mourning for the dead plays down my joy." Like so many people in former occupied countries, she went from one heartbreaking funeral to another as there was word of the fate of those who were incarcerated.

An additional document of surrender, effective immediately, was also signed by Generalfeldmarschall Wilhelm Keitel in Berlin on May 8, which became officially known as V-E, or Victory in Europe, Day. American President Harry Truman's 61st birthday happened to be that day. He dedicated the surrender to FDR, saying that his "only wish was that Roosevelt had lived to witness this day."

The 9th Air Force Commander Lieutenant General Hoyt S Vandenberg issued the "Order of the Day" on May 8 which said, in part:

"The unconditional surrender of all German forces marks the attainment of our objective in Europe. It follows the complete defeat of the enemy on land, sea, and in the air. From friends and enemies alike has come evidence of the tremendous role of air power in accomplishing this historic success. Each man who fought and died is inseparable with those who fought and lived. By the strength of our faith and in your determination you have come thousands of miles to drive a powerful enemy from the skies, then turned your weapons against the foe on the ground to destroy his ability to resist. To each one of you is due this credit."

A simple memorial service was held by the 391st Bomber Group and attended by all those in the organization. At the open-air assembly, the unit commanders read the honor roll of crewmen who had been killed, wounded, or named missing during the 17 months of action against the enemy. In all, 44 of the 391st Bomber Group's planes were lost and 1,341 damaged in battle in the European Theater of Operations. The total number of Allied bomber crewmen killed was estimated to be at least 100,000.

George, of course, was relieved that the long war was over and eagerly participated in the victory celebrations. On the other hand, like so many career soldiers since the beginning of time, he also felt a certain let-down. Peace-time jobs in the military just don't have the same sense of urgency or importance. "There's something about the exhilaration of war," admitted Jack Kolb. "It's something you can't understand unless you've lived it. When the war had been over a few months, and normality had set in, George and I used to sit around in Paris and say to each other, 'It wasn't a good war. But it was better than no war at all.'"

Simone had always dreamed of getting married in the Catholic Church so she had one stipulation for George – he had to take Catechism classes and convert to Catholicism. He agreed and Simone didn't waste any time scheduling him for his first class on May 16, just a little more than a week later.

On June 8, the two had what Simone calls a "special dinner" at the Ritz to celebrate a solemn anniversary. Simone revealed, "It's one year ago today that I walked out of that terrible German prison." In remembrance, she took what she called a "barefoot pilgrimage" to the Notre Dame de Laguet Cathedral, a distance of 8.4 kilometers or 5.2 miles to "give thanks for my liberation." Walking barefoot as a religious gesture is considered a sign of innocence, humility, and servitude. In the chapel are hundreds of plaques that people have put up giving thanks to God for being rescued from disaster.

George was baptized as a Catholic and confirmed by Father O'Grady at the St. Joseph Chapel in Paris on June 23. But there was a problem. "We wait with big anxiety for the paperwork certifying this whole thing," said an exasperated Simone. "I didn't make him get baptized only to have to cancel our church wedding. Now they say we need more paperwork from the American Chaplain. Father O'Grady is also saying that the baptism of a Protestant of his denomination is not recognized as valid. I spend my time trying to fix that."

Another issue arose at the same time. Simone explained, "I feel sick as a dog. My belly aches. I am annihilated by vomiting. I know something is wrong."

There's yet an additional factor that adds to their stress. At first, Simone described it simply as "Such fatigue for George. He has lost weight." Then it quickly escalated to, "They tell me George is in the hospital. I go crazy. The doctors can't say what it is. I know at once it is meningitis. I take the responsibility for it." Simone hadn't been feeling well with those stomach problems so she assumed that she had somehow transmitted the disease to George.

Meningitis is caused by the inflammation of the protective membranes, known as the meninges, that cover the brain and spinal cord. It's usually caused by an infection of the surrounding fluid. Although it can be contagious, there was really no reason for Simone to conclude that she was responsible for George contracting it. Yet, she took on that guilt.

She claimed, "It's my independence crisis, my fear of getting married, and the paperwork problems with the Church that made him sick. My little treasure, I am responsible for all your troubles. He deserves so much to be happy. I need to heal him, caress him, give him back his taste for life. I am sick with anxiety. If anything happens to him, I will stop living." Fortunately, George recovered after several weeks of being bed-ridden and on medication.

After that, Simone made an appointment for herself and, not surprisingly, reported, "On June 29, I finally go to Doctor Kipiaco in Paris. I find out that I am pregnant. I worry about telling George but he is an angel about it. He's my darling and he comforts me."

Years later, their daughter Claire said skeptically, "My mother always put forward a 'life without sin' kind of persona but sitting around the table one night, we kids were discussing their marriage with them. We put some dates together and 'Voila!' We realized my brother Jerry was born seven months after their wedding ceremony. My mother broke into tears and told us the 'reason' that happened. My Dad had come down with meningitis and they didn't think he would live. So Jerry was conceived. I still don't know how my dad did that, sick as he was."

Things still weren't settled with the wedding preparation. On July 13, Simone wrote, "I go to see Monseigneur Renion. Such contradictions. I am tired of the church. Every time he says something different." Finally, things get straightened out. George's conversion became official and they finally were informed that they could be married in the Catholic Church.

Being pregnant while also trying to plan for the wedding continued to take its toll on Simone: "I am sick. It's horrible. It's non-stop torture. The fitting of my wedding dress is terrible. I run outside to throw up."

George accompanied her to the gynecologist's office. Simone happily reported, "We went to see Doctor Sureau, 11 Rue Portalis, behind Saint Augustine Church. Together we are reassured. Everything is OK. Every day we are more and more in love. We find out the birth of our child is expected between February 27 and March 2nd of 1946. We are so happy!"

Back in the United States, the first atomic bomb test was conducted in the desert near the Los Alamos research facility on July 16, 1945. Dr. J. Robert Oppenheimer, the project's director, solemnly watched the enormous mushroom cloud rise into the New Mexico sky. Recognizing the historical significance of the event and the terrible destructive power he helped unleash, he recited a passage from an ancient Hindu text: "Now I am become death, destroyer of worlds."

A second major summit of the Allied nations was held, this time in Potsdam, from July 17 to August 2 to negotiate additional terms for post-war construction. A plan was formulated for Germany to be divided into four Zones with each of the major Allied nations occupying one of them.

There was agreement that there would be "a complete disarmament and demilitarization of Germany." This included an elimination of all German military and paramilitary forces, a dismantling of all aspects of German industry that could be utilized for military purposes, and the banning of production of all military equipment. Other provisions included the establishment of a democracy, the elimination of the national policy of racial discrimination, and the conducting of a war crimes trial. Democracy was to be established at the state and local levels but there would be no federal government for the immediate future.

On August 6, 1945, President Harry Truman made the agonizing decision to unleash the atomic bomb on Hiroshima. Nicknamed "Little Boy," the weapon had an equivalent of 15,000 tons of TNT and was dropped by the Enola Gay, a B-29 Superfortress bomber named for the mother of Colonel Tibbets. The initial blast and subsequent firestorm killed an estimated 80,000 people.

Major General Charles Sweeney piloted an observation plane which released a specially-encased measuring instrument with a letter included which was meant for Japanese physicists. The message was, "Now that you have seen that we can do this, tell your leaders to stop this war. We regret that this major new discovery is being used this way, but the war has to stop."

The Japanese didn't surrender, however, and another B-29, nicknamed Bockscar, also known as Bock's Car, piloted by Sweeney, dropped another bomb three days later, this one on Nagasaki. "Fat Man," the second bomb, had an equivalent of 21,000 tons of TNT and produced approximately 75,000 casualties. The intended target was actually Kokura but the city was shrouded in smog and smoke. Nagasaki, which had clear weather, was the back-up target, giving rise to the phrase "Kokura luck" in Japan.

On the other hand, Tsutomu Yamaguchi, an oil tanker designer, could be a symbol for bad luck. He was on his way to the airport returning from a business trip to Hiroshima for Mitsubishi Heavy Industries when he realized he had forgotten his hanko (travel pass.) He returned to the city and reported, "There was a great flash in the sky and I was blown over." It turned out the first atomic bomb was dropped just 2 miles (3.2 kilometers) from him. Somehow, he survived, suffering just upper body burns and losing the hearing in his left ear.

Despite the injuries, he returned to his home town of Nagasaki and reported back to work. The second bomb was dropped, once again exactly 2 miles or 3.2 kilometers from him, just as he was in the middle of describing the terror of what he experienced in Hiroshima. This time, Yamaguchi was unhurt. Would it have been possible for him to have been both the unluckiest and luckiest person in the world at the same time? At any rate, he's the only one to have survived both atomic explosions. Living to age 93, he finally succumbed to stomach cancer on January 4, 2010.

President Truman concluded that the alternative to using the bombs, a D-Day type of invasion of Japan, would have cost an untold number of American lives. In preparation for this option, however, the War Department had 1.5 million Purple Hearts made. Though "Operation Downfall," the invasion of Japan, was never necessary, those same Purple Hearts are still being issued today.

Survivors of the atomic bombings in Japan were called *niju hibakusha* or "explosion-affected people." The American conventional fire-bombings of densely-populated Tokyo actually resulted in upwards of 100,000 deaths, more than the death total from either the Hiroshima or Nagasaki atomic bombings.

V-J, or Victory over Japan, Day, is celebrated as either August 14 or 15, depending on the time zone differences, the day that Japan announced its intention to surrender. The official ceremony was held on September 2, when the document of surrender was executed aboard the USS Missouri, anchored in Tokyo Bay. Japan and Russia, however, to this day haven't officially signed a peace treaty to end World War II due to a continuing dispute over the Kuril Islands.

The six seemingly-endless years of World War II that began with Hitler's invasion of Poland were finally over. The conflict took more lives and destroyed more property than any war in history. General Douglas MacArthur provided a fitting eulogy: "Today the guns are silent. A great tragedy has ended. A great victory has been won. The skies no longer rain death. The seas bear only commerce. Men walk everywhere upright in the sunlight. The entire world is quietly at peace."

Exact numbers of war-related fatalities are always difficult to calculate because many of them come from disease, famine, or lingering injuries. The figure cited most often for total people killed in the war is, as has been mentioned, 58 million, although estimates range from 45 to 60 million. Approximately 80% of those deaths came from just four countries - Russia, China, Germany, and Poland. On a percentage basis, Poland suffered the most deaths, losing a staggering 20% of its population.

Over 100 million soldiers served from more than 30 countries during the course of the war. A total of 407,000 Americans were killed. French casualties were 217,600 military personnel and 350,000 civilians for a total of 567,600 people. The British lost nearly 384,000 troops and an additional 70,000 civilians. The Soviet Union suffered the most losses with, including numbers for the Ukraine, over 18 million soldiers and 7 million civilians killed, close to 14% of the population.

According to Stub Miller, "In August, as the war came to an end, I was ordered to report to Fort Sheridan, Illinois where I was discharged on August 29, 1945. Bess and I celebrated by dancing the night away to the Lawrence Welk band at the Aragon Ballroom and drinking our first champagne. The next morning, we arrived back home in Benton Harbor to begin our life again in a new home with a two-and-a-half-month-old son."

Like the rest of the world, George and Simone were thrilled that the war in the Pacific was over and much of the world could start the rebuilding process. After their whirlwind romance, they were married in a civil ceremony on September 3. The next day, the marriage was consecrated at the historic *Église du Sacre'-Coeur* or "Sacred Heart

166

Eglise du Sacre'-Coeur in Nice, France

Church" on 22 France St. in Nice which was built in 1872 by the Fathers of the African Missions of Lyon.

The priest began the ceremony by asking those in attendance to rise and said to George and Simone, "You have come together in this church so that the Lord may seal and strengthen your love in the presence of the Church's minister and this community. Christ abundantly blesses this love. He has already consecrated you in baptism and now he enriches and strengthens you by a special sacrament so that you may assume the duties of marriage in mutual and lasting fidelity. And so, in the presence of the Church, I ask you to state your intentions. George and Simone, have you come here freely and without reservation to give yourselves to each other in marriage? Will you love and honor each other as man and wife for the rest of your lives? Will you accept children lovingly from God and bring them up according to the law of Christ and his Church?" They responded affirmatively to the questions.

The priest continued, "Since it is your intention to enter into marriage, join your right hands, and declare your consent before God and his Church." George stated, "I, George Stalnaker, take you, Simone de Cruzel, to be my wife. I promise to be true to you in good times and in bad, in sickness and in health. I will love you and honor you all the days of my life." Simone responded, "I, Simone de Cruzel, take you, George Stalnaker, to be my husband. I promise to be true to you in good times and in bad, in sickness and in health. I will love you and honor you all the days of my life."

The priest concluded with, "May the Lord in his goodness strengthen your consent and fill you both with his blessings. What God has joined, no man must divide."

The couple exchanged rings and vowed to each other, "Take this ring as a sign of my love and fidelity in the name of the Father, and of the Son, and of the Holy Spirit." George and Simone kissed, the priest pronounced them husband and wife, and those gathered applauded as the newlyweds walked back down the aisle.

After the wedding, George and Simone lived at one of the most famous residences on the "Rive Gauche" or "Left Bank" – the Hotel Lutetia, 45 Raspail Boulvevard, Paris. No ordinary luxury hotel, the Lutetia became home to many artists and musicians. Featuring a welcoming statue of Gustave Eiffel in its courtyard and offering a spectacular view of the Eiffel Tower, the 230-room hotel was built in 1910. Its guests have included Pablo Picasso, Charles de Gaulle, Peggy Guggenheim, and James Joyce, who wrote part of *Ulysses* while staying there. Many of their portraits hang on the Art Deco and Belle Epoque walls of the hotel. The crystal chandeliers, period furniture, and soft jazz music playing throughout the building give the distinctive feel of being in the heart of Paris.

When the French government abandoned the city on June 14, 1940, the hotel was commandeered by the Abwher, the German counter-espionage organization, and used to house officers in charge of the occupation. The Germans moved out of the Lutetia when Paris was liberated and it was taken over by the French and American military. From then until after the end of the war, it was used as a repatriation center for prisoners of war, returnees from concentration camps and other displaced individuals. It has changed ownership and been renovated a number of times and is currently undergoing a three-year renovation, scheduled to be completed in 2017.

In all, the 391st Bombardment Group flew 294 missions in the ETO (European Theater of Operations) with a cumulative total of 62,178 crewmen participating. Of these, 29 were killed, 67 wounded, and 198 listed as missing in action or taken POW. A total of 15,841 tons of bombs were dropped on German targets. The official date of the Group's deactivation was October 25, 1945.

Only a half-dozen B-26's have survived through the years. One is now at the Air Force Museum, Dayton, Ohio, and another can be seen at the Musée de l'Air in Paris. Probably the most famous Marauder is Army Air Forces serial number 41-31773, nicknamed "Flak-Bait," which flew 207 combat missions over Europe, more than any other American aircraft in World War II. This historic plane is currently undergoing restoration at the Steven F. Udvar-Hazy Center, Chantilly, VA. More than a thousand patched holes in the fuselage bear witness to the fact that this plane was appropriately named.

In a letter to B-26 Marauder Historical Society in 1991, President George H.W. Bush acknowledged, "The Marauders legacy involves some of the greatest campaigns, leaders, and pilots in the history of military air power."

George & Simone Stalnaker's Wedding

A happy couple

Chapter 17 – "Sometimes I Cry & Would Love to Disappear"

On November 20, 1945, the Nuremberg Trial of Major War Criminals began before an international tribunal at the Palace of Justice in Bavaria. Joseph Stalin favored the summary execution of 50,000 to 100,000 German staff officers. However, after negotiations, the Allies agreed that criminal proceedings requiring documentation of crimes and sufficient evidence would be more in keeping with international law.

The Charter of the International Military Tribunal issued in London on August 8, 1945 specified three categories of charges:

- **Crimes against peace**, including planning, preparing, starting or waging wars of aggression or wars in violation of international agreements.

- **War crimes**, including violations of customs or laws of war, including improper treatment of civilians and prisoners of war.

- **Crimes against humanity**, including murder, enslavement or deportation of civilians or persecution on political, religious or racial grounds.

Twenty-one of the twenty-four defendants were found guilty of committing crimes in at least one of the three categories.

The "Subsequent Nuremberg Proceedings," consisted of twelve additional trials conducted from December of 1946 to April of 1949 in the same location before U.S. military tribunals. Here, 185 Germans were indicted and 97 convicted.

Simone was not impressed with the "I was just following orders" defense used by those on trial bluntly claiming, "All they want is pity. I think I dislike them more now than during the war."

Hitler's successor was supposed to be military leader Hermann Goering. He was the dominant personality at the Nuremburg trials but failed to convince the judges of his innocence. They found him guilty in all three categories - crimes against peace, war crimes, and crimes against humanity. Goering was sentenced to death by hanging. On October 15, 1946, the night before his scheduled execution, he commited suicide in his cell, taking a capsule of cyanide poison that he had succeeded in hiding from the guards.

Back in the United States, Bess Miller reported that, "Jobs were hard to come by after the war since so many of the troops returned home. Stub knew a job was available as a plumber but you had to be certified. So, he read two books over the weekend, took the test, and passed the exam. He went on to become a Master Plumber and eventually ran the company. That's how he was. Very ambitious. Everyone admired him. He was hard-working. A perfectionist."

According to Stub, "After the war was over, a package from the Olivos in France arrived which contained the wooden shoes that Marinette had promised to send. That began a friendship that was to last for a lifetime. Papa Olivo died shortly after the war. Marinette married but, unfortunately, lost her husband early."

In 1945, George was sent from Paris on a two-year assignment as Deputy Director of Combat Intelligence for Air Force headquarters in the city of Wiesbaden in the central western part of occupied Germany. Not far from Frankfurt, it's the capital of the federal state of Hesse. The name "Wiesbaden" comes from "meadow baths," referring to its famous 26 hot springs, fourteen of which are still active.

Although Wiesbaden is also known as the "Nice of the North," primarily for its mild climate, it would not have been a good idea to say that in Simone's presence. Comparing anything about Germany to France, especially to her home town, would anger her.

Simone counted the days until George's German deployment was over. Living outside of France for the first time, she lamented, "How much I regret leaving my beloved country. Any time I get a chance, I know I'll go back home with pleasure. There was a splendid sky today when we woke up that gave me nostalgia for Nice and its sun. But, of course, the weather becomes grey and cold by 11 a.m. What a nasty country Germany is, just like its people!"

On the other hand, Simone was understandably tired of living in a hotel room remarking, "At last we have our first home, even if it's just temporary while we wait for better housing. We move to Handel Strasse. There's even an electric oven, although it sometimes makes the electricity in the house shut down. We clean and unpack. We're tired but happy. I feel like we can breathe. We have room to live and start to calm down. Little by little, the house comes along as we furnish and decorate it."

Showing she was just as feisty as ever, Simone became incensed when the German man who formerly owned their Wiesbaden house was allowed to come back and cultivate the garden. "It is outrageous. When the Germans came into France, they took everything in our gardens and gave it to their own men," she exclaimed. A German worker in their home, not knowing the background of either of them, began talking about the good old days of Nazism and was subjected to a bitter tongue-lashing by Simone. He almost immediately regretted bringing the subject up and, not coincidently, was relieved of his duties shortly thereafter.

Many of the things Simone took for granted as a child growing up in a well-to-do family she learned to appreciate as an adult. She commented, "We get our food at the base commissary. The huge range of goods is unbelievable. We have the opportunity to buy marvelous things. No restrictions on rice, chocolate, meat, sugar, coffee, gelatin, etc. I think about other poor French women who walk for miles to try to find food on the black market. I can't believe how lucky I am to have all that I do."

As the baby's due date got closer, she made a bold decision, insisting "No child of mine is going to be born on German soil!" George recalled with a laugh, "I flew her back to Paris, just a month before Gérard was born." Known as Jerry, he said, "My dad got with Jack Kolb, his buddy in the OSI (Office of Special Investigations), and arranged to taxi a C-45 Beechcraft Expeditor down to the end of the runway where my mom was in a car. They opened the door, she got in, and he flew her to Paris." Simone stayed at familiar surroundings, the Lutetia Hotel, while awaiting the birth of their child.

George traveled back and forth between Paris and Wiesbaden, a distance of about 448 kilometers or 278 miles. As much as he would have liked to stay with her, he knew he couldn't shirk his military responsibilitie. Simone often felt lonesome, particularly when she didn't feel well due to her pregnancy. "When he is away, I miss him so much. What an angel. What a treasure of a husband the Lord has sent me," she gushed.

On January 28, she confessed after a flight delay, "George has to leave a plane stuck in Vélizy-Villacoublay because of bad weather conditions. I am so happy to be able to keep him with me a little bit more. Hoping that bad weather last as long as possible. Every day we are more and more in love."

As you might expect, George had certain duties to perform when his wife experienced food cravings: "I ask George to buy oysters for me because he plans to leave tomorrow morning on his flight. There is no hope that I'll be able to see him before February 15th. After he goes, I have lunch by myself at the brasserie. I'm really feeling down. It's impossible for me to fall asleep even though I am really tired. This room seems so empty. I already wrote George three letters today. Finally, on February 2, I make myself a little soup, take a hot bath, and go to bed at 8 p.m. I am sore and I'm just exhausted. George calls at 2 a.m. I am very sad and long for him."

It's not hard to imagine how difficult it was for her being in the late stages of her pregnancy and alone at the hotel. Fortunately, she was able to have her mother stay with her part of the time. A typical entry in her journal was this one just before Valentine's Day of 1946: "I am exhausted. I have a headache. I am sore. I go to bed early. Very bad night. George being blue calls me late which makes me blue in turn. My physical look is ugly. Full of stretch marks."

February 12 was a particularly stressful day for Simone as she revealed, "I have a 5 p.m. appointment with Doctor Sureau. My emotions are out of control in the doctor's office. He thinks I might have twins. I go to radiology in the hospital and then have to wait for the results. I am very nervous. The results show only one baby. What a relief!"

She gave George the news when he arrived in time for Valentine's Day. She recalled, "He was two hours late. I find him in front of my door, more attractive and adorable than ever. He wears a new raincoat and a new beret. He offers me a beautiful coat with hood made with English wool. It's splendid. I just give a picture frame and an ashtray. I am really spoiled. We stay in bed. Despite my big belly, we are much in love. My darling desires me. We are completely happy."

George knew exactly what would make his wife feel better – more oysters. "We have a big fancy meal with oysters, asparagus a la crème, champagne, apértifs, etc. We go see *La Folle de Chaillot* (*The Madwoman of Chaillot*.) It is really zany. It's tiring for me but takes my mind off things," she said. The satire, written by Jean Giraudoux, was first introduced in Paris in 1945.

Unfortunately, George had to return to Germany the next morning. After a routine check-up, he was distraught to learn that they found a spot on his lungs. He didn't want to needlessly worry Simone but he also didn't want to keep anything from her. He decided to call to tell her. "He is really sad. I try my best to comfort him on the phone. He's worried he will have to leave the army. I went to the doctor today. He said that the baby has dropped into place and childbirth will probably be early next week," said Simone anxiously.

Several days later, Simone got some good news: "George calls. He is much more optimistic. He announces a great surprise. He has good results from the lung X-Ray. Nothing is wrong. It's a relief for me to know my darling is OK."

Simone finally goes into labor on March 4. She said, "Childbirth begins. My water breaks at noon. I am in horrible pain. It's non-stop.

175

It's awful. Our son Gérard is born at 5 a.m. on March 5. He is 4½ kg (a little over 9 pounds, 14 ounces.) He is lovely and healthy. He is so exactly the baby of my desires that I thank God for such an adorable baby."

Jerry's birth happened to fall on Shrove Tuesday, the day before Ash Wednesday. The holiday is better known as "Mardi Gras" in French which means "Fat Tuesday," referring to the practice of eating rich, fatty foods such as pancakes before the ritual fast of Lent. Mardi Gras is famous for feasting and celebration in places with strong French influence, such as New Orleans.

Jerry reported, "After I was born, my dad came back to get my mom in a B-17 Boeing Flying Fortress when he was on a tour of U.S. Airfield Facilities in Europe." Admittedly, it was a bit outside of military regulations when George excused himself to go to the bathroom and handed the controls of the Flying Fortress over to Simone who was sitting in the co-pilot's seat holding Jerry. At least George remembered to put the plane on automatic pilot and, since the war was over, Simone didn't have to engage the enemy in combat, something she probably would have done with enthusiasm. They arranged to have another car waiting when they landed back in Germany.

Tata, the girl from the farmhouse where members of George's crew were hidden, recalled excitedly, "We got news from George about his marriage to Simone de Cruzel. They seemed so happy! I remember learning that they were living at the Lutecia in Paris and then that they had a little 'Gérard.' My Mom, with all her heart, knitted a layette for the baby."

In the weeks that followed Jerry's birth, Simone believed she was experiencing the post-partum depression familiar to most new mothers. She confessed, "Got the baby blues. Feel so depressed. Jerry cried from 3 to 6 am. Then he became nice again. We are exhausted." Fortunately, she had George by her side saying, "He takes me in his arms and I feel better. George is like a nurse, he heals me. When he leaves, I panic. I am terrified. The nights last forever."

What kept Simone going through this period is her love for her newborn son and the support she received from George. "Our kid gets cuter every day. He looks like a two-month-old baby. Everybody admires how precocious and how healthy he is. As for George, he is a treasure of patience. Always paying attention to me. He treats me like a queen." The result of the addition to their little family according to Simone was, "We are more in love than ever."

In truth, things were far from perfect. George drank too much and was jealous not only of men who paid too much attention to Simone but even of anyone who tried to hold the baby. Simone, strong-willed as ever, told George to "get over it." In a revealing entry in her journal, she wrote, "I wonder if the jealousy of George is not going to ruin our happiness some day and won't force me to end this. There are perpetual scenes that drive me insane."

On the other hand, there were signs that Simone's wartime ordeal was continuing to affect her. She didn't have the nightmares that George did but seemed to be bothered in other ways. The depression that she thought was just "post-partum" wasn't going away.

According to Simone, "George and I have a big fight. He accuses me of always being anxious and nervous. I cry a river." As usual, they reconciled over drinks at the bar. But later, in a moment of self-reflection, she wrote, "I got the blues again. Years and months go by, but I don't change. It's always the same despite the time flowing. I become very irritable and I cannot help it."

After what she went through during the war, it's understandable there would have been some lingering negative affect, especially the "survivor's guilt" of being able to live through the prison ordeal while so many others were not as fortunate. There were times she simply felt overwhelmed admitting, "George is sleeping and that gets on my nerves. The food is burning and I have also to take care of Jerry. How can I do all of it?" In today's world, Simone would likely be a candidate for, at a minimum, a series of discussions with a qualified therapist.

Simone was sensitive to the fact that George was experiencing his own symptoms caused by what he had experienced. His screams during his nightmares understandably frightened her. Her dilemma, though, was that she didn't want to burden him by sharing too much of her own issues. She explained, "George is suffering and I feel I am going to turn crazy. I know the disappointment I am causing him and I regret so badly to have to hide that with the goal to make him suffer less. Sometimes I cry and would love to disappear. But he is so sweet that he calms me down."

Simone was thrilled that George was able to take two days of leave for Easter and the baby's baptism. She was feeling better about herself saying, "On April 19, I decide I have no clothes to wear so I go buy a simple black dress. The weather is beautiful, George arrives by plane, and I am crazy happy. At the end of the day, we cannot stop our desire and we make love. I belong to him for the first time since Jerry's birth."

George Stalnaker after another sleepless night

She downplayed the problems they were having by rationalizing, "My mother always says that a marriage without arguments is boring."

The next day, Father Vittone performed the baptism ceremony in front of 15 friends and family members. Simone reported, "We have a reception for the guests at the Le Monseigneur Restaurant, 94 rue d-Amsterdam (near the famous Moulin Rouge). It's fantastic. We feel so relaxed. Just like a first date all over again."

By the beginning of May, Simone was getting ready to move to base housing in Wiesbaden. Still as outspoken as ever, she remarked, "George calls to say things are falling into place for the housing. I will be a translator one day a week. The US Army is insane with stupid instructions that change every week."

Two months after Jerry's birth, Simone claimed, "I am tired but happy to be on base with George and to have lost my belly. George organizes the move so well that I have zero stress. I have a German woman, Maria Shultz, to help me. Thanks to George, everything is comfortable. The officers and their wives are nice. The vibes are good and relaxed. George is patience incarnate. He is more and more sweet all the time."

Among the entries in her journal was: "It's May 12, Mother's Day for the Americans. My mother-in-law Margaret never stops sending me parcels. I feel embarrassed. I'm glad to know we can count on George's parents when we eventually get to the USA. He doesn't want us to ever live with them in Des Moines, though.

Jerry is now interested in playing with his fingers. He can keep his head straight. He stretches his arms and legs while smiling. He is a good little guy. Sleeps all night long now. But always hungry. He is a little scamp. Everybody is under his charms. We take Jerry for a check-up to see Doctor Schwartz. Everything is OK.

On May 16, I start my massage sessions with a big German woman. She knows her job. She says I will feel much better. I do physical exercises regularly. I have ten more kilos to lose.

It's May 23 and today is George's birthday. There's no way to get fresh flowers so I make some paper flowers for him. I improvise a celebration. I get him a Roff pipe and a tobacco pouch. I would love to spoil him much more but there is not much to buy in Germany. We have Brandy Alexanders and champagne.

Today is May 30, Memorial Day for all the Americans killed during the war. It's a beautiful day, we think of them, and sit outside to get grilled by the sun.

179

It's June 5. Jerry is three months old. Our little man makes us very happy. Everybody says he's beautiful and joyful. When he cries, we imitate him and he immediately calms down and smiles. He grabs his sheet to suck it and grabs my cheeks, my lips, and anything he can reach. At his check-up, the doctor says he is wonderful. He predicts teeth will be coming soon because he drools a lot. He advises me to start to give him spoons of mashed vegetables. He is like a six-month-old baby. He smiles during the medical check-up. Everybody turns around to look at him. So much has happened since June 6 of last year, D-Day."

On August 6, Simone celebrated her birthday saying, "I am 26 years old today. I get a bunch of flowers offered by the maids. Also there is a big cake with 'Happy Birthday' written on it. The German women get on my nerves the way they fight with each other. But, George is wonderful, treating me so sweetly. He gives me a white purse. Jerry, meanwhile, is teething and crying a lot.

Today, September 3, we celebrate the first year of our civil ceremony and tomorrow will be the anniversary of our religious wedding. No, I don't regret having married him. I just hope that his jealousy crises will go away."

Simone looked forward to George's next assignment which they were told would be back in the United States. "We were invited to dinner over Dally and Frank Hunt, a couple of our friends from the base. We have an American dinner of Virginia baked ham and apple pie, sweet potatoes, and Manhattan cocktails. I am very amused by these new tastes for me. I like very much being among my American friends. Then we are invited for dinner at the home of Ralph and Dee Freeze. They have new furniture and it's charming. I admire it. What a kitchen! I dream of one just like it. George promises me to get one as sophisticated when we get to the USA."

Sounding very much like the first time mother she was, Simone was fascinated with everything that Jerry did. On September 24, she wrote, "Our little phenomenon is always in action. He can now say, 'buduboudida.'" That might not mean anything in French or English but she's thrilled to report on October 14, "Jerry said, 'Mama' for the first time." That certainly meant something in any language.

Then a long-awaited event occured on October 26. "I got to go back to Nice for a vacation," she beamed. "I was glad to leave Germany to go anywhere, even if it is just for a few days. Furthermore, when it's for Nice, it's wonderful. The blue sky, the sea, and the climate is like paradise. The air is so pure. What a joy it is to be home again. You appreciate something much more when you have been away from it and then come back. All the family is there. Maman didn't want us to stay in a hotel so she gave us her room. Gérard is immediately adored."

George's jealousy continued to annoy Simone, however, who said, "While in Nice, I receive a terrible letter from George. He's having a horrible jealousy crisis. He wrote mean sentences. I am so sad that I would like to die. I write back. I am desperate. Maman tries to comfort me but I am very sad."

As usual, Simone forgave George and things went back to normal for a while. They focused on the business of being parents as well as being a couple. January 1, 1947 came with Simone commenting, "It's the New Year. My George and I celebrate with a long kiss. It's our second New Year's Day but the first one that Jerry is alive for. The first Santa Claus for him. And we begin this year being three of us."

18 – "Praying for a Miracle"

According to daughter Sylvie, her father George and Jack Kolb were known for playing "Russian Roulette" at parties. That's the game of holding a gun loaded with one bullet to your head, spinning the cylinder, and pulling the trigger. They would laugh while others around them gasped. It's not a good idea to play that game a lot of times. The odds tend to catch up with you. The spy business, being involved in the mysterious world of intelligence-gathering, was another type of "Russian Roulette" that could be just as dangerous.

As the chill of the Cold War began to take hold, virtually everyone working for the American government in or out of uniform seemed to be focusing on the activities of the Soviet Union. Heads turned with whiplash speed from paying attention to a real war with actual fighting to the cerebral war of combating their propaganda with your propaganda and trying to capture their information while safeguarding your information. Most of the globe was divided into two camps – the US-led Western Bloc and a Soviet-led Eastern Bloc of nations. Few countries were able to maintain neutrality.

The Office of Strategic Services was disbanded by President Truman after the war and the CIG (Central Intelligence Group), supervised by the NIA (National Intelligence Authority), established. They lasted less than two years as both the CIA (Central Intelligence Agency) and NSC (National Security Council) were formed in 1947. The CIA went dark two years later when the "Central Intelligence Agency Act" exempted it from having to disclose information about its activities or use of funds.

Larry's Kolb's father's full name was "Lewis Jackson Kolb." He was known as "Jack" when he and George first met in Paris. Later, he was referred to as "Lew." According to Larry, most people in Georgia pronounced "Kolb" as "Cobb" and so his father also sometimes called himself "Jack Cobb." So it was with many of their friends who were in the espionage business. Names were often temporary and disposable.

George was always known as George, though. Larry knew the members of the intelligence community who would come to the house for meetings with his dad as his "uncles." "They used to say that Uncle George was an honorary spy because of his association with Auntie Simone, who was a real spy. That was good enough for them," he recalled with a laugh. He would sometimes refer to George as "My favorite uncle of all."

Adding to the already tense relationship with the Western nations, the Soviet Union in 1948 declined to participate any longer in the four-zone administration of Germany. They also drove the democratically-elected government out of its seat in the Soviet sector, installed a communist regime in East Berlin, and blocked access to the sectors of Berlin that were under the control of the Western Allies.

In response, the Berlin Airlift was organized to drop supplies to the people of West Berlin. The United States, Great Britain, Canada, New Zealand, Australia, and South Africa risked a confrontation with the Soviets by flying more than 200,000 flights, providing as much as 9,000 tons of supplies per day.

The following year, the two German states came into being. West Germany, officially the Federal Republic of Germany, was formed as a democracy and East Germany, the German Democratic Republic, was created as a communist state. Germany quickly became the center of espionage activity for both the western and communist powers. Timely, relevant information on enemy activities became a commodity as valuable as precious metals and jewels.

The Cold War never heated up because the United States and Soviet Union had nuclear deterrents leading to a Mutually Assured Destruction (appropriately forming the acronym "MAD") policy. Either side built the capability to destroy the world many times over. Instead, there were smaller proxy wars fought between countries loyal to one side or the other and enough espionage and political subversion to provide fodder for the plots of television series and movies for decades to come.

American Secretary of State George Marshall initiated the Marshall Plan, officially called the European Recovery Program, an ambitious effort to help stimulate a new beginning for the war-torn European economy, remove trade barriers, and prevent the spread of communism. Beginning in 1948, $13 billion in food, machinery and other goods were given to a total of 18 nations.

Formerly the leading European power behind Great Britain, France had its economy significantly weakened by World War II. The country's infrastructure was badly in need of repair as factories, bridges, railway lines, highways, etc. had suffered enormous damage. An estimated 1.2 million buildings had been either destroyed or damaged. The Marshall Plan also helped stimulate the French economy with an outright grant of $2.3 billion.

The Blum-Byrnes Agreement gave France a jump-start on the road to recovery. The debt payments to the U.S. from both World Wars of $2.8 billion were forgiven with a new loan of $650 million extended to the French. The agreement was signed by U.S. Secretary of State

James F. Byrnes and French politician Léon Blum, who had served three times as France's Prime Minister.

The country then took off on an extended economic boom, commonly called the "Trente Glorieuses" or "Thirty Glorious" years. In conjunction with other Western European countries, France founded the European Coal and Steel Community which later evolved into the European Common Market and then the European Union. Western Europe became a model for economic co-operation, eventually introducing a common currency, the Euro, on January 1, 1999.

In turn, the United States enjoyed remarkable economic growth in the post-war period. The automobile industry converted back from producing military vehicles and equipment to producing cars, many industries based on new technologies were born, and a housing boom was driven by low-cost G.I. mortgages. The nation's Gross National Product of $200 billion in 1940 grew to $300 billion in 1950 and to more than $500 billion in 1960. At the same time, the jump in postwar births known as the "baby boom" significantly increased the number of consumers and members of the middle class.

After the two years in West Germany, George and Simone got their state-side assignment in 1947. Simone, in particular, was thrilled to be out of the German turmoil. They spent four years living in Prairie Village, Kansas. George was given a prestigious teaching appointment at Fort Leavenworth's U.S Army Command and General Staff College, a graduate school for military officers from all branches of the service, interagency representatives, and international military officers. The family lived in an on-base apartment and celebrated the birth of their first daughter, Claire, followed by their second, Sylvie.

The couple moved to Levittown, New York when George was assigned to Mitchel Field's Air Defense Command Headquarters, located on the Hempstead Plains of Long Island. Simone, a high school French teacher at this point, was proud to become a naturalized American Citizen. She qualified because she was a foreign national who had been both a permanent resident and married to a U.S. citizen for three years; showed that she was able to read, write, and speak English; and demonstrated a basic knowledge of U.S. history and government in a written examination. On June 16, 1950, she took the Oath of Allegiance required for citizenship by raising her right hand and saying:

"I hereby declare, on oath, that I absolutely and entirely renounce and abjure all allegiance and fidelity to any foreign prince, potentate, state, or sovereignty of whom or which I have heretofore

been a subject or citizen; that I will support and defend the Constitution and laws of the United States of America against all enemies, foreign and domestic; that I will bear true faith and allegiance to the same; that I will bear arms on behalf of the United States when required by the law; that I will perform noncombatant service in the Armed Forces of the United States when required by the law; that I will perform work of national importance under civilian direction when required by the law; and that I take this obligation freely without any mental reservation or purpose of evasion; so help me God."

George's father, Dr. Luther Stalnaker, spent most of 1949 through 1951 in Japan as Advisor to the U.S. Military Occupation Headquarters. As temporary President of Drake University, the 61-year-old Luther visited California on an inspection tour of the university's ROTC (Reserve Officers' Training Corps) students at Norton Air Force Base in San Bernardino on July 12, 1954. With him was Lt. Col. Richard E. Armstrong, a Drake Professor of Air Science and Tactics.

At about 9 p.m., as he was crossing U.S. Highway 101 on the outskirts of San Rafael, California while walking back to his motel, Luther was struck and killed by an auto driven by a drunk driver, a 24-year-old San Francisco City College student. The Drake community mourned his loss and Stalnaker Hall was named in his honor. To this day, there is an annual Stalnaker lecture series of distinguished speakers that is one of the highlights of the Drake school year. In addition, all of Luther's current and future grandchildren were given automatic admission to Drake.

According to Drake Dean, Ron Troyer, "Luther W. Stalnaker was one of the most impressive academic figures in the history of Drake University. His memory continues to live on campus and in the minds and hearts of many alumni. I have had the opportunities to meet and talk with alumni. Invariably, those who were there during Luther W. Stalnaker's era remark that he was an inspiration, an example of the consummate scholar. His reputation as a person who cared for students and was concerned about their intellectual development is unmatched."

George and Simone moved back overseas and lived in Washington Heights, a United States Armed Forces housing complex located in Shibuya, Tokyo. Among his responsibilities were to act as the chief negotiator for the return of Haneda International Airport (later known as Tokyo International Airport) and other large air fields to Japan. Promoted to full Colonel on April 11, 1957, George was named Director of Plans, Programs, & Requirements for the 5th Air Force. After three years, he was transferred to Johnson Air Force Base in

Sayama, Tokyo as Director Of Operations for the 3rd Bomb Wing. While in Japan, Jerry attended Johnson High School and George and Simone had a second son, Marc, followed by a third, Eric.

Despite the passage of time, Simone's feelings about Germans did not change. Daughter Claire explained, "While we were in Japan, I remember my mom's family coming for a visit from Nice. It was an international flight and as people from the different nations deplaned, the waiting families applauded as the names of their countries were announced. I was little and clapped for everyone. But my mother held my hands down and shushed me when it was the turn for the Germans.

The happiest my parents ever were as a couple was when we lived in Japan. They were more affectionate and more demonstrative with each other. Was it the fact that they could afford help around the house? That may have contributed toward a more stress-free environment."

Jerry concurred, "My mom cried when my dad was assigned to Japan but she cried again when he got orders to move back to the states. She fell in love with the good life in Japan. So much so that my dad extended for a fourth year. That was a very happy time for my parents. Besides having a gardener and maids, my mother liked Japan because my dad had become a full Colonel and had considerable status as the Director of Operations. There were cocktail parties all the time. My parents went to see the geishas dance and often went out on the town. They were very active. Everyone in our family was happy and healthy."

The experience in Japan was the closest Simone would ever come to the privileged life-style she enjoyed growing up in Nice. She thrived being in the limelight and loved the active social life that came with being the wife of the Director of Operations.

George returned to the United States and joined the Air Force's Air Command and Staff College, Air Defense Command, Maxwell Air Force Base, Montgomery, Alabama. After spending a combined six years, five months, and 16 days while deployed in England, France, Germany, and Japan, George remained state-side for the rest of his career.

Larry Kolb commented, "George was my father's best friend, and I always loved having him around, though as I recall the only time after I was born that my father and George were stationed on the same base was from about 1962 to 1964 at Maxwell. We lived three houses away on a street called Inner Circle."

Their favorite pastime was playing golf at the course at Maxwell Air Force Base. Larry remembers being with them when they shot 54 holes in a day. Although the course was crowded with people waiting to

186

The Stalnaker Family in Japan
L to R children are Jerry, Eric, Marc, Claire, and Sylvie

tee off, the starter gave them priority status by putting them at the head of every line.

"George went up to the first tee for the second round," Larry reported. "He took off this expensive gold watch. I recall my father telling me it was a Rolex worth about $300. That was back in 1962 so it would cost thousands of dollars today. Anyhow, George wanted to get serious about the golfing so he took off the watch and gave it to me for safekeeping. I checked my pocket every few minutes to make sure it was still there. I was a little kid and was nervous about being entrusted with something so expensive."

Jack loved to tell the story of how he once hit what he thought was a pretty good shot on a Par 3, 170-yard hole. It was a bright sunny day with a lot of glare so he and George lost sight of the ball. Despite looking everywhere, they couldn't seem to locate it. It wasn't in the rough. It wasn't in the bunker. Finally, George walked up to the hole, saw the ball was sitting in the cup, and yelled out, "I found it! It's here!" Jack, of course, bought drinks for everyone in the clubhouse and the Maxwell Golf Club gave him a trophy to commemorate the hole-in-one.

"There were many other times when George flew in and visited my family when we lived on Okinawa, in Nebraska, in Virginia, and in east central Florida. I travelled with my parents to visit the Stalnaker family in Tokyo when we lived on Okinawa, in Maryland, and in the Florida Panhandle. Uncle George would surprise us at dinnertime sometimes, tell me great stories, and drink hi-balls with my dad," recalled Larry. Along with their bourbon and water drink, of course, they'd smoke Camel cigarettes.

"Uncle George managed to drop in for dinner with us at least once in every place on earth we ever lived," continued Larry. "When he was around, it was like a national holiday for my family. He and my father would get at least a little tipsy together. George would joke and tell stories. I remember his always talking about his kids. He had a strong affection for his family."

According to George's son Jerry, "My dad and Jack Kolb were very close. In fact, he spoke highly of the whole Kolb Family. One time when I was in high school in Montgomery, my parents were out of town and my house was a wreck after I hosted a drinking party. I looked up early in the morning, all hung over, and there was Jack. My mom and dad had asked him to look in on me. He asked, 'Do your parents know about this?' I answered, 'No, sir.' He just shook his head and told me to get the place cleaned up before my parents got home. He said, 'Get this place ship-shape if you don't want your parents to find out. I did and he never ratted me out. He scared the hell out of me. He was a big guy and I knew he was a big deal in the OSI."

"Sylvie Stalnaker and I were about the same age and were in the same class in elementary school for a couple of years, so I knew her best," recalled Larry. "I was sitting right beside her in Mrs. Solem's fifth grade class, when, right after lunch, she informed us that President Kennedy had just been assassinated. Sylvie raised her hand and said, 'My dad is a Republican and he doesn't like President Kennedy much, but even he's going to be sad about this.' I raised my hand, announced that my father was an investigator, and said I was sure that, of course, he would soon be on his way to Dallas to solve the case of who murdered our President."

After attending Johnson High School in Tokyo for two years, Jerry graduated from Montgomery Catholic High School in Alabama in 1964. Before he received his B.S. in Business Administration from Auburn University, he got a draft notice ordering him to report for service in the French Foreign Legion. Jerry automatically held dual citizenship because he was born in France to an American military officer and French mother. With assistance from the State Department, he avoided his obligation to France and instead joined the U.S. Air Force.

George became Deputy for Operations HQ Command at Bolling Air Force Base in Washington, D.C. "What I remember most about Bolling is that my dad owned a speedboat and would let it out full-throttle. I'd be scared and crouch down and he'd be laughing," recalled youngest son Eric.

According to Marc, "My brother Eric and I played for the same football team, the Clinton Boys' Club in Maryland, as kids. You could always hear my mom in the stands with her thick French accent yelling, 'Go, Clinton, Go!' The other kids would pick up the chant and call out, 'Go, Clean-tawn, Go!' using the same accent. It kind of became the motto for our team."

George's final appointment was as Base Commander of Andrews Air Force Base, perhaps the country's best-known airfield. Traditionally, that command has been given to respected senior officers on their last assignment before retirement. Construction began at Camp Springs Army Airfield, in late 1942. The base became operational on May 2, 1943 with the arrival of a Republic P-47 Thunderbolt. By the end of May, 75 other P-47's arrived and the field began its mission to train fighter pilots for overseas combat.

Camp Springs was renamed Andrews Field in 1945 to honor Lt. General Frank M. Andrews, one of the Air Force's founding fathers. He was killed in an airplane crash on May 3, 1943, the day after the base opened. After the Air Force separated from the Army in 1947, the name was changed to Andrews Air Force Base. That year also marked the arrival of an F-80 Shooting Star, the first permanently assigned jet aircraft.

In June of 1950, Andrews was the center of combat readiness training for B-25 medium bomber crews. In later years, it served as headquarters for Continental Air Command, Strategic Air Command, Military Air Transport Service, Air Research and Development Command, and the Air Force Systems Command.

Nicknamed the "Gateway to the Capitol," Andrews is best known for the transportation of world leaders such as kings, queens, presidents, prime ministers, popes, and many of the highest-ranking military officials from other countries. Harry Truman was the first President to fly from the base on November 24, 1946. Then, in 1959 an upgrade to the runway and addition of a parallel runway prepared the base to be the port of entry and departure for foreign dignitaries.

In March of 1962, President John F. Kennedy's official aircraft, a C-118, had transferred its base from Washington National Airport to Andrews, thus making it from that time forward the "Home of Air Force One."

Andrews has been the site of many historic events including the greeting of Soviet Premier Nikita Khrushchev by President Dwight D. Eisenhower in 1959, the welcoming of the first Prisoners of War back from Viet Nam in 1973, the return of the Iranian hostages to the U.S. in 1981, and the landing of rescued Prisoner of War PFC Jessica Lynch from Iraq in 2003. On Oct. 1, 2009, Andrews Air Force Base, along with Naval Air Facility Washington, became known as Joint Base Andrews Naval Air Facility.

"I remember one night, when Uncle George came to our house on Langley Air Force Base, in Virginia, around 1968," said Larry Kolb. "Dinner was over and just George and I were sitting in the living room, and he yawned and apologized to me, and said he'd had a long day. I asked him what he'd done that day, and he matter-of-factly told me he had flown from an Air Force base somewhere in Maryland, over the Atlantic, to where he could see the coast of Spain, watched several Soviet bombers and gotten so close to one, flying side by side for a minute so close that he and the Soviet pilot had seen the whites of each other's eyes and nodded at each other, met up with a couple of tankers to refuel over the Atlantic, and then, because of weather at his home base, he had chosen to land at Langley, so he could have dinner with us. I asked him if he often had days like that and he said yes.

George was about to retire. He was still a pilot, but didn't actually do much flying anymore. Just enough to keep his hours up. Part of the job of being Base Commander at Andrews was to see the President off each time he took off and greet the President each time he landed there. The problem was that he wasn't exactly a fan of Lyndon Johnson.

'In fact, Larry,' Uncle George said to me one night over dinner, 'the President wouldn't know it - because I'm an Air Force officer and he's the Commander-in-Chief, so I show him perfect respect - but I can't stand the son of a bitch.'

'Oh, George!' my mother said. 'That's just because you're such a Republican.' 'No, it's because he's such an asshole,' Uncle George said. 'Last month, they sent us this nice young steward from Ohio. Twenty-one years old, just out of tech school, and such a great kid that, for his first assignment as a steward, they sent him straight to Air Force One. On the kid's first day on the plane, I was right behind the President heading down the aisle, and the kid was just beaming with pride. He stepped up, introduced himself to the President, said how much he admired him and what an honor it was to be able to serve him.

Then he stuck out his hand to shake the President's hand, and do you know what the son of a bitch did?' Uncle George didn't wait for an answer. 'The President looked at that poor young steward and said, 'Get the fuck out of my way!' It had a certain admirable directness and simplicity. To this day, it remains my favorite Presidential quote."

George retired on July 31, 1969 at the age of 52. In all, he gave 28 years, one month, and 20 days of service to his country. The official address on his DD214 Retirement Record was 7100 Archery Drive, Upper Marlboro, Maryland. The nearby streets in the Sherwood Forest Development were called Nottingham Drive, King Richard Drive, Shield Drive, Arrowhead Way, Jousting Lane, and Robin Hood Drive. Coincidently, Stub and Bess Miller settled down on a street also called Robin Hood Drive, next to Nottingham Lane, in Stevensville, Michigan. Bess lives there to this day.

In addition to the Silver Star, Bronze Star, and Purple Heart, George's medals include the Legion of Merit, Air Medal with 6 Oak Leaf clusters, two Commendation Medals, French Legion of Honor, and French Croix de Guerre with Palm.

Son Marc recalled, "My dad would tell stories about the war but my mom never did. She was tight-lipped. She never said much. I don't think she wanted to relive any of it. I do remember we went back to Nice once and she pointed out some signs on lamp posts that had the names of the people she was imprisoned with who were killed. That's all she ever said about it, though."

Something totally unexpected happened as Simone had to fight one last courageous battle, one which she could not win. It began as breast cancer which she developed at just 45 years of age in 1966. She had a breast removed. Eric said, "My mom had a radical mastectomy when I was six years old. I don't remember much about it but I do remember that they didn't do any cosmetic surgery back then. I can still picture the gaping hole she had in her chest."

Simone asked just one thing of George - that he quit both drinking and smoking. He agreed and, to his credit, kept that promise.

According to Marc, "I remember my mom would take us with her to doctor's visits and hospitals when we were young because my dad was gone a lot. My brother was just a year younger than I was. Maybe that's why she always hoped we would become doctors. Instead we wound up hanging around airplanes like our dad."

Adding to Simone's stress was the news of Jerry's deployment to Viet Nam, a place with which the French were all-to-familiar. "The phone rang in 1969," said Eric, "when Jerry's orders came through for Viet Nam. My mother just couldn't handle that. She just couldn't stop crying. We were living in base housing at Andrews. They didn't have enough housing for everyone who was going to be shipped to Viet Nam so they slept in tents. That was the last place she'd want any of us to go."

"I don't think of my parents as heroes," admitted Claire. "I worshipped my dad until, as a teenager, I recognized he had a drinking problem. I realized that he was human and not the man I had believed him to be. Don't get me wrong. He was the smartest person. The one who could make me understand the happenings of the world around me. I was proud of him and like to feel that I am a lot like him. My mother must have suffered living with a man whose drinking caused so much pain."

After a short time when she was believed to be in remission, Simone suffered a recurrence of the disease and had her other breast removed. Eventually, she developed bone cancer and finally succumbed on January 23, 1976. "She died a slow, painful death at Andrews Air Force Base Hospital. It was quite a shame," recounted Jerry with understatement.

Marc said, "The thing I remember most about her when I was a teenager was that she knew she wasn't going to be around for long so she taught the five of us to iron, sew, cook, etc. so we'd be self-sufficient. I was just 16 years old at the time. It really helped me when I

192

got to college. She was a fighter until the very end. It's hard to think of my Mom as a bad-ass on the streets with a rifle in her hands chasing Nazis around but I know that's who she was. She was a warrior. An amazing woman. I have a great deal of admiration for her.

My mom was in a coma towards the end and a priest came over from St. John's Church. She hadn't spoken for a day or day and a half. We didn't think she'd wake up. Suddenly, her eyes popped open and she said, 'Father, there's someone else here in the room.' He said, 'That's the Lord Jesus." I guess that satisfied her because she closed her eyes again. I was in the room with my brother Eric and we witnessed that."

"We were all raised as Catholic and I kept crossing myself and praying for her every night. I was just praying for a miracle that never happened," admitted Eric. "I'll always remember we got the call that she had died. My dad packed us into the car and we all rushed to the hospital. It was like a dream sequence. Like it wasn't real."

"It became increasingly clear to me that my mother was the real hero of the family," admitted Jerry in tribute to her.

Among the many prestigious awards she received for her contributions to the war effort were the *Médaille de la France Libre*, *Médaille du Combatant Volontaire de la Résistance*, *Croix du Combatant*, and *Médaille de la Guerre*.

There's a Native American saying by an unknown author that seems to describe Simone quite well: "A strong woman is one who feels deeply and loves fiercely. Her tears flow as abundantly as her laughter. A strong woman is both soft and powerful, she is both practical and spiritual. A strong woman in her essence is a gift to the world."

"She died when I was half-way through my junior year and Eric was half-way through his sophomore year in high school," recalled Marc. "The two of us were always together. We hung out with the same group of friends. That's when our older brother Jerry really stepped up and took on a leadership role in the family. He was 13 or 14 years older than us. He was just fantastic. He really helped the family out."

Eric concurred, "Jerry was stationed in Okinawa. He came home and arranged to get transferred to Bolling Air Force Base. He stepped up big-time. Looked after us. Told us what military life was like. Marc and I followed in my dad's footsteps but, really, Jerry's, too."

"Like so many from that generation, my dad had undiagnosed PTSD. When he woke up from a nightmare screaming, it affected all of us," lamented Marc. "In addition, he would be coughing terribly because of his smoking habit. He and my Mom had their problems. I always remember their arguing. After he found out she was terminally ill, he stopped drinking and spent more time at home. After she died, he was really in a funk. He was down for a while. We were worried about him."

Following Simone's death, George taught English as a Second Language, was active in the First United Methodist Church of Niceville, Florida, and contributed to cultural and charitable causes. Niceville, a quiet city that is apply named, has a population of about 12,000 and is located in Okaloosa County, close to Eglin Air Force Base on Boggy Bayou which opens into Choctawhatchee Bay. It's best known as the home of the annual Boggy Bayou Mullet Festival, which refers to the common ray-finned fish found worldwide in coastal temperate and tropical seas and not the 1980's-style hair style that featured a short cut in the front and long in the back.

Chapter 19 - The Return to France

George was always grateful to those who helped him and his crew evade capture proclaiming, "The French were wonderful to us and courageous. I will always love them. We couldn't have had better treatment. I can't praise too highly the courage and loyalty of these brave people."

Other members of the flight crew expressed similar feelings. Stub Miller fondly recalled going back to see the Olivo family: "In 1972, Bess and I were with a tour group going to visit London and Paris. We decided to fly from Paris to Nantes, where Marinette lived, and see the family. We only had 24 hours but we really made every minute count. It was very difficult for us to understand each other and Bess and Marinette spent just about the whole night passing an English-to-French dictionary back and forth. We went to Poligne to Maman Olivo's and visited the old barn. They had a seven course dinner for us and all the family assembled to greet us. What a wonderful time!

Marinette and her 16-year-old nephew Francois came to visit us in 1975. Francois brought his violin with him and practiced every day. We introduced him to bowling, water skiing, and baseball. He excelled in all of them.

In 1978, we again visited our friends in Nantes. We stayed with Marinette and saw many famous spots such as Port de Nantes, Cathedrale, St. Pierre, and the La Loire Valley with many famous chateaus. Then we went on to Cognac and visited a friend of theirs who owned a home built during the French Revolution and the family owned a distillery where cognac is made. We drove up the coast of Brittany, saw the town of Rennes, went out to Mt. St. Michel and could see Normandy Beach.

We had dinner with Joseph Bodard's family and also saw Victor and André, who were all with the Underground. We then spent the next week with Tata and her family. We saw many German fortifications from the war. We celebrated her daughter Claire's 16th birthday and Maman's 80th. Even though Maman could speak no English, she learned the words of the Star Spangled Banner and sang it to us!

One of the highlights of our visit with Tata was when she brought out the stick I had whittled for her while in the barn. It said, 'TATA 1944.'

In 1980, Marinette had an education seminar in Quebec and then flew in for a visit. She enjoyed shopping and spending time with our grandchildren. She was a teacher of young children and was so good with them. They really loved her, too. She spent two weeks with us and then flew on to Washington, DC to see George Stalnaker. By this time, she was speaking very fluent English."

Marinette spent time not only with George but also with his new wife, the former Celeste Boswell, a Niceville resident whom he married in 1977. Celeste had no children of her own.

Stub went on to say, "Tata's daughter Claire came to spend a year with us in 1981. She adjusted to American life quickly and became part of our family. She attended Lake Michigan College, made excellent grades, and made friends easily. As the time neared for her to go back home, she didn't seem to be quite ready. Claire turned 20 and began to hoard things she wanted to take back for her parent's 25th anniversary party and recipes so she could cook 'American' when she got back. She was very reluctant to leave her friends. Also, our children and grandchildren had accepted her as one of them and she felt sad to be leaving them. She thought that one day she might like to live in the United States.

Near the end of June, we took Claire to Chicago to catch her plane. She was loaded with seven pieces of luggage which we thought she wouldn't be allowed to take but she managed to get them all on board. It was a tearful goodbye and our home seemed very lonesome without her."

President Ronald Reagan went to Normandy on June 6, 1984 to dedicate a monument commemorating the 40th Anniversary of D-Day. Standing on the spot on the northern coast of France where Allied soldiers had stormed ashore, he spoke these words to an audience of veterans gathered at Pointe du Hoc:

"Forty summers have passed since the battle that you fought here. You were young the day you took these cliffs; some of you were hardly more than boys, with the deepest joys of life before you. Yet, you risked everything here. Why? Why did you do it? What impelled you to put aside the instinct for self-preservation and risk your lives to take these cliffs? What inspired all the men of the armies that met here? We look at you, and somehow we know the answer. It was faith and belief; it was loyalty and love.

The men of Normandy had faith that what they were doing was right, faith that they fought for all humanity, faith that a just God would grant them mercy on this beachhead or on the next. It was the deep knowledge - and pray God we have not lost it - that there is a profound, moral difference between the use of force for liberation and the use of force for conquest. You were here to liberate, not to conquer, and so

196

you and those others did not doubt your cause. And you were right not to doubt.

You all knew that some things are worth dying for. One's country is worth dying for, and democracy is worth dying for, because it's the most deeply honorable form of government ever devised by man. All of you loved liberty. All of you were willing to fight tyranny, and you knew the people of your countries were behind you.

When the war was over, there were lives to be rebuilt and governments to be returned to the people. There were nations to be reborn. Above all, there was a new peace to be assured. These were huge and daunting tasks. But the Allies summoned strength from the faith, belief, loyalty, and love of those who fell here. They rebuilt a new Europe together.

It is good and fitting to renew our commitment to each other, to our freedom, and to the alliance that protects it. We are bound today by what bound us 40 years ago, the same loyalties, traditions, and beliefs. We're bound by reality. The strength of America's allies is vital to the United States, and the American security guarantee is essential to the continued freedom of Europe's democracies. We were with you then; we are with you now. Your hopes are our hopes, and your destiny is our destiny."

Following the rousing speech, President Reagan and First Lady Nancy thanked and shook hands with each of the veterans who were present.

During the 40th anniversary ceremonies, Staff Sergeant Duane "Pinky" Pinkston, who served with the 505th Parachute Infantry Regiment of the 82nd Airborne Division, proudly showed visitors a clearing station that he created at La Fiere Bridge, less than 20 meters from the front. Using a crawl space under a house with less than three feet of clearance, he provided initial triage and treatment for more than 100 soldiers from June 6 to 9, 1944. The area was left intact by the house owner, complete with plasma bottles, syringes, dried bandages, and torn pieces of clothing.

The Normandy American Cemetery holds the graves of U.S. servicemen who died on D-Day and in subsequent fighting. The Cemetery and Memorial is a tribute to those Americans who gave their lives to help bring an end to World War II. A Visitor's Center was opened in a wooded area of the cemetery which now hosts about a million tourists per year.

The site, at the north end of a half mile access road, covers 172.5 acres and contains the graves of 9,387 soldiers who lost their lives in the

D-Day landings and ensuing operations. On the Walls of the Missing, in a semicircular garden on the east side of the memorial, there are an additional 1,557 names listed. Rosettes mark the names of those who have since been recovered and identified.

The memorial consists of a semicircular colonnade with a loggia at each end containing large maps and narratives of the military operations. At the center is the "Spirit of American Youth Rising from the Waves" bronze statue. An orientation table overlooking the beach depicts the landings in Normandy. A reflecting pool faces west at the memorial. The burial area has a circular chapel and granite statues representing the United States and France.

A month after President Reagan's visit, there were more celebrations along the Normandy coast, this time involving the crew of the "Miss Take." Bess Miller described the trip this way: "We arrived at the Charles De Gaulle Airport in Paris at 10:30 a.m. on July 25. We went to City Hall in Rennes where a large crowd had assembled and wondered what they were waiting for. Imagine our surprise when we found out they were waiting for us!

We participated in placing flowers on a memorial and a service commemorating the liberation of France by the Allied Forces. The American airmen were given medals and the wives were given beautiful bouquets of flowers. There was a reception held in a huge hall which was beautifully decorated. Many people greeted us along with newspaper and television cameras. We had lunch there as guests of the Mayor. In the afternoon, they gave us a tour of Rennes. In the evening, we went to the Mayor's home for a very elegant dinner, then he invited us to join him at the Tour de France bicycle races. This is a very famous race and we were there for the trophy presentation. We had a police escort and seats at the finish line. That was all just the first day of the reunion tour!"

Tata Olivo said, "To mark the 40th Anniversary of D-Day, old members of the Resistance had found and invited the crew members and their spouses. My daughter Claire was the interpreter. She had spent a year in the U.S., mostly with Stub and his wife Bess whom she now calls her American mother.

During a four-day period, the crew was celebrated as heroes everywhere they went. Together with the members of the French Resistance, they were honored by the Mayor of Rennes, the capital of Brittany, during a banquet for which our whole family was invited. At Coësmes, the inhabitants gave a little bag containing a piece of the fallen plane and George was given back a French bill that he had given to one of the members of the Resistance. At Poligné, the village was jubilant and everyone gathered in front of the barn for a picture. Maman told me afterwards that it was the best four days of her life. She was so happy to see again the men whose lives they had saved!"

George claimed proudly, "In 1984, the French invited us to come back with these same people for a reunion. Except for Papa Olivo, all of the Underground people they could find were still living. They took us to all the places we had been hidden and all the routes we had covered. Most had survived the years as had we. They gave us parts of our crashed aircraft and pieces of our chutes and took us to our hiding places and routes of escape. We took some plaques over and gave it to them in appreciation. I had pilot wings put on each one of them. It also had their French Underground name and real name. We presented it to each one of these people. I must say it was highly emotional." The plaques were engraved with the phrase À Cause de Vous, Nous Vivons! which means "Because of You, We Live!"

Four members of the flight crew, Gene Squier, Jim Clark, Stub Miller, and George, stood for quite a while staring out at Omaha Beach and the English Channel when they, like President Reagan, visited the Normandy American Cemetery. They were reminded of D-Day, the final flight of the Miss Take the following month, and the time they spent behind enemy lines. It seemed so long ago. As is often the case with war veterans, they didn't say much to each other. It was as if words weren't necessary or sufficient.

According to Jan (Squier) Andersen, Gene Squier's daughter, "The city of Rennes, near where the plane crashed, invited my father and members of the crew back to France for a celebration. There were parades, ceremonies, banquets, television coverage and speeches. The villagers gave the crew pieces of their plane that had crashed. My father received a very burned tail gun. The children in town even asked for autographs. The men and their wives were treated like celebrities."

Stub Miller recalled, "We went back to relive our experiences of 1944. We met Gene and Ev Squier in Paris on July 26 of 1984 and drove to the Hotel Frantel in Rennes where we were met by Marinette and Claire. We were joined there by George and Celeste along with Jim Clark and his friend, Mabel. It was a great reunion!

We met Dr. Andre Pothier, President of the Resistance, who along with Marinette, had put the reunion together. We were greeted with lovely bouquets of flowers in our rooms sent to us by the Mayor of Rennes, Monsieur le Minister Edmond Herve.

The next day we went to the Hotel de Ville (City Hall) where we were welcomed by the Mayor as well as the Council Municipal. There was a huge crowd of people gathered around and we were very surprised that they were all there to greet the American fliers. There was a memorial ceremony where flowers were placed on a memorial by the Resistance and George who represented our group. The TV and newspapers covered the activities. An elaborate reception followed with champagne, flowers, and lunch. The Mayor presented each of us with a bronze medal engraved for the occasion.

In the afternoon, we were taken on a tour of 'Old Town,' with cobblestone streets and a beautiful park. We were guests of the Mayor at his home and the food was excellent. Afterward, a police escort took us to the bicycle races which were going on that night, a very important event in France. We were introduced to the crowd and, for a few minutes, they made us feel as if we had won the war all by ourselves.

The morning of July 28, we attended a reception at the Coësmes Town Hall and Fire Station which was hosted by Mayor Paul David. This was the village where our plane went down and each of us was given a piece of our plane salvaged from the farm and placed in a velvet bag tied with a red, white, and blue ribbon. The ladies were presented with bouquets of flowers. We placed flowers on a memorial and walked through the village to the field where our plane had crashed. Tents had been set up in the spot and 70 or 80 people turned out for our luncheon. We could still see the indentations in the ground where our plane had crashed. After lunch, we were invited to the Mayor's home for champagne. Little kids asked for our autographs.

In the afternoon, our schedule took us to the village of Poligne where we attended a reception in the Town Hall. This was the village where the old barn was and the Olivos lived so it was very meaningful to us. We placed flowers on a memorial and there was a very impressive ceremony with the band playing the French National Anthem and then the American National Anthem. Bess became very emotional here and the newspaper reporter interviewed her about her feelings.

As we walked to the old barn, we were shocked to see what they had done to it. It was decorated in red, white, and blue with American flags flying. The inside had been set up for a cocktail party and reception. They even had electricity in it. There was much reminiscing about our stay in the barn. We were escorted to the Town Hall for dinner where 50 to 60 people joined us. There was music and dancing afterward and each of us was presented with a watercolor portrait of 'The Old Barn' done by Marcel Olivo.

On Sunday, July 29, we drove to Langon to attend a Catholic Mass honoring the French Resistance. It was very impressive. It was held outside in a field and afterward we joined in a military parade to the cemetery. There was a memorial of nine stones where nine soldiers had been killed. A ceremony was conducted with many speakers and, as usual, covered by the press and TV. Then we were ushered to another field where large tents had been set up for lunch. There were 100 to 150 people attending. After many courses, there was a program and our group got up to sing 'Auld Lang Syne' which seemed to thrill the French people. They were delighted!

On July 31, we were guests of the Bodard family honoring Joseph's 80th birthday. He was with the French Underground, helped us escape, and housed Gene Squier while we were in the barn. We ate for five hours. There were many courses, singing, dancing, opening of gifts, and toasts.

Later, we drove to Vitré where we had hidden after leaving the barn. The town was very quaint and picturesque and we enjoyed a long walk after so much food! We all had crepes at Claude Bodard's summer home.

We attended another reception at St. Ganton Town Hall on August 1. We were greeted by the Mayor and 40 to 50 villagers. After a nice lunch, we toured the village and surrounding countryside. We saw the old mill where bicycles had been stolen during our escape and drove through the pretty little village of La Gacilly.

The lady Mayor greeted us at Pipriac and we were her guests for a buffet dinner where the entire town of 75 people turned out. Everyone was anxious to talk to us and, in some cases, it was very difficult without an interpreter. They were all so kind and treated us like celebrities. This was the last stop on our itinerary and we were a pretty weary bunch since our schedule had been very hectic.

I took a walking tour of Rennes on August 2 taking pictures while Bess packed. At 2 p.m., Marinette met us at the hotel and we bid a final goodbye to all our friends. They brought us photographs, newspapers, and souvenirs to take home. On our way to Nantes, we stopped in Poligne to have cakes and champagne with Maman and to take a last glimpse at the old barn. We visited Papa Olivo's grave and it was very emotional. The next day, Marinette invited the eight of us to her home for dinner and then we spent the night in a hotel. We spent the next two weeks with the Squiers touring France, Monaco, Italy, and Switzerland. What an experience, never to be forgotten!!!

Because of the war, we are now like a family. Certainly the shared events of July, 1944, the efforts to escape from the Nazis, and the dangers experienced by all helped cement an unforgettable friendship."

Each flier was given some pieces of the calcified B-26 Marauder as well as pieces of their parachutes. At the time, the Germans had threatened to punish severely anyone who would keep a fallen plane's debris but many did. George was surprised when two 100 franc bills he had on his person when he landed were shown to him. This money was for eventual use if shot down in occupied territory. Forty years later, the money, kept for safekeeping, was returned to him. One bill was kept by the fliers and the other for the archives in Coësmes.

Visiting the barn in Poligne was a moving experience for the crew. "This is the first time that I've seen the outside of it," admitted Jim Clark. "I did not realize that the Germans were so close on the road."

Meeting other people involved in the rescue brought tears to people's eyes. George humorously summarized their odyssey by declaring that July 8, 1944 "was not the date of one of my best landings."

In front of a large gathering in Saint-Ganton, Marinette, the Master of Ceremonies for the flight crew reunion events, recalled the events during the flight crew's evasion and escape forty years earlier: "Here we are at the final phase of an odyssey that took you from Poligne to here in Saint-Ganton. Remember, the night is dark. Crouched in the ditch, you wait for the rumbling of a motor. Here comes the car driven by Pierre Aubron. It is a vehicle from the Todt enterprise (the German organization that built D-Day fortifications on the coast.) Pierre and Emile Pinot found the car near a light pole sabotaged by the Underground forces. Pierre Aubron seized it and arrived toward you, all lights out. You pile into the car, all six of you, and you ride and ride on small country roads to avoid the German troops that are everywhere on the more important roads.

Pierre Pinot (known as André Bedard to the Resistance) and a few friends have the duty to protect your car when you come to the railroad crossing watched over by the Germans. The Underground's mission is to open the barrier. Luckily, you pass through without any problem.

What a relief when you arrive at Francois Massiot's house, Mayor of the small village of Saint-Ganton, where the car stopped. And how welcome is the champagne that helps you overcome your emotions. The room, ten meters square, where you settle in is quite peaceful and the food that Pierre and his friends bring you is mighty good. You can even go out a little at dusk, sit under the trees and smoke a cigarette. I am told that one night you seal your friendship with your hosts by drinking this rum left by the English in Redon four years before. You drink the whole jug! I will not mention how much rum it contained!

Days pass. Over at the front in Normandy, the German defenses fall apart. It is time to take the American fliers to Pipriac. It becomes an urgent decision to make when we learn that the Germans are getting ready to search the town of Saint-Ganton. At the Moulin du Tertre, (the mill) you find bicycles to help you rejoin the Allied troops around Vitré. But there are only five bicycles for six people. Pierre Pinto must go look for a sixth bicycle at the Mayor's house which is surrounded by Germans. He is caught. They lock him in the garage and put a sentry at the door. Eventually, they check his papers, identity card, etc. He has those and shows them to the officer in charge. They turn him loose! Of course, the papers are false. If they had searched him, they would have found the knife that Stub Miller had just given him!

You leave Vitré with two French leaders, one of whom you remember as Jean Marion, along with two brave boys you nicknamed Silver Streak and Turtle Neck. We would call them in French, 'La Trace d'Argent' and 'Col Roulé.'

And then you meet the American troops. It is the end of your nightmare, of the fear of being discovered and taken by the enemy. Now you know the hope of seeing this long four-year war come to an end soon. You dream of rejoining your families who still only know that you are missing in action.

In France, you left many friends who will always have a special place for you in their hearts. This has been like a friendship chain with all the links being tied together, forty years later! How to express to you the emotion that we feel when we see you among us, evoking all those remembered experiences? We are privileged to be here. Others are not, forever gone in the shadow of death.

Someone also was looking forward to seeing you again and if you are here today it is because this someone started the whole thing going. I was asked, 'Do you think the American fliers could come to France to help us celebrate the fortieth anniversary of the Liberation?' I said, 'Of course. Why not? I'm going to write to them. We'll invite them for all the celebrations commemorating the Liberation.'

As they began, these festivities end in joy and emotion. They will remain in our memories as a living testimony of universal brotherhood, peace, and freedom. Our 'Partisans,' our members of the Underground, worked toward that end. Now, because of their dedication, we can enjoy these hours of happiness. I close with the words of the theme song of the Resistance – 'Sing, friends, in the dark...Freedom is listening to us in the night.'" (The words are from the *La Chant des Partisans* or "The Song of the Resistance" which was used as a rallying song after *La Marseilles* was banned by the Nazis.)

Just three and a half-years later, in February of 1987, Marinette died suddenly. This is an excerpt from the eulogy delivered at her funeral:

"We call her "Marraine" (Godmother) because although she loved children, she never knew the joy of being a mother and throughout the years, she has become Marraine for many of those who are here today. Olivier, the husband she never ceased loving, had left her alone only to be reunited with her today after a separation of almost 30 years. It was a painful experience that changed her life and, in remembrance of him, she went towards others. She was asked to be Godmother to children within the families of her sister, brothers, cousins, and friend.

Risking her life, she generously helped take in and hide for three weeks the crew of a fallen American airplane. She maintained a strong friendship with the crew members, a friendship that has grown stronger and stronger throughout time, despite an ocean's distance, a friendship that death cannot conquer. Her greatest wish was to see those around her loving one another, as she had loved others throughout her life. This is, perhaps the most beautiful and greatest role of a Godmother. So, in her memory, those of you who have come here today to be with her because you, too, love her and because you realize that the slightest sign of affection fills her with joy, you can also call her 'Marraine' now that we must say goodbye."

Chapter 20 – Treasures in the Attic

"I went with my dad to the 50th Reunion of the 391st Bomber Group at Norfolk, Virginia," said son Marc. "It was great not just to spend time with him but to meet some of the others he went to war with. I'll always remember how they asked the airmen to stand up if they had ever been shot down or held as a POW. It was amazing. There was hardly anyone left sitting down. What a group of guys!

One of my fondest memories is when I was a pilot during the Gulf War in Iraq after completion of my 36th and 37th missions. My dad had flown 35 of them in World War II and I remember his being really proud of me that I had passed him. I wasn't a hero the way he was. I was never shot down behind enemy lines or anything like that. It wasn't like I exceeded him in any way. It was just a big personal moment for me. Like I measured up."

After two heart bypass operations, diabetes, prostate cancer, colon cancer, and a broken hip, George finally succumbed to heart failure at age 83 on September 4, 1999 in his home with a hospice nurse at his side.

According to Jerry, "My dad told me once, 'Nobody wants to be 83 except the guy who is 82.' He had open heart surgery several years before. He fell in the shower & damaged vertebrae in his back. The pain was excruciating. He gave up and his body shut down about two months after that." Right to the end, he had those recurring nightmares where he would call out in his sleep to his soldiers to warn them of danger.

"He had a lot of friends at his memorial service," said Marc. "We went to Arlington Cemetery where a West Point liaison person took us in hand & guided us through the formal burial with the caisson (a horse-drawn, two-wheeled cart which bears the casket of the deceased), troops marching, and 21-gun salute. It was very moving. My father was put to rest alongside my mother, who was already buried there." The experience at Arlington Cemetery was something that really affected me. I knew I had to do something. Just going there, even as a visitor, tends to make you more patriotic. I think that's why all three of us – myself and my brothers - served."

George was buried in a grave next to Simone's in Section 11, Row 0, Site 64-2 of the Arlington National Cemetery, located directly across the Potomac River from the Lincoln Memorial. More than 300,000 people are buried in the 624-acre veteran's cemetery, the nation's largest and most prestigious which is called "America's Most

George Stalnaker's Final Flight

Hallowed Ground" and is also known as the place "Where Valor Proudly Sleeps."

As a full colonel, George, carrying an O-6 rank for the sixth highest officer pay grade, was eligible to be buried with full military honors. At the time, only E-9's (enlisted soldiers with the ninth highest pay grade) and above were eligible. The Army has since changed its policy so that all service members, regardless of rank, who die from wounds received resulting from enemy action and are being interred, inurned, or memorialized at Arlington National Cemetery, can receive those honors.

His funeral included a caisson with riderless horse, consistent with the tradition for high-ranking officers, symbolizing that a leader has fallen. His obituary read: "Col. George Stalnaker, USAF retired, made a 'full stop' landing – mission completed. After a lifetime of service in and out of uniform, the Des Moines, Iowa native left a legacy of leadership, compassion, and achievement few have equaled."

According to Bess, "Stub passed away on July 6, 2006. He was everything to me. Our daughter died first of cancer and then our son had a brain aneurism and died about a year after Stub. As you can imagine, it was a very difficult time. I still have one daughter, Mary Ann, who is wonderful. I don't know what I'd do without her. She's given me three grandsons. I divided up Stub's medals to give to each of them." Stub had received the Distinguished Flying Cross, the Purple Heart with one oak leaf cluster, the Air Medal with one silver and four bronze oak leaf clusters, and the European Theater of Operations Ribbon.

I'm 93 years old now and my daughter and her husband plan to move in with me when I get old enough to not be able to take care of myself. Right now, I'm fine. I'm just a little hard of hearing, that's all. I still take care of my house, drive a car, and use my computer to keep in touch with some of the people in France like Tata's daughter Claire who lived with us. I've had a good life."

Jerry Stalnaker received a Master's Degree from Troy State University in Montgomery, Alabama and started his Air Force career in September of 1967 in the back seat of a two-man F-4 Phantom jet. Like all Air Force navigators, he had the nickname of "GIB" which stands for "Guy in Back."

"When I became a fighter jock backseater (another term for navigator), most of the back seat guys were actually pilots," he said. "The Air Force decided to use only navigators in the back starting in the

George Stalnaker Funeral Caisson, Arlington National Cemetery

late 60's. Once we were all navigators, we were referred to as WSO's (Weapon System Operators.)"

Both Jerry and his pilot were awarded the Distinguished Flying Cross for back-to-back missions to rescue a company of Republic of Korea troops pinned down by the Viet Cong. Flying the F-4 for the 557th Tactical Fighter Squadron with a call sign of "Shark Bait" out of Cam Ranh Bay, they dropped bombs on the enemy and used their air-to-ground 20 mm gun. When they ran out of ordnance, they diverted to Chu Lai, a nearby Marine Corps Base. They shut down one engine, hot-pit refueled, quickly uploaded a new set of bombs, and then went back to the fire-fight, completely destroying the enemy.

Hot-pit refueling is similar to a lightning-fast NASCAR pit-stop. As a plane lands after a sortie, it taxis into a "flow," a semi-circular shelter open at both ends. With the plane's engines still running, a crew hooks a fuel line to the aircraft and fills it up preparing the plane for a quick relaunch. The only thing that wasn't done according to the book is that a Marine got up on the jet and handed both crewmembers a Coca-Cola during the refueling operation. Jerry explained, "The Air Force guys are a little more safety-conscious and would never do that. But it was a welcome treat."

"I wised up and went to pilot training," he added, "coming in first in my class & becoming a full-fledged fighter pilot. My dad & I used to go round & round about fighter pilots versus bomber pilots. In his era, the bombers took most of the flak. In Viet Nam, the fighters took most of the flak. My dad said they would have fighter escorts on some missions. He joked that when the shooting started, the fighters left and were nowhere to be seen. In Viet Nam the B-52 bombers flew way high up and rarely got shot at although they did lose a few to SAM's (Surface-to-air missiles)."

Flying 163 combat missions in all, Jerry received that Distinguished Flying Cross along with nine Air Medals, one for every 20 missions plus an extra one for a particularly challenging mission flown in bad weather with bombs dropped directly on target thereby saving many American lives by, as he calls it, "getting our grunts out of a bind."

He went on to pilot the North American Aviation T-39 Sabreliner out of Andrews Air Force Base, became a Maintenance Officer, commanded a Maintenance Squadron, and retired after 30 years in September of 1997 as a full Colonel, like his father. Jerry then worked as a Condominium Manager in Destin, Florida for 18 years. He has a daughter Terri and he and his wife Davia have two sons, Zack and Jake.

209

"I was one of the original "Crispy Warriors," boasted Jerry, referring to a group of seniors in Destin that met for the first time for breakfast on his birthday, March 5, 2007 at "the big round table" in the Harbor Docks Restaurant.

The veterans, many of them pilots, began a practice of meeting weekly to exchange war stories. "There's not too many places you can go and be 65 years old and one of the youngest people," he joked. The name comes from the food the group ordered – they would all have the Fisherman's platter with very crispy bacon. The waitresses begin referring to them as the "Crispies" which eventually became "The Crispy Warriors." They later re-deployed to "Another Broken Egg Café."

"When we moved to Neptune Beach on the outskirts of Jacksonville, Florida, I formed the same kind of group," claimed Jerry. "We call it the 'Jax Vets.' We started with just four guys and now we are up to close to 50. One of the guys is a 94-year-old who flew fighters in WWII."

The group currently meets for breakfast at Denny's Restaurant on Third Street every Thursday at 7:30 a.m. An American flag is positioned right by the "Table for 40," the typical number that attends on any given day. The attendees drink black roast coffee and will consume 20 pots of it before the morning is over. The meeting starts with a prayer, is followed by the Pledge of Allegiance, and then announcements are made about local and national veteran's issues. Other than that, the group is very informal.

"We aren't a service organization," Jerry said. "We just get together for the camaraderie." He works off breakfast at the Mayport Naval Station gym, a place he frequents typically three times a week.

Another pilot in the family who served with distinction, Dick Hosman was born in Spencer, Nebraska on May 8, 1919 and attended Iowa State University. He was a member of the Sigma Phi Epsilon fraternity and Pershing Rifles but, most importantly, met George's twin sister Josephine there. They both graduated in 1941 and he was commissioned as a 2nd Lieutenant in the Army by the ROTC (Reserve Officers' Training Corps.) Dick and Jo, as she was called, married on September 27 of that year and spent 65 years together.

After graduating from flight training school, he was assigned to the 398th Bomber Group in England, where he flew B-17 bombers on 35 missions, earning the Distinguished Flying Cross in the process. After the war, Dick received his Master's degree from the University of Minnesota. Like George, he was transferred to bases across the United States and Japan in increasing responsibilities, retiring as a full colonel.

He received the Air Medal with four oak leaf clusters, three Bronze Stars, the Korean Service Medal, and both the Army and Air Force Commendation Ribbons. He then served as Assistant Dean of the College of Engineering at the University of Wisconsin at Madison.

In retirement, Dick and Jo loved to travel and spend time at their cabin on Found Lake in St. Germain, Wisconsin. Jo died on April 18, 2007 at 89 years old and Dick on September 28, 2012 at 93. They had three girls – Margaret Lee, Nancy, & Debbie.

George's brother Howard began a commercial broadcasting career with the Meredith Corporation as soon as he came home from the war. After managing a number of radio and television stations, he was named to the Nebraska Broadcaster's Hall of Fame in 1976. He passed away from cancer on July 18, 1994 at the age of 75.

In addition to son James, Howard and his wife Martha had a second son, Thomas, and two daughters, Sally and Susan. Martha passed away on August 28, 2008 at the age of 89.

Following in their father's footsteps, both Jerry and Marc went on to train at MacDill as Air Force pilots. Jerry flew an F-4 and Marc an F-16.

Youngest daughter Sylvie (Stalnaker) Patrick helped care for Simone until her death and, after that experience, chose to become a Registered Nurse. A graduate of the University of Maryland, she was a neonatal and cardiac intensive care unit nurse for twenty years. Finally, she worked with the elderly at The Lowman Home in White Rock, South Carolina. Her own breast cancer diagnosis came in 2010. The 58-year-old died suddenly on March 19, 2012 at her home in Niceville, Florida. She was survived by her husband John and two sons, Kevin and Scott.

Her obituary included the following: "Sylvie was passionate about flowers. Her yard is a riot of color, representing Sylvie's outlook on life. She mixed her bulbs, perennials and annuals like an artist. She also created beautiful pottery. Her large heart made her easy to befriend."

Larry Kolb said of his former classmate, "Despite the fact that Sylvie was 37 years younger than my mom, they always maintained a close relationship, frequently writing to each other. Sylvie was spunky, friendly, and smart. Like all the Stalnakers, she was a close friend of our family."

"I remember I had my cell phone off, lamented Marc. "When I turned it on, there were nine missed calls about my sister. It was just one of those things. She was taking medication for sleep apnea, for her back, for a bronchial infection, and for her cancer. Her body couldn't handle it all."

George and Simone's oldest daughter, Claire, was diagnosed with Parkinson's Disease, a progressive disorder of the nervous system that affects movement, in 1993. It develops gradually, often starting with a slight tremor in one hand. The degenerative disorder causes stiffness as well as tremors. There is no cure.

Claire now has trouble with her balance, is prone to falling, and has consequently had both her shoulders replaced. Currently living in a rehabilitation center in Florida, she doesn't have the dexterity any longer to type on a keyboard so she can't use e-mail. Wanting to contribute to this book, she did so by texting a number of short messages on her cell phone. She still has use of her thumbs.

Claire obviously inherited some of her father's athletic ability. George, as you recall, won the State Half-Mile Championship in high school. "I felt a lot of pressure to do well," she admitted. "I was one of the trainers for the Auburn University track team. I had worked with my high school's track team and saw nothing to keep me from doing the same in college. So, I learned about track in a class that consisted of all men and me and was conducted by no less than Mel Rosen."

Mel was head coach of Auburn's track team for 28 years, from 1963 to 1991, during which time the team won four consecutive Southeastern Conference Indoor Track & Field Championships along with an outdoor championship. During his career, he coached seven Olympians and 143 All-Americans. Claire was obviously in some pretty "fast" company.

Mel went on to become coach of the U.S. Olympic men's track team and was elected to both the USA Track & Field Hall of Fame and the U.S. Track & Field & Cross Country Coaches Association Hall of Fame.

"This was 1969 and there wasn't a women's track team so I became the only woman in the SEC to manage a men's team. One day for fun, Coach Rosen let me run the 220 (half a lap on a standard track) with the men, even though I was no sprinter. The football team and band practiced on the same field and with them rooting me on, I beat a group of the best runners on the team."

There were plenty of laughs and snickers among those members of the track team who watched this scene unfold. Some joked about the runners "being beaten by a girl." Coach Rosen saw this and then challenged the rest of them to race against Claire. She demonstrated that her victory was no fluke. The result was the same in the second heat. Claire came in first place. She had beaten all the men on that vaunted team. This time, instead of snide comments and taunts, the members of the track team stood in stunned silence.

"Then I cramped up," remembered Claire. "When there's too much lactic acid in the muscles, it is very painful. I can still hear Coach Rosen in that nasal New York accent saying, 'Stawlnakah! Whatsa mattah?'"

Unfortunately, Mel didn't say, "We should start a women's team. You'd be the star." He also didn't say, "You're good enough to run with any of the men. I'm going to petition the NCAA to get an exception to allow you to be the first collegiate woman competing against men."

According to Claire, "You would think Auburn would want to take advantage of the fact I was a woman and say yes to the magazine and newspaper coverage. But NOOO! They didn't at all. In fact, they kicked me off the travel team as a manager as a cost savings. What it amounted to was Auburn no longer would pay my way. I still went to the meets, though. They weren't going to stop me." Claire obviously also inherited a lot of her mother's determination.

So, not only was she denied the ability to run herself because there was no women's team but Claire even had to pay her own travel expenses to work as manager of the men's team.

Obviously born a few years too soon, she could have benefitted from the change produced by Title IX of the Education Amendment. A law was enacted in 1972 prohibiting discrimination on the basis of sex in any federally funded education program or activity. In other words, if Auburn were going to have a men's track team, it ought to have a women's track team, as well. Claire likely would have been of significant value to that team. From the way it sounds, had she been allowed to run on the men's team, she would have been of considerable value there, as well.

After graduating from Auburn, Claire needed a job but found much more than that on a different kind of track. She took the recommendation of a neighbor and drove to the Bowie Race Track in Maryland. The one-mile track is part of the Belair Stud Farm, known as the "Cradle of American Thoroughbred Racing." It was love at first sight. The first thing Claire heard was the rhythmic breathing and the sound of hooves in the pre-dawn darkness. That was followed by the shouts of the handlers and the sight of the early morning steam rising off the horses' backs after their post-gallop bath. She was captivated.

"It was sensory overload," Claire enthused. "I got a job walking hots (cooling down horses after workouts and races) right away and never looked back. I went to work seven days a week for 100 hours a week. I walked miles every day. This was a culture all its own. I just lucked into this job with the leading trainer. I learned about the care and feeding of these equine athletes and went from hot walker to groomer where I was placed in charge of four horses.

As a groomer, I was responsible for mucking out the stalls. This consisted of using a pitchfork and disposing of all the feces and urine these big animals could manufacture. The groomer deposited this in a piece of plastic or burlap called a muck sack in a wheelbarrow. When the sacks were full, we emptied them in a muck pit. These in turn were emptied out by huge trucks that would deliver them to one of the many mushroom farms. It was a messy and time-consuming job.

The other duties included putting the horses feed tubs in which is not as easy as it sounds. A healthy horse is usually an aggressive eater. After they ate, an exercise rider would bring the tack (bridle, saddle cloth, and saddle) which was placed on the horse and the halter placed back on so you could tie them up. Most of the horses wore galloping bandages which we placed on their legs to prevent injury. All this was done as quickly as possible. You'd feed your horses, brush them, remove bandages from the night before, tack the horses up, start cleaning the stalls, get buckets full of warm soapy water ready for when they came in from the track, bathe the horses, and put fresh water out so the hotwalker can let the horses sip it slowly as they cool off. Then, you'd make sure the horses have been fed, exercised, cleaned up, and hay placed in the clean stall.

You'd also have to administer any first aid the horse required. It could be anything from whirlpooling, hosing down a swollen limb, or applying a poultice." The latter involves wrapping a soft, moist material typically containing clay, bran, or herbs to a horse's knees, legs, or ankles.

She continued, "Then, you'd take a breath and rake up the shedrow (A covered walkway along the row of stalls in a horse barn) in front of the stalls. Any extra maintenance like pulling the manes, trimming hairs around the face, making new bandages, laundering the old bandages, etc. is done at this time. Most horses wear at least four standing bandages.

Looking back, that was a lot of work for $200 a week! But, I always loved horses and I was happy! I'm sure I'm writing too much but there's so much to say! How I wish I was still there!"

Claire went on to marry John Hayden who flew OV-10s (a light armed reconnaissance aircraft called the Bronco made by North American Rockwell) in Viet Nam and retired as an Air Force Lt. Col. They had two girls, Taylor and Kari.

"I'm sorry that I can only write a little at a time," said Claire. "My thumbs lag behind my thoughts. Being able to text my story has been so cathartic for me." She certainly doesn't need to apologize for anything.

Brother Marc comes to check on Claire and take her on outings. He was captain of the Rugby Team at the University of Maryland. After graduation, he became an F-16 pilot rising to the rank of Major and flew combat missions in support of Desert Storm in 1990. Formerly a member of the Air Force Reserve, he is now a Captain flying Boeing 717's for Delta and is married to Vicki. He has a son Kyle and three daughters, Samantha, Kelly, and Rachael.

Youngest of the Stalnaker siblings, Eric was in the Marines and left after nine years as a Staff Sgt. He learned how to fix airplanes there and went on to do the same for NASA. After that he started working for Bank of America as an aircraft mechanic on their fleet of Gulf Stream jets. He lives in South Carolina with his wife Teresa. They have three sons, Chad, Lucas, and Noah and a daughter Stephanie.

Clearly, George and Simone's family has grown and prospered. According to Eric, "My parents were great people. They were heroes. They both risked their lives fighting for their respective countries. I couldn't be more proud of them."

Did George have any regrets? "Just one," admitted Eric, "My dad said he always regretted giving up smoking."

Pleased by many things but particularly his family's service to America, George claimed, "My three sons were all in the military. One (Jerry) fought in Viet Nam, one (Marc) in Desert Storm in Iraq, and one (Eric) was in the Marines. My brother Howard was an Aircraft Carrier Pilot in WWII, my brother-in-law Dick was a B-17 pilot flying out of England in WWII, and I have a son-in-law John who flew in Viet Nam as a Forward Controller getting shot at from everything from B-B guns up to the big caliber stuff. And also my nephew Jim, my brother's son, who flew F-18's in Desert Storm. I'm very proud of all of them."

According to Jim, a Marine Colonel, "It's sad that we Baby Boomers never really understood what the Greatest Generation went through. Now that we have discovered from recent conflicts more of what veterans have to wrestle with on a daily basis, it gives you a different perspective on the sacrifices they made. There are still things that I will never talk about from my experiences in combat. I flew 103 missions over all the conflicts I served in and have never shared the details with my wife, my soul-mate and love of my life for 37 years. She is smart and knows it's better to never ask. I have a son Joe who is a Marine Captain and Cobra pilot who served in Afghanistan. He and I can quietly look at each other, knowing that it does not need to be discussed."

World War II veterans are now being lost in record numbers. In the United States, about 900 of them pass away every day. During the three years, seven months, and 30 days of American involvement in World War II, a total of 291,557 soldiers were lost, or about 218 per day.

Most of those in America's Greatest Generation didn't talk about their war-time experiences. They were quiet, unassuming heroes. Unfortunately, the only images that those in subsequent generations had were from bloodless, antiseptic Hollywood movies. Some, however, like George and Simone Stalnaker, left their priceless words behind for us to discover. Those letters, journals, and notes are like treasures in our attics, waiting to be discovered. For most of us, they provide a window to an unknown, private world of courage and sacrifice.

A Final Tribute

Tata Olivo declared, "George Stalnaker was a great man who was so smart, so grateful, and so sensitive. It was a privilege for us to have known both him and the members of his crew. Alas, in 1947 my Dad passed away. He at least got to see the personal letter of gratitude that was written to him by General Eisenhower and the French Interior Minister after the war. In 1986, Marinette at 61 years old and Maman at 90 years old left us as well. My youngest brother Emile was 72 years old when he died in 2006. Marcel and I are the only ones remaining.

I don't speak English well enough to truly express the emotions that I feel. We will always be grateful to the American people for freeing France from the Germans. We will thank to our last days the young soldiers who, often at the cost of their lives, came to fight on our soil. A great thank you from the bottom of our hearts."

George's feelings, in turn, were well-expressed in what he had engraved on those plaques he awarded to the members of the French Resistance who helped him and his crew - "Thanks to You, We Live!" They are among the estimated 5,000 Allied airmen who were shot down over occupied France who can say that.

French President François Hollande characterized the close relationship that endures between the two countries as, "We were friends at the time of Jefferson and Lafayette and will remain friends forever."

In recent times, America and France have, unfortunately, shared the experience of being targets of horrific and senseless violence. After the July 14, 2016 Bastille Day truck attack in Nice that killed 84 people and injured more than 200, President Obama declared, "We stand in solidarity and partnership with France, our oldest ally, as they respond to and recover from this attack. On this Bastille Day, we are reminded of the extraordinary resilience and democratic values that have made France an inspiration to the entire world, and we know that the character of the French Republic will endure long after this devastating and tragic loss of life."

Catastrophe struck Orlando, Florida the previous month as a lone gunman killed 49 people and injured 53 at Pulse, a gay nightclub. The Eiffel Tower was lit with the colors of the rainbow flag the following night and Paris City Hall was decorated with both American and rainbow flags. President Hollande commented, "It is America that was hit but freedom that was targeted" after signing a book of condolences at the American Embassy. He vowed to toughen the fight against the attacks on innocents "at the side of the American people."

After the Islamic State terrorist attack in Paris seven months prior to that which killed 130 people and injured 368, American President Barack Obama condemned France's deadliest incident since World War II and reaffirmed the unbreakable ties between the two countries by declaring, "France is our oldest ally. The French people have stood shoulder to shoulder with the United States time and again," and added, "Paris itself represents the timeless values of human progress. Those who think that they can terrorize the people of France or the values that they stand for are wrong. The American people draw strength from the French people's commitment to life, liberty, the pursuit of happiness. We are reminded in this time of tragedy that the bonds of liberté and égalité and fraternité are not only values that the French people care so deeply about, but they are values that we share. And those values are going to endure far beyond any act of terrorism or the hateful vision of those who perpetrated the crimes."

The two countries seem to be inextricably tied in times both of triumph and tragedy. Hopefully, the times of triumph will soon return.

Bibliography

Air Forces Escape & Evasion Society, http://airforceescape.org/nazi-warning-to-helpers-of-airmen, retrieved March 21, 2016.

Aglion, Raoul, *Roosevelt and de Gaulle: Allies in Conflict: A Personal Memoir,* The Free Press, New York: 1988.

Allen, Trevor, B-26.com, *General Crew Stations/Box Formation,* http://www.b26.com. Retrieved August 8, 2015.

Argunners, August 9, 2015, *Tsutomu Yamaguchi: Survivor of two Atomic Bombs.* Retrieved December 26, 2015.

Binney, Marcus, *The Women Who Lived for Danger: The Women Agents of SOE in the Second World War,* Hodder & Stoughton, London: 2002.

Briehan, Mason, *Martin Aircraft 1909-1960,* Johnston Thompson, Santa Anna, CA: 1995.

Beevor, Antony, *The Second World War,* Back Bay Books, New York: 2013.

Carter, Ian, Imperial War Museums, iwm.org.uk, *The German Response to D-Day,* Retrieved March 10, 2016.

Clark, Jim. 1991, 1992, 1994. "391st Bomb Group Association". *Wings Of Courage.*

Cobb, Matthew, *The Resistance: The French Fight Against the Nazis,* Simon & Schuster UK, London: 2013.

Davison, Phil, January 26, 2014, The Independent, *Captain William Overstreet: Pilot who claimed to have chased a German fighter plane under the base arch of the Eiffel Tower in 1944.* www.independent.co.uk. Retrieved September 5, 2015.

Deák, István, *Europe on Trial: The Story of Collaboration, Resistance, and Retribution during World War II,* Westview Press, Boulder, CO: 2015.

The Destin Log, March 11, 2011, *The "Crispy Warriors"*, http://unified-communications.tmcnet.com. Retrieved June 20, 2015.

"Escape And Evasion". 1944. Washington, D.C. War Department, U.S. Adjutant General's Office.

Feltman, Rachel, The Washington Post, https://www.washingtonpost.com/news/speaking-of-science/wp/2014/12/15/no-carrots-dont-make-your-eyesight-better. Retrieved February 3, 2016.

The Florida Times Union, May 22, 2015, Table for 30: Weekly meet-ups are a time for vets to laugh, swap stories, remember, http://jacksonville.com. Retrieved June 22, 2015.

Fourcade, Marie-Madeleine, Noah's Ark: *A Memoir of Struggle and Resistance,* Dutton, New York: 1974.

Francis Devon, and Carroll, Gordon, *Flak Bait: The Story of the B-26's and the Men Who Flew Them in WW II,* Zenger Publishing Co., Washington: 1979.

Freeman, Roger A., with Allen, Trevor J. and Mallon, Bernard, *B-26 Marauder at War*, Charles Scribner's Sons, New York: 1978.

Gammell, Charlotte, November 1, 2010, The Telegraph, *Eileen Nearne: British Spy Gave Rare Interview,* http://www.telegraph.co.uk. Retrieved September 8, 2015.

George Stalnaker Life Story. 1992. DVD. Niceville, FL: Stalnaker Family.

Gilbert, Martin, *The Second World War: A Complete History*, Henry Holt & Co., New York: 2004.

Green, William, *Famous Bombers of the Second World War*, Doubleday, New York: 1959.

Gunston, Bill, *Jane's American Fighting Aircraft of the 20th Century*, Military Press, New York: 1989.

Haffner, Sebastian, *The Meaning of Hitler*, Orion Books, London: 1983.

Hamby, Alonzo, *The Man of Destiny: FDR and the Making the American Century,* Basic Books, New York, 2015.

Harkins, Clyde, *Marauder Pilot to Pilot*, B26.com, http://b26.com. Retrieved August 8, 2015. Used by permission.

Hart, Liddell, London Daily Mail, February 4, 1947, *Was the Maquis Worthwhile?* Retrieved February 11, 2016.

Harwood, William B. *Raise Heaven and Earth: The Story of Martin Marietta People and Their Pioneering Achievements*, Simon & Schuster, New York: 1993.

Hastings, Max, Inferno: *The World at War, 1939 – 1945*, Vintage Books, New York: 2012.

Hickman, Kennedy, January 11, 2015, http://militaryhistory.about.com/od/1900s/p/World-War-I-Marsha-Ferdinand-Foch.htm. Retrieved February 20, 2016.

Jackson, Julian, *France: The Dark Years: 1940-1944*, Oxford Univ. Press, New York: 2003.

Johnson, David, *The Man Who Didn't Shoot Hitler: The Story of Henry Tandey VC and Adolf Hitler,* The History Press, London: 2014.

Kaiser, Charles, CNN.com, *2015/05/06/opinions/Kaiser-ve-day-french-resistance.* Retrieved February 17, 2016.

Kampka, Erich, *I was Hitler's Chauffeur*, Pen & Sword Books Limited, South Yorkshire, England: 2010.

Kazel-Wilcox, Anne & Wilcox, PJ, *West Point '41: The Class that Went to War and Shaped America,* University Press of New England, Lebanon, NH: 2014.

Kolb, Larry. 2016. George and Simone Stalnaker Len Sandler Interview by author. On telephone. Westford, MA.

Kolb, Larry J., *Overworld: The Life and Times of a Reluctant Spy,* Riverhead Books. New York: 2004.

Miller, Bess. 2016. George and Simone Stalnaker Len Sandler Interview by author. On telephone. Westford, MA.

Miller, Stub Memoir. 1993 Len Sandler Interview by author. On telephone. Westford, MA.

Moench, John, *Marauder Men: An Account of the Martin B-26 Marauder*, Malia Enterprises, Longwood, FL: 1989.

Moorhead Joanna, March 30, 2013, The Guardian, *My Aunts, the Unlikely Spies*, http://www.theguardian.com. Retrieved September 9, 2015.

Newborn, Jud, *Sophie Scholl and the White Rose,* Oneworld Publications, Oxford: 2006.

Nimitz, Chester W., Admiral, *Reflections on Pearl Harbor*, The Admiral Nimitz Foundation, Fredericksburg, TX: 1985.

North, David, *Word War II: The Resistance*, New World City, New York: 2015.

Olivo, Tata and Marinette. "Letters To Jerry Stalnaker". Letter.

Ottis, Sherri Greene, *Silent Heroes: Downed Airmen and the French Underground*, University Press of Kentucky, Lexington: 2014.

Ouest-France,. 1984. "Fortieth Anniversary Of The Port-De-Roche Massacre".

Ouest-France,. 1984. "A Gift For The American Fliers Shot Down At Coesmes: Parts Of Their B-26 Marauder".

Paxton, Robert O., *Vichy France: Old Guard and New Order, 1940-1944*, Columbia University Press: 2001.

Phillips, Larry, AC3, The Air Force Times, December 23, 1964, *Exploits in French Underground Recalled by Woman in Bolling,* P. 6.

Rees, Lawrence, *The Nazis: A Warning from History,* BBC Books, London: 2006.

Rings, Werner, *Life with the Enemy: Collaboration and Resistance in Hitler's Europe, 1939-1945,* Doubleday and Company, New York: 1982.

Rosbottom, Ronald, *When Paris Went Dark: The City of Light Under German Occupation, 1940-1944,* Little Brown, New York: 2015.

Ryan, Cornelius, *The Longest Day: The Classic Epic of D-Day,* Simon & Schuster, New York: 1994.

Sauras, Emile. "Letter To Celeste Stalnaker". Letter.

Schlesinger, Arthur, Jr., *The Letters of Arthur Schlesinger, Jr.,* Random House, New York: 2013.

Schofield, Hugh, BBC News, August 23, 2004, *Eyewitness: How Paris was Liberated,* Retrieved November 25, 2015.

Sedgwick, John, March, 2005, *The Harvard Nazi,* http://www.bostonmagazine.com. Retrieved August 17, 2015.

Simbeck, Rob, *Daughter of the Air: The Brief Soaring Life of Cornelia Fort,* Grove Press, New York: 1999.

Stalnaker, Claire. 2016. George and Simone Stalnaker Len Sandler Interview by author. On telephone. Westford, MA.

Stalnaker, Eric. 2016. George and Simone Stalnaker Len Sandler Interview by author. On telephone. Westford, MA.

Stalnaker, Jerry. 2016. George and Simone Stalnaker Len Sandler Interview by author. On telephone. Westford, MA.

Stalnaker, Jim. 2016. George and Simone Stalnaker Len Sandler Interview by author. On telephone. Westford, MA.

Stalnaker, Marc. 2016. George and Simone Stalnaker Len Sandler Interview by author. On telephone. Westford, MA.

Stalnaker, Simone. "Diary Of Simone Stalnaker". 1945-1946 Diary.

Tannehill, Victor C, *The Martin Marauder B-26*, Boomerang Publishers, New York: 1997.

Toliver, Raymond, *The Interrogator: The Story of Hanns Joachim Scharff, Master Interrogator of the Luftwaffe,* Schiffer Publishing, Atglen, PA: 1997.

Vinen, Richard, *The Unfree French: Life Under the Occupation,* Yale University Press, New Haven: 2007.

Yenne, Bill and Greene Michael J.L., *Black '41: The West Point Class of 1941 and the American Triumph in World War II,* John Wiley, New York: 1991.

Wagner, Ray, *American Combat Planes of the 20th Century: A Comprehensive Reference,* Jack Bacon & Co., Reno, Nevada: 2004.

Washington Post, February 9, 2014, *"Obama and Hollande: France and the U.S. enjoy a renewed alliance."* Retrieved October 20, 2015.

Index

Anderson, General Samuel, briefing before D-Day, 79; comments by Clark, 50; message to 391st, 142, 143.

Belcher, Larry, D-Day aftermath, 82, 83.

Bodson, Henry, trained Audie Murphy, 40

Brandon, Lt. Col Donald K., 391st Bomber Group, Squadron 574th, 63.

Chamberlain, Neville, appeasement, 10, 14; replaced by Churchhill, 16.

Clark, Jim, arrival at MacDill, 48-49; at Omaha Beach, 199; background, 46; beginning serious action, 65, 66; bombing V-1 sites, 66, 67; celebrating arrival of Americans, 128, D-Day, 81; dedicates memorial, 147; escaping, 110; first ride in B-26, 49; getting restless, 119-120; in battle, 94, 99, 118; missions, 90; not at reunion, 109; not getting caught with his pants down, 128; organizing the 391st, 49-50; parachute landing, 101-104; re-visits Poligne, 203.

Colsch, Smiley, ill-fated second tour, 83.

Corniglion-Molinier, Brigadier General Édouard, background, 24-27; offer to Simone, 26; *photograph of,*

25; what he saw in her (Simone de Cruzel), 26-27.

Churchill, Winston, Battle of Britain, 20; Churchill and Stalin, 157; "Churchill's Secret Army", 28; Dunkirk speech, 17; first speech as Prime Minister, 16; Pétain rejects Churchhill, 18.

De Gaulle, Charles, airport named after, 198; Hotel Lutetia guest, 168; promotion to Brigadier General, 17; rallies French to resist, 21, 22, 24, 87, 149.

Donovan, William, beginnings of CIA, 48.

Doolittle, General Jimmy, modifications of B-26, 58; Tokyo bombing raid, 47.

Dooley, Jr., Major Joseph E., 391st Bomber Group, Squadron 573rd, 63.

Eisenhower, General Dwight, deceiving Hitler, 77; D-Day, 78, 81; Five Star General, 41; greets Khrushchev, 190; jacket, 66; Liberation of Paris, 149; praise for 391st, 79; priority not Paris, 148, surrender of Germans, 160, writes letter, 217.

Foch, General Ferdinand, warning about Versailles Treaty, 12.

Fourcade, Marie-Medeleine, code name "HEDGEHOG", 88, 89.

81; death, 206; discharge, 165; first buzz bomb, 69; found equal to the task, 67, 68; Gestapo HQ, 98, 99; going overseas, 62; helped by the Resistance, 99-101; introduction to Army, 51, 62; leaving the Olivos, 123; martyr's ceremony, 147; missions, 90; the "Miss Take" 95, 96; off-duty activities, 68, 69; the Olivos barn,116, 117; on bicycle, 111; plumber, 173; R&R, 83; Redistribution Center, 138, 139; reunion, 109; Silver Star, 137; stares at Omaha Beach, 199; visits to France, 193-195.

Murphy, Audie, trained soldiers, 40

Murphy, Frank, in forest, 104; in hiding, 109; in transit, 134; injured, 99; missions, 90; prays, 94; reunion, 103; whore house, 133,134.

Mussolini, Benito, cult of personality, 158; declares war, 18; rise to power, 11.

Nearne, Eileen, code name "ROSE", 87, 88.

Nimitz, Admiral Chester, tour of Pearl Harbor, 43-44.

Obama, Barack, U.S. relationship with France, 217-218.

Olivo, Marinette, death, 201; hiding the Americans, 115-117, 123; package, 173; Resistance reunion, 199-201.

Olivo, Tata, hiding the Americans, 115-117; love for George Stalnaker, 217; returns to France, 195; tribute to U.S. soldiers, 198.

Oppenheimer, Dr. J. Robert, atomic bomb test, 164.

Overstreet, Captain William, flight through Eiffel Tower, 145.

Pétain, Philippe, Vichy government, 18, 19.

Philippe, Marcel, Port-de-Roche massacre, 146, 147.

Reagan, Ronald, speech at Normandy, 196-197.

Roosevelt, Franklin, background, 7, 8; death, 157-159; declaration of war, 43; establishes OSS, 48; four terms, 160; increases defense spending, 41; neutrality, 16; New Deal, 7, 8; pact with Churchhill and Stalin, 157; presents medals, 40; response to Pearl Harbor attack, 43, 45; salute, 127; Truman, 50; Truman praises, 161.

Sauras, Emile, D-Day, 77; hiding George Stalnaker, 106-110; reaction to plane crash, 105.

Scharff, Hans, Master Interrogator, 157.

Schlesinger Jr., Arthur, assistant to JFK, 48; liberation of Paris, 149.

Scholl, Sophie, White Rose, 155.

228

About the Author

Over the past 28 years, Len Sandler has successfully developed and delivered close to 3,000 leadership seminars for such organizations as IBM, NASA, GEICO, General Motors, EMC, Siemens, AT&T, Disney, Lockheed-Martin, McKesson, Citigroup, Liberty Mutual, General Electric, Lucent Technologies, Fidelity Investments, Johnson & Johnson, the U. S. Navy, Hertz, Blue Cross/Blue Shield, Honeywell, Abbott Labs, Motorola, Staples, Verizon, Merck, and Oracle. Formerly an adjunct professor at Boston University's School of Management, he holds a B.S. in Psychology, an MBA, and a Ph.D. in Organizational Behavior. Len lives in Westford, MA, with his wife Marilyn. He has four children - Lori, Melinda, Scott, and Craig - along with three grandchildren - Elizabeth, Louisa, and Oscar.

Sandler is also the author of *Becoming an Extraordinary Manager: The Five Essentials for Success* and *See You on the High Ground: The Jared Monti Story.*

232

Made in the USA
Charleston, SC
05 January 2017